MW01241721

Intellectual Helplessness in America

Thinking Clearly

A N D

Acting Rationally

STEVEN A. DANLEY

ISBN: 978-1-4834-8625-3 (sc)
ISBN: 978-1-4834-8623-9 (hc)
ISBN: 978-1-4834-8624-6 (e)

Library of Congress Control Number: 2018906334

Because of the dynamic nature of the Internet, any web addresses or links contained in this book may have changed since publication and may no longer be valid. The views expressed in this work are solely those of the author and do not necessarily reflect the views of the publisher, and the publisher hereby disclaims any responsibility for them.

Any people depicted in stock imagery provided by Getty Images are models, and such images are being used for illustrative purposes only. Certain stock imagery © Getty Images.

Scripture taken from the King James Version of the Bible.

Scripture taken from the New Testament in Modern English by J.B Phillips copyright © 1960, 1972 J. B. Phillips. Administered by The Archbishops' Council of the Church of England. Used by Permission.

Scripture quotations taken from the New American Standard Bible® (NASB), Copyright © 1960, 1962, 1963, 1968, 1971, 1972, 1973, 1975, 1977, 1995 by The Lockman Foundation Used by permission. www.Lockman.org

Scripture quotations marked (NIV) are taken from the Holy Bible, New International Version®, NIV®. Copyright © 1973, 1978, 1984, 2011 by Biblica, Inc.™ Used by permission of Zondervan. All rights reserved worldwide. www.zondervan.com The "NIV" and "New International Version" are trademarks registered in the United States Patent and Trademark Office by Biblica, Inc.™

Lulu Publishing Services rev. date: 7/17/2018

To the republic: one nation under God, indivisible,
with liberty and justice for all

Contents

Preface

Thinking is primarily for the sake of action. No one can avoid the responsibility of acting in accordance with his mode of thinking. No one can act wisely who has never felt the need to pause to think about how he is going to act and why he desires to act as he does.
—L. SUSAN STEBBING

How the Book Came About

Last year at this time, I was reflecting on the significance of opening day at the 2017 Masters golf tournament—without Arnold Palmer. This year, I have been reflecting on evangelism without its master, the Reverend Billy Graham. And now, on journalism without Master Charles Krauthammer. I have that same feeling about America. Just as "the King" is gone from golf, the servant king is gone from the pulpit, and the prince of probity is gone from the newsroom, to a large extent so is rationality from the individual and collective consciousness of America. Our steadfast oracles are fading away. Collectively, we have fallen and can't get up—without help. I believe this book can help.

I suspect that many of you are having the same dilemma. You love America but are deeply troubled by its current condition. America is not healthy, and we know it. We are stuck in the mud of our own mixing. There are those with integrity, energy, and wisdom who can and are willing to help. But by and large, their help is not wanted by an elitist minority.

This minority is extreme (leftist), entrenched (in bureaucracy, courts, media, academia, Hollywood), overconfident ("moral betters"), exclusive (hence the moniker "elite"), and authoritarian (assimilate or expire). Their rise to power was based on calculated fabrications aimed at the heartstrings of America: give some of us power and some of us will transform culture into a Disneylandian society where your every desire will be fulfilled (for the price of admission). They reached into their sorcerer's bag and pulled out the oldest of fables: we are smart enough and good enough to rule ourselves. Their method of implementation is, of course, to have you sign the conservatorship papers, thereby making "me in charge of you."

But that concept is not American. It is utopian and always ends in totalitarianism. Give *me* the power, and *I* will (pretend to) make you satisfied. In America, our prescribed model is just the opposite: give *us* the power, and *we* will safeguard it against all we know about human nature. Those of us who have been dutifully taught our profound political heritage take great pride in the genius of America's governing model. We are grateful for its originality, the genius of mixing human aspirations with nature's practicality, the incredible courage and resolve that was sacrificed to bring it about, and the beautiful and delicate fragility of its continuity. It reminds me of the china and crystal that Mom wanted us kids to be careful around because it was beautiful, because it had been passed down by those she loved, and because it couldn't be replaced if broken.

Today, this loyal and incompetent minority is still roughhousing among the china and stemware despite warnings to play elsewhere. They are rebelling against the heritage that gave us the potential for life, liberty, and the ability to pursue happiness of a qualitative and collective sort. The rejection of our heritage has in many ways resulted in "America the Homeless." We are losing our sense of family built around common virtues and values. As a result, as a country, we have made poor decisions that have nearly bankrupted our political, economic, and moral-cultural systems and are pushing us out on the street. Many of our institutions are now factories that largely produce despair. As evidence of this morass, birth rates are down, suicide and substance-abuse rates are up, justice is unequally administered, language is vulgarized and indistinct, loyalty is purchased rather than earned, and anger is boiling over into increased instances of violence.

There are many reasons and root causes for this crisis. I want to explore the one that has placed a large segment of the population and our institutions into an intellectual funk and has resulted in a long-term hangover from poor choices and actions. The primary thesis of this book is that, individually and collectively, many of us have rendered ourselves intellectually helpless in addressing the critical issues of our day because we have refused, forgotten, or never been taught how to think well, which is the basis for acting rationally. The shocking fact is just how long this has been going on. It's like a bad, intensely depressing movie where everyone knows what's going to happen, and be said, long before it happens and is said. There are no surprises in monotony.

This book has been asking me to write it regardless of whether I want to. It is in response to an internal whisper of "you have to do something." I don't know you; you don't know me. But I know that we ought to care about each other. And, in that vein, this is a book not about telling anyone what to think but reintroducing classical methods of how to think rationally and logically so that better choices can be made that conform to reality and utilize common sense. If we think clearly, we will provide ourselves with increased opportunities for agreement, ideas will converge that provide a basis for negotiation and compromise, and we will be able to disagree with each other respectfully after taking the time to understand and thoughtfully consider each other's perspectives. We will allow each other to remain faithful to our just consciences, without attempting to utilize government coercion or reputational assassination to force-feed or "culturize" anyone against their will.

Introduction

As a kid, I loved to eat sloppy joe sandwiches. For those who haven't had the pleasure, you combine ground beef with ketchup, worcestershire sauce, brown sugar, and onions; heat it; and then slap this loosely joined concoction onto a hamburger bun. These sandwiches are easy to make, delicious, and extremely messy. You can't eat one without it oozing onto and drying up in your fingernails, covering the outside of your mouth, sticking in your teeth, spilling on your shirt, and possibly returning later as unwanted reflux.

Much the same can be said for sloppy thinking. Intellectual fast food can taste good going down because it agrees with our taste buds, but it usually bubbles back up after it has trouble being digested. Unfortunately, since actions are the outflow of a person's thought processes, the reflux is typically the exhaust of bad ideas implemented. Without help, we just wind up rechewing our intellectual cud.

A critical aspect of thinking clearly is to accept one of the axiomatic facts of life, that truth accurately describes reality as it is. The world was and is established by truth, and no amount of spin will change that. That is why untruths, whether based on ignorance or manipulation, are a hard stop and are painful. They are detrimental to the sender and the receiver. When false ideas are internalized and lived out, it results in predictable distortion, pain, conflict, and chaos. Unity is only possible when we submit to fundamental truths, such as "all men are created equal, that they are endowed by their Creator with certain unalienable [cannot be taken or given away] Rights, that among these are Life, Liberty and the pursuit of Happiness." When these realities are not predominately accepted, we collectively get what we have today: fragmentation and polarization to the point where we would rather fight for what we want than compromise for what we need. Over time, this mess sticks and hardens, removable only by cutting out the knots.

Given our current state, I think that it is fair to say that no one would mistake us for the greatest generation. The greatest generation's hallmark was sacrifice; today's hallmark is self-indulgence. As a result, we are in danger of finally extinguishing the flame of history's greatest experiment in ordered liberty. The cognitive malware has been launched and stupidity has gone viral. As English writer and philosopher G. K. Chesterton once said, "A despotism may almost be defined as a tired democracy."

What I Want to Accomplish

My goals for this essay are as follows:

1. Document how prevalent and serious America's current state of intellectual helplessness is. We are in a crisis the magnitude of which we have not seen since the Civil War. We are in real danger of dying an undemocratic death.

2. Identify the intellectual impediments that have deadened our ability to think logically and make rational choices, and break the stranglehold of bankrupt philosophies and the charlatans who use them to keep their elevated status by pushing everyone else down. They are intellectual terrorists and extremely dangerous. They will go to any lengths to extinguish anyone who does not agree with them.

3. Provide suggestions for thinking clearly and acting rationally that give us a fighting chance to regain our intellectual and thus motivational capacity. Love without truth is simply not love. I want to offer the intellectually homeless a bath, shelter, and a meal so an environment for learning is provided. People today are overwhelmed by the anxiety of uncertainty, incoherence, double standards, and hate. Thinking clearly can calm the spirit and soothe the soul.

4. Keep the American story of governing by reflection (thinking) and choice (acting) alive and well.

Book Themes and Structure

These are some of the basic themes that have guided my thought processes in this book:

1. There is a wholeness and order to reality, human life, and thought.

   This wholeness and order brings integrity, connectedness, beauty, and unity. Many of the world's greatest discoveries have resulted precisely from believing in, and therefore searching for, this wholeness and order. For example, this concept is present when examining the word *university*. The Latin word is *universitas*, which is a combination of *uni* (one) and *versus* (turn)—thus, the idea of "turned into one." Put another way, one may consider viewing *university* as the combination of two ideas: *unity* and *diversity*, the search for unity among a diversity of subjects. This unity is critical for both individual mental health and societal peace. When we see things for what they are, we are individually sane and collectively cognizant that we are all in this together. The value of thinking logically and acting reasonably is that it enables us to effectively integrate our individual lives and collective culture with reality.

2. The genius of America's founding, as detailed in the Declaration of Independence and the US Constitution, is that it matches reality, and it is a better foundation than we could make for ourselves today.

   The founders were presented with circumstances that cannot be re-created: a new and vast open territory, a physically distant government, a pioneer mentality, and an overriding desire for a new start built on initiative and fundamental freedoms. Out of these humble beginnings, a group of practical intellectuals began the work of creating and combining, from scratch, a new type of governmental system (a republic based on democratic principles) and a new type of economic system (capitalism), undergirded by specific moral principles and fundamental truths about humankind. They did so under the extreme duress of knowing they would be charged with treason and sedition, for which they could easily lose their lives. For those who say we could have built a better foundation, consider the entire 2016 presidential election process.

3. Collectively, the choices and subsequent habits of many Americans and our institutions have produced a culture and citizenry that has predictably gone into an intellectual stupor with a diminished capacity for sound decision-making.

    It is doubtful that there is an American alive today who would not agree that our ability to think rationally has been compromised by our culture. This reality has resulted in an extremely polarized society across a variety of ideological lines (politics, religion, identity, race, etc.). The galvanizing force of a constitutional republic "of, by, and for the people" has given way to the separating force of extreme individualism. And, as always, there are those at the ready to exploit this dissention to their benefit.

4. There is a way back home, but it will require the concerted, collective efforts of every part of society.

    For many, this will require a complete about-face and recommitment to the ideals of our founding documents. It is the narrow path of admission, respect, obedience, and commitment to our heritage.

To facilitate the exploration of this book, its contents are organized in the following manner:

Part I: The Case for Our Intellectual Helplessness

I suspect that the reality of intellectual helplessness in our culture is not a surprise. The revelation may be just how prevalent the epidemic is, having spread into every facet of life and American culture. After grasping the full extent of the problem, it is a wonder and a mercy, to me at least, that the United States of America still exists at all.

Part II: Consequences and Examples of Our Intellectual Helplessness

Have you ever poured soda into a clear glass filled with ice chips and watched as it wiggles its way around the chips? Eventually, every crevice is filled with soda and the ice begins melting. Similarly, intellectual helplessness is the caustic soda that envelops and then decays the solid foundations of society, eventually diluting the soda. The cumulative consequences of our intellectual and practical shortcomings are ubiquitous and life threatening.

Part III: Turning the Lights Back On

As a good American, I will only suggest productive ways of thinking and acting that are intended to assist us in regaining a solid intellectual and action-based footing for repairing our culture. No personal credit is warranted here as I am primarily borrowing suggestions established since the beginning of human time. It may be the first time, however, that the current younger generation has been schooled with this sort of knowledge. They have been too busy being told that society can't offer definitive ways of thinking; that would be oppressive and might make one feel bad.

Part IV: Concluding Remarks

The last chapter looks behind the curtain of today's American society to identify and discuss a current and present danger: the perceived attempt to form an American monarchy of an entrenched elitist minority.

Definition of Significant Terms

The following definitions are intended to assist the reader in understanding the intended meaning of the author as he uses the following terms:

- *intellectual helplessness*—having false ideas about reality that render one incapable of efficiently and effectively thinking about or taking action to address conditions/events
- *reality*—the way things actually are
- *truth*—a belief or idea that accurately describes reality

- *thinking*—the activity of searching out what must be true, or cannot be true, in light of given facts or assumptions
- *knowledge*—justified, true belief; being able to deal with things as they are on an appropriate basis of thought and experience
- *wisdom*—the integral comprehension and application of truth.
- *intelligence*—one's ability to grasp the truth of things
- *rationality*—the human ability to see an existent relationship between real or possible facts and other real or possible facts, such that if you have the one, you have the other
- *logic*—methods for reasoning correctly from premises to conclusions; apprehending things clearly, judging truly, and reasoning conclusively
- *fact*—an entity, regardless of type, that has an unchanging particular property or relation
- *belief*—dispositions or a readiness to act as if something were the case or a fact
- *virtue*—habits of moderate action; acting with restraint to one's impulses, due regard for the rights of others, and reasonable concern for distance consequences
- *character*—the pervasive and long-range governing tendencies of feeling, thought, and will that one has acquired through the experiences and choices that determine one's life as a whole, and of which one's actions are only a very partial expression
- *will (human spirit)*—the decision center of the body that identifies and considers alternatives and chooses a course of action
- *desire*—the wanting and active seeking of something for oneself
- *emotions*—spontaneous strong feelings generated by one's reaction to circumstances, mood, or relationships with others
- *love*—not the emotional affection for another but the will to seek out and implement the good for another person
- *personhood*—a combination of the mind (thinking, feeling), the will/spirit (decision-making), the soul (transmitting and receiving), and the physical body (implementing)
- *pluralism*—a governing system that allows for differing views to be presented, considered, and negotiated with the final decision resting on a vote of majority opinion

- *autonomy*—seeing humankind as a sufficient and self-contained entity able to effectively rule him/herself without assistance or interference

Author's Parameters

As I began the planning process for the writing of this essay, I realized just how broad a scope of information I was tackling. I became increasingly aware of the importance of keeping its content in the realm of direct knowledge and experience. My background and experience lend themselves to analysis of issues from a variety of fields and perspectives: government, business, and the moral-cultural institutions of family, media, philosophy and religion, education, and sports. I worked in regional county government for thirty-three years in a variety of executive/management positions (including chief human resources officer and performance audit director); lecture at the University of California Irvine (UCI), teaching a "Business and Government" course; volunteered as a patient/family adviser for St. Joseph hospital; served as a thirty-year NCAA and high school basketball referee; and in 2016 coauthored a critically acclaimed book entitled *Management Diseases and Disorders: How to Identify and Treat Dysfunctional Managerial Behavior.* Academically, I earned a master's degree in business and public administration and a bachelor's degree in political science from UCI, and I am a graduate of the Colson Fellows Program for a Christian worldview.

As such, the content of this essay is not postulated by a scientist or a full-time academic. It comes from a practitioner and cultural observer with multiple occupational and avocational passports (in leadership and line positions) who seeks knowledge for practical and beneficial use. It is not knowing for knowing's sake, or to impress anyone by using big philosophical or epistemological (whoops, sorry) terms. It is an attempt to find and speak truth to the heart of all of us (especially to me), to make us better as individuals, a community, and a nation. Its purpose is not to divide but to bring us together. It is not about taking sides and fighting about politics, religion, money, or anything else. It's seeing where the truth takes us and being willing to take the journey with an open mind and heart. Once we have done that, we can politely let the chips fall where they may.

As I take on this task, I do so with a sense of inadequacy as an imperfect human being who cannot possibly know everything necessary about myself, others, or society. But it is an honest practicum based on fifty-plus years of observation, participation, trial and error, and error resulting in subsequent trials. I know what works and what doesn't, and I have the scars and successes to prove it.

In today's environment, this book may be viewed by those who profit from the status quo as an unmasking of sorts. They are right. But I believe it will be change for the better from which all of us can benefit. With that, I humbly invite you to consider taking an intellectual and practical journey with me to affirm and discuss the root causes of what ails America and suggestions for how we might clearly think and intelligently act our way back home.

PART I

The Case for Our Intellectual Helplessness

Chapter 1

The Fundamentals of Democratic Capitalism

What duty is more pressing ... than ... a plan for communicating knowledge
to those who are to be the future generation of the liberties of this country.
—GEORGE WASHINGTON

As we all know, the first requirement for change is to acknowledge that one has a problem. In making that assessment, it is helpful to know what "healthy" looks like to properly gauge one's condition. To accomplish this, I will use a helpful analytical framework developed by Professor Michael Novak that details America's political-economic system of "democratic capitalism."[1] Below is a depiction of that model:

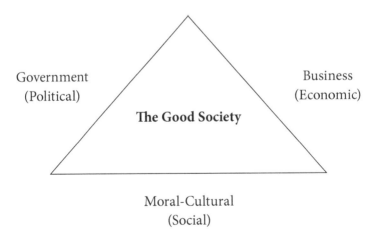

Government
(Political)

Business
(Economic)

The Good Society

Moral-Cultural
(Social)

---

[1] Michael Novak, *Three in One: Essays in Democratic Capitalism 1976–2000* (Lanham, MD: Rowman & Littlefield Publishers, Inc., 2001).

The basic idea is that the goal of every legitimate society is to secure the "good society" or "common good" for its citizens. To achieve this, each major component of society must cooperate by staying within its assigned roles and coordinating its efforts. In the graphic on the previous page, achieving the good society requires that America's business, government, and moral-cultural institutions individually accomplish their missions and then balance their contributions among the other two. Novak likens this model to a three-legged stool. If one of the legs is knocked from the stool, it falls over; if one leg becomes longer or shorter (more or less important) than the others, the stool ceases to be a safe resting place.

In this chapter, we will quickly walk through Novak's model to better understand democratic capitalism. Let's start first with the goal of the system: achieving the "good society."

The Good Society

The concept of the good society is intrinsic to each person and therefore varies. As such, in each era, it is necessary to build a consensus about what represents the good society for the most number of people. Building that consensus involves a balancing of the common good (group desires or "universals") with personal liberty (individual desires or "particulars"). More succinctly, how does society balance what I want versus what everyone else wants? This consensus is best achieved through the interplay of competing ideas in a well-functioning democracy, or pluralism. Novak states that the key is to find an image of the good society that will survive over the long term, even when free individuals have quite different ideas about it. It is important that we hear this because this is not what's happening today, and it is jeopardizing our entire system.

I have intermittently taught a university course entitled "Business and Government" over the past fifteen years. In each class, I have discussed with students the concept of the good society. Here is some of what I have learned from the students over this period:

- The students never question that the goal of every legitimate society is to secure the good society for its citizens. It appears to be intrinsically understood.

- When asked to brainstorm about what a word image of the good society would look like, the students typically identify such terms

2

as community, justice, environmental responsibility, tolerance, freedom, health, security, shelter, opportunity, and wealth. When asked to vote on which word best describes the good society, two words consistently reach the top of the list: *justice* first and *freedom* second.

These two words have important implications. *Justice* is a moral term that has prerequisites. One prerequisite is that for justice to exist, it must first be possible to find and know the truth. Why? Because if anything can be true, it is difficult to see how criteria can be developed for judging what is better or worse, just or unjust. The truth is therefore mandatory for justice to be accomplished.

Today, *freedom* is a term that is often not thought of or used in a manner consistent with America's founding. In the context of our founding, freedom is not the *license* to do what one pleases, but it is rather the obligation and the unfettered ability to do what is good and right. That is so because American democracy is a voluntary *covenant* established between the people and their elected government representatives. The government agrees to uphold and protect the unalienable rights of its citizens in exchange for its citizens agreeing to be bound by agreed-upon obligations to sustain that liberty (things like consenting to majority rule). In essence, it is a living relationship between a government and its people, which is beautifully personalized by Lady Liberty. Today, many of our thoughts and behaviors suggest that what we mean by using the word *freedom* is an unfettered license to do as one pleases in many areas of living (e.g., driving, identity preference, keeping one's word, civility of speech, truthfulness).

The Moral-Cultural Component

The moral-cultural component is positioned at the base of the triangle because it is the foundation of the system, providing the philosophical and motivational basis of the democratic-capitalistic system. This component is concerned with foundational thinking that seeks to answer humanity's most fundamental questions in such areas as existence, meaning, good and evil, and human rights (what we believe and why we believe it). We have a natural instinct and intellectual necessity to know the philosophical "why" of things so we can have a logical reason for acting.

The moral-cultural component of our system is developed through a progression:

Ideas	→	Worldviews	→	Values	→	Actions	→	Roles of Business and Government
evolve into		shape our		determine our		have consequences for the		

Ideas

To productively engage the world in the moral-cultural, economic, and political arenas, it requires that we understand the great ideas that compete for people's hearts and minds. These ideas provide theories on how life works. In examining these ideas that best explain life, we find a smorgasbord based on every conceivable intellectual food group from a variety of thinkers: truth and virtue (Socrates), subjectivism (Protagoras), reason (Plato), logic (Aristotle), metaphysics (Augustine, Aquinas), empiricism (Descartes), natural law and social contract (Locke), skepticism (Hume), synthesis (Hegel, Kant), economic inequality (Marx), existentialism (Kierkegaard), evolution (Darwin), nihilism (Nietzsche), psychoanalysis (Freud), secularism (Sartre), pragmatism (Dewey), justice as fairness (Rawls).

Worldviews

A worldview is the sum total of our beliefs about the world and our place in it. It is a way of seeing and comprehending reality, the lens we look through to interpret what we see. And everybody has one. It is the GPS for one's journey.

Worldviews are not static. Each person has the capacity to develop, edit, and reboot one. Because worldviews come from webs of interconnected ideas and beliefs, it changes with and in response to continual examination and alterations of one's seminal beliefs.

After taking a reasoned look at the myriad of ideas, they can be consolidated and summarized into three summary worldviews for consideration, based on Etienne Gilson's analysis referred to as Gilson's Choice[2]:

<u>Theism</u>	<u>Naturalism</u>	<u>Nihilism</u>
God matters	Man matters	Nothing matters

---

[2] Etienne Gilson, *God and Philosophy* (New Haven: Yale University Press, 1941).

Each worldview takes the individual down a different road to different destinations. To avoid being in a "prison of isms," one must choose a worldview. The American founders did. They chose theism with idea splashes from the Socratic method, dashes from Aristotelian logic, pinches from Platonic reason, a sprinkling of Augustinian metaphysics and Aquinian proofs, tablespoons of Iroquois participatory democracy, and cups of Lockean natural law. These choices led them to design, build and administer the American system of democratic capitalism. It is an engine designed for a specific purpose, with specific inputs (moral-cultural, business, political) that hope to yield specific outputs (justice, freedom, pursuit of happiness). Like any other machine, it will not work if one puts sugar in the gas tank.

America today suffers excruciatingly from the polarization resulting from the culture war between theism and naturalism. It is a question of who drives the car: the unchanging principles of theism or the dynamic musings of humankind.

Individual and societal decisions on worldview are extremely important. Having inadequate ideas causes us to run into reality in painful ways (e.g., the earth is flat, drink the Kool-Aid, the master race, might is right, the goal of life is to maximize pleasure, eugenics, and so on). An even more disturbing consideration is that the principle cause of violent conflict is not the desire for new markets or new territories, but the desire to crush those who have a different worldview (1940s Germany, Bosnia, Kashmir, Sudan, Iraq, Palestine/Israel, as well as liberal vs. conservative). Unfortunately, most of the world distinguishes and separates people based on fear rather than commonalities. We tend to hold down or exterminate what we do not understand or cannot control.

If we are to engage the world in its economic, political, or moral-cultural activities, it requires that we understand the great ideas and worldviews that compete for people's hearts and minds. The moral-cultural component of the triangle is made up of the following institutions that will be discussed in more detail later in the book: family, philosophy (religion), education, and the media (news/arts).

Values

A "value" is a principle, standard, or quality considered worthwhile or desirable that we choose to live by. Values are the natural outcome of one's worldview. If one holds to a theistic worldview, one would expect to see values like searching for truth, institutionalizing morals, and being focused on others and driven by a future fulfillment outside of an earthly realm. If one holds a naturalistic worldview, one would expect to see more focus on the here and now, pragmatism, the maximization of pleasure and the minimization of pain, more self-focus, scientific dogmatism, and the search for the right social, political, and economic structures as the means to achieve the good society.

Over the past several decades, American society has seen significant movement toward a naturalistic worldview and its corresponding values. One such example is in education. A traditional understanding of institutions of higher learning was that one of its primary goals was to improve the character of its citizens/students. This is easily confirmed by examining the inscriptions and murals on public buildings or the seals and mottos at heralded universities. Harvard's motto is "Veritas" or truth; Princeton's seal contains the phrase "Vet Nov Testamentum" (Old and New Testament); and Yale's seal contains a picture of Hebrew scripture. Sadly, over the past twenty years, I have never encountered a student who could say that a primary stated goal of the university was to make him or her a better person.

A second example is the changing manner in which knowledge is pursued. In the past, understanding the philosophical and moral underpinnings of why things were pursued was an important part of *knowing* something. Today, it has increasingly become common to focus primarily on understanding the business and technical side of issues with little emphasis on the values that created the motivation to seek change. As a result, in many halls of academia and corporate America, it has become commonplace to ignore or claim that one cannot discuss the philosophical or moral reasons why change was sought. Take, for instance, the snubbing of religious motivations. There have been an untold number of improvements to society and culture that were pursued and discovered due to specific religious convictions and motivations that "placed an extraordinary faith in reason."[3] Just a handful of examples include Newton, Kepler, and Galileo seeing themselves as "pursuing the secrets of creation;"[4] the birth of capitalism in European monasteries; and the moral propositions concerning fundamental human rights, such as liberty and freedom underlying

---

[3] Rodney Stark, *The Victory of Reason* (New York, Random House, 2005), x.

[4] Stark, 16.

Martin Luther King Jr.'s efforts. Yet, in each of these cases, it is a rarity for the discoverer's religious motivations to be communicated to students.

Such an environment encourages rampant revisionism. Over time, unbridled revisionism resulted in so many incompatibilities that it required being given a name: *syncretism* (the fluid combination of disparate and sometimes opposing beliefs that have been combined into something completely new and sometimes illogical). I try to explain this concept to my students by using analogies, such as falsely believing that one can have total moral freedom and then expect to see low health care costs—or that a boss who irresponsibly damages a subordinate's reputation can then expect to receive loyalty, cooperation, and friendship from them.

Actions

Our choices are based on our ideas, worldviews, and value system. Things are never fully theoretical because people act the way they think. This is a valuable truth in today's world. If someone tells you, "You really don't want to date me right now," you should believe that person. Or if a terrorist group tells you they want to wipe you off the face of the earth, you should protect yourself. Or if an FBI agent tells colleagues that he/she will stop a political candidate from becoming president, we should be concerned about the health of our democracy.

The Governmental (Political) Component

In my university class, I ask students to state everything they did before they got to school. The resulting list includes things like brushing one's teeth, taking a shower, going to the bathroom, getting dressed, eating, driving, taking the trash out, paying bills, and so forth. Then I ask them if government was involved in any of these activities. To their surprise, government has a role in each activity. For example, government has health standards for food, air, water, and sanitation; requirements for formal registration of all births, marriages, and deaths; minimum decency codes for dress; traffic laws for transportation, and more. After a brief discussion, the quiet realization sets in that government is ubiquitous and a necessary occupational (humanitarian) hazard.

As much as we hate to admit it, we need some form of government. Several thousand years of human history prove that unless there is some consensus over the rules and goals of a group, the people will undermine their own well-being. There are simply too many human interests, wills to power, or passions that will not confirm to the dictates of reason and justice on their own.[5]

Like any new venture, America's republic began as a series of concepts:

- **Means** concept: Fundamentally, democracy is a system or vehicle to take you where you want to go. As such, it is a means and not an end. The end is the good society.

- **Legitimacy** concept: A government's legitimacy depends on its willingness and capacity to preserve and promote the common good for all citizens.

- **Civil society** concept: This is a larger and deeper concept than government. The task of how best to devolve power from the state to its citizens is a moral idea at the heart of the experiment in self-government. Self-governing citizens first try to meet their social needs by creating their own social organizations and, only as a last resort, through turning to the state.[6]

- **Experiment** concept: In the late 1700s, when America was attempting to form its own government, nearly everything about it was new and experimental:

  o the rule of law rather than monarchy
  o democratic self-government by representation rather than ruler decree
  o limited government rather than expansive dictatorship
  o separation of powers rather than unitary control
  o private property rather than state ownership
  o equal protection rather than protection of the elite
  o freedoms of speech, press, assembly, and religion

---

[5] Alexander Hamilton, *Federalist No. 15* (December 1, 1787), 90–98.
[6] Novak, *Three in One*, 100.

America's new government "of, by and for the people" instituted the following vision and mission statements for the country:

> *Vision statement* (as found in the *Declaration of Independence*): "We hold these truths to be self-evident, that all men are created equal, that they are endowed by their Creator with certain unalienable Rights, that among them are Life, Liberty, and the pursuit of Happiness."

> *Mission statement* (as found in the *US Constitution*): "We the People of the United States, in Order to form a more perfect Union, establish Justice, insure domestic Tranquility, provide for the common defense, promote the general Welfare, and secure the Blessings of Liberty to ourselves and our Posterity, do ordain and establish this Constitution for the United States of America."

The Business (Economic) Component

The father of capitalism is Adam Smith. The book most typically associated with Smith is *The Wealth of Nations*. However, in actuality, the full title of the book is An Inquiry into the Nature and Causes of the Wealth of Nations. It was published in March 1776. Does the year 1776 ring a bell? The implications send shivers up and down my spine. At the same time the Founding Fathers were designing the world's first democratic republic to serve as the United States' governmental structure, it was also choosing the new theory of capitalism for its economic system. Smith promoted the ideas of an invisible hand of competition, free markets, incentives, and private property rights to fulfill the following new roles of a capitalistic economy:

- maximize profit
- provide goods and services
- create new wealth and promote invention and ingenuity
- diversify the interests of the republic

A reading of the US Constitution makes it clear that one of the founders' primary goals was to establish a strong and wide commercial base to provide economic sustainability for the country and its individual citizens, and as a further check and balance against government power. The Constitution specifically provides for commercial liberties to protect the marketplace and allow unlimited participation in it by all parties. The founders also saw an opportunity for commerce to create a formal (economic) mechanism to backstop the reliance on the unsteadiness of virtue in sustaining the republic. Through business, self-restraint is a voluntarily necessity for the realization of economic self-interest. For an economic system to be profitable and sustainable, all parties must voluntarily agree to keep contractual commitments, respect intellectual property, and refrain from creating artificial barriers to participation and competition (e.g., monopoly, collusion).

The Interrelationships between the Components

While we don't have time to fully discuss or develop the interrelationships between the moral-cultural, government, and business components, I believe it is helpful to write a few words about each one.

Moral-Cultural (Social) to Government (Political)

Moral and social considerations are part and parcel of the political process and governmental actions. Laws get made and regulations are promulgated and enforced because of the way people feel about the rightness, wrongness, or fairness of attitudes and behaviors. People vote for elected officials based greatly on their moral-cultural convictions. A 2016 national survey on voting choices conducted by the Barna Group, demonstrated that among ten different sources of influence (e.g., religious beliefs, family members, news media, friends, advertising, political commentators), the most likely influence on who people voted for in the 2016 presidential contest was their religious beliefs.[7]

Political scientist James Q. Wilson also noted the highly moral objective of democratic government: "It is acknowledged in almost every important area of public concern, that we are seeking to induce people to act virtuously not only because it is desirable, but because it now appears it is necessary if

[7] Barna Group, "Religious Beliefs Have Greatest Influence on Voting Decisions," Research Releases in Culture & Media, October 27, 2016, https://www.barna.com/research/religious-beliefs-have-greatest-influence-on-voting-decisions.

large improvements are to be made in those matters we consider problems. Under our conception of democracy, the function of democratic institutions is to serve as mechanisms by which people act to fulfill their moral-political responsibilities: to protect the weak and innocent; promote public health and safety; secure the overall common good. Our founding documents (i.e., the Declaration of Independence and US Constitution) are chalked full of moralistic phrases and words regarding the duties of democracy. Even our concept of the separation of powers is a highly moral concept. It seeks to square two competing themes: man is capable of incredible good and at the same time every person is fallible and under the right temptations is susceptible to self-indulgence over the common good."[8]

Even our money is inscribed with the phrase *Novus Ordo Seclorum* (the New Order of the Ages). The founders clearly saw the United States as more than just the formation of another country. They viewed it as a unique opportunity in history to reach beyond themselves and strive for the highest aspirations of humankind: the freedom to govern themselves by *reflection* and *choice,* rather than by propaganda and fiat.[9] The United States was not a lucky wager. It was created by deliberate, definitive choices to establish, stabilize, and preserve a nation. "As [political theorist] Hannah Arendt and others have pointed out, the American experiment is the most intellectually neglected social reality. Nowadays, almost no one grasps it originality or can articulate its specific moral vision, its table of virtues."[10]

Moral-Cultural (Social) to Business (Economic)

Social issues necessarily impact commerce in several ways. Take for instance the marketing of goods and services. A business needs to know the moral-cultural climate in which it operates. Is the business's target population largely theistic, naturalistic, or nihilistic? Does it have a traditional view of family, or is it open to alternative models? What are its views on race, gender, and sexual orientation? Social issues also impact how a business chooses to operate internally. Does the business prioritize technology over its employees or employees over its technology? Does the business

---

[8] James Q. Wilson, *On Character* (Washington, DC: The AEI Press, 1995), 22.

[9] Michael Novak, *On Two Wings* (San Francisco: Encounter Books, 2002), 11.

[10] Michael Novak, "Controversial Engagements," *First Things*, April 1999, https://www.firstthings.com/article/1999/04/002-controversial-engagements.

value employee skills over customer service? Does the business value profits over social responsibility?

Businesses that deny the relationship between moral-cultural convictions and business decisions typically find themselves having sustainability issues. Consider the consistent myriad of ethical failures in the business world: Enron, Worldcom, Tyco, Subprime Mortgages, Mylan's EpiPen, British Petroleum's Deepwater Horizon, Volkswagen, or Wells Fargo. The moral-cultural deficiencies of some businesses have been so egregious that a term had to be invented to address it: "corporate social responsibility."

Many are not aware that the relationship between morality and business was the primary concern of capitalism's founder, Adam Smith. Smith's motivation for creating capitalism was not wealth for wealth's sake, but wealth to provide for social health. In his time, the world was necessarily concerned with *distributive justice*: when there were far fewer resources, the overriding question was how to fairly distribute that wealth. Smith hoped to create an economic system whereby all citizens could become their own owners of production and share in the expanded opportunities for wealth. As a result of these efforts, the concept of *productive justice* was created: if one knows there is need, and one has the ability to meet that need, then there is a moral imperative to meet that need.

Additionally, at its essence, economics is the means of exchange for a given culture. As such, it is a question of value, as well as moral obligation to uphold agreed upon transactions. Likewise, corporations are considered legal "entities" and thereby are granted certain privileges, such as limited liability, indefinite life, and special tax treatment. In exchange for these privileges, corporations have an ethical responsibility to the society that granted them.

Government (Political) to Business (Economics)

Virtually all the major problems that preoccupy government involve economic issues, including these:

- condition of the economic environment and markets
- food and fuel
- employment and inflation
- productivity and expanding populations
- development and justice

- cost of war and security
- reasonable credit availability
- taxes
- health care costs

Our founding documents demonstrate that the founders understood this connection:

- The second part of the Declaration of Independence identifies that one of the primary reasons the colonists rebelled was due to the economic hardships they suffered from British laws regarding the colonies.
- Article 8 of the US Constitution bestows the business rights of government: to levy and collect taxes, to borrow money on the credit of the United States, to regulate commerce, and to coin money and regulate its value.

In addition, the primary goal of the governmental regulation of business is to benefit consumers. One of the ways it accomplishes this is by protecting competition through antitrust legislation, such as the Interstate Commerce Act of 1887 (provides for the federal regulation of interstate commerce), the Sherman Act of 1890 (addresses unreasonable restraints on free trade and monopoly restrictions), the Clayton Act of 1914 (addresses anticompetitive actions by firms against new firms trying to establish themselves in the same market, provides for government authority of mergers, and allows for private lawsuits), and the Federal Trade Commission Act of 1914 (addresses unfair methods of competition or unfair or deceptive acts or practices).

Balancing Moral-Cultural, Government, and Business Components

As we have seen, the United States has a democratic-capitalistic structure made up of the following components:

- The *moral-cultural* component is based on the unalienable rights of humankind and the pluralistic expression of those rights in the public square.

- The *political* component is based on the consent of the governed, power vested in elected representatives, and government institutions of due process.
- The *economic* component is based on open markets, incentives, and private property.

As Novak described, "Each of these three components has its own institutions, rituals, procedures, social base and social strength. Each has its own tendencies, ambitions, achievements and distortions. Each for its own well-being requires the health of the other two. Yet each one has a tendency to seek its own self-aggrandizement at the expense of the other two. The whole point of the democratic-capitalistic model is to develop a healthy competition between the three components in which people of quite different psychologies and learned skills participate. It is designed that way. The whole notion is to divide power. It is a question of how to give us liberties, then how to protect them against everything we know about human nature."[11]

Accordingly, there are three ways to destroy our system. One can destroy its economic genius. One can destroy its political genius. Or one can attack its cultural genius. To attack any one of these is to attack the other two, as they are all interrelated, each one necessary for the other's existence. Indeed, the most devastation occurs when any event or crisis negatively impacts all three areas. Consider, for example, that the following catastrophic events had failures in each of the moral-cultural, government, and business arenas:

- slavery and racism
- labor exploitation
- corporate economic scandals
- Catholic Church sex scandals
- Iraqi weapons of mass destruction
- prison scandals
- IRS targeting scandal
- false and biased media coverage
- the Holocaust

---

[11] Novak, *Three in One*, 60.

- environmental disasters
- fake news

This is what makes democratic capitalism so powerful. It matches life (reality). Each one of us is an economic agent. Each is citizen. Each of us seeks meaning, follows conscience, and pursues truth and understanding.[12]

---

[12] Novak, *Three in One*, 45.

Chapter 2

Intellectual Helplessness in the Moral-Cultural (Social) Arena

Moral-cultural issues impact our identity, our sense of placement in the universe, our concepts of right and wrong, and our sense of what's important. The four institutions addressed below that make up this component are philosophy, family, education, and media (news and arts).

One needs to look no further to understand why intellectual helplessness engulfs the moral-cultural arena than the *reordering* and *redefining* of these institutional priorities over the past several decades. During the formative years of my life (1960s to early 1980s), it was common to hear influential adults routinely use the phrase "God, country, family" in reference to an appropriate ordering of life priorities. Once these intrinsic (internal) areas were addressed, it was believed that other nonintrinsic (external) priorities, such as media and education, would take care of themselves and reinforce the intrinsic priorities. At that time, media and technology had a much smaller influence due to a smaller selection and availability of vehicles to carry the message, as well as the nonimmediacy of the receipt and distribution of news. Media existed primarily in terms of newspapers, books, VHF television, and radio during waking hours. Inventions such as the cell phone, personal computer, internet, and cable television were unavailable. In the same vein, although educational philosophies were changing greatly during this time, the mass marketing of these ideas outside of the educational environment was limited as well.

These limitations are unrecognizable in today's culture. Technology has made information distribution instantaneous, worldwide, and continuous. It is so ubiquitous today that, if for nothing else but to keep one's sanity, we must search for ways to periodically unplug ourselves from this bombardment of information, marketing, and opinionated persuasion.

This informational explosion has dramatically impacted the ordering of the life priorities of "God, country, and family." To illustrate, consider an internal, informal poll I have taken with my university classes over the past fifteen years, in which I asked students to rank the current priority order of each of the four moral-cultural arenas (philosophy, family, education, and media). For fifteen years, the consensus ranking has consistently been media first, followed by education, family, and philosophy. Recent studies confirm this changing environment, particularly among different generations. A 2016 Barna study indicated the following sources as having "a lot, some, or a little" combined influence on the choice of a presidential candidate: news media, 60 percent; family members, 49 percent; religious beliefs, 46 percent.[13] A 2015 Pew Research Center study identified an increase in religious unaffiliation for all demographic generations from 2007 to 2015 (silent generation, from 9 to 11 percent; boomer, 14 to 17 percent; Gen X, 19 to 23 percent; and millennial, 25 to 34 percent).[14] A June 2017 study by Barna ranked the following priorities as being central to the identity of those polled: (1) family, (2) being an American (country), (3) my religious faith (philosophy), and (4) my ethnic group.[15]

As such, today many are being increasingly influenced by nonintrinsic external and group influences, such as media and education. To further exacerbate this change, many are not just changing their ordering of these priorities but also are revising the definition of and views about each individual institution. In the arena of philosophy, morality and truth have increasingly been moving toward relativism, religious affiliation has declined among all age groups, and the occult is capturing more attention in our culture.[16] In the arena of family, traditional family structures are being liberalized, and permanent identity attributes are being discussed as malleable preferences. In education, technology is being implemented with less consideration of its social implications, and exclusive indoctrination

[13] Barna Group, "Religious Beliefs Have Greatest Influence of Voting Decisions," October 27, 2016, https://www.barna.com/rserach/religious-beliefs-have-greatest-influence-on-voting-decisions.

[14] "The Whys and How of Generations Research," Pew Research Center, September 3, 2015, http://people-press.org/2015/09/03/the-whys-and-hows-of-generations-research/.

[15] Barna Group, "Forming Family Values in a Digital Age," June 27, 2017, https://www.barna.com/research/forming-family-values-digital-age/.

[16] John Stonestreet and G. Shane Morris, "Millennials Spellbound by the Occult," BreakPoint, November 21, 2017, http://www.breakpoint.org/2017/11/breakpoint-millennials-spellbound-by-the-occult/.

is increasingly being used as a technique over inclusive learning opportunities. And in the media, the presentation of unbiased facts is consistently being eclipsed by agenda-driven opinions.

Media and educational institutions are keenly aware of this transition and are taking full advantage of it, seeking to retain and expand their increased status and influence. Today's generation is attached at the hip to their computers and smartphones. A neurosis is created if one attempts to take our electronic "blankey" away from us. Many are hardwired to accept what the elitist minority tells us, whether it be in a classroom or various media outlets. Today, people acquire many of their values from a screen rather than a person or a good book. Tragically, however, this self-indulgent, nonstop marketing is not meant to *make* a better society, but to *take* your money.

As a result, on today's moral-cultural train, the previous forward-looking engines of philosophy and family are and have been repositioned to the caboose, looking backward and reacting to what education and media have dictated. In this changing environment, intellectual helplessness has naturally flourished, as these changes have substantially taken place in an environment of muted protective boundaries (e.g., morality, sanctity of life, rule of law, professional ethics), and with an insufficient availability of customized tools (e.g., freedoms of speech and religion, scientific method, feasibility studies) necessary for the efficient and effective implementation of the changes. In essence, we have analogously given people airplanes without flying lessons, medical options without ethical moorings, and mortgages without sufficient monthly income to pay the bills.

Intellectual Helplessness in Philosophy

*Philosophy is an attempt to figure out the best way to
live, what the best ways to be and to do are.*
—DALLAS WILLARD

General Philosophy

So, philosophically, how is America doing? I think there is general agreement that we are a mess. Part of the reason for this is that while having a solid worldview is a prerequisite to choosing wisely among values, virtues, and actions, students are rarely taught the basics of philosophy anymore.

Understanding the importance and practical application of philosophy is practically gone. Perhaps this is intentional. If an educational institution does not teach you *how* to think, it is easier for it to tell you *what* to think. For example, replacing traditional core courses with unhelpful and nonunifying courses—solely to be able to describe one's institution as "diverse"—denies students the ability to acquire the more critical philosophical tools that lead to life-changing revelations (i.e., learning). Take for instance Hunter College in New York City. It is reportedly requiring its political science majors to take a course entitled "The Abolition of Whiteness," which appears to be little more than an attempt to shame anyone born Caucasian.[17]

I realize that the mention of the word *philosophy* is off-putting to many young people. "Do we really have to talk about what a bunch of old dead (white) guys thought? How is that pertinent to my technologized life?" But here is where it becomes intensely pertinent. Our philosophies delineate our views on the origin and value of life, the cause/effect relationships of our actions, and the obligations to a particular morality that guides our actions. Ultimately, our philosophy dictates a level of hope for us as individuals and as a global community. We can get a glimpse into the world of today's youth by viewing pop culture. In a 2017 article in *Vox*, Constance Grady chronicles the replacement of dystopian novels and films (e.g., *The Hunger Games*, *Divergent*) by stories of teen suicide. One such new story is *13 Reasons Why*, a TV series in which a seventeen-year-old girl kills herself and leaves behind cassette tapes for thirteen people she blames for her death, outlining each one's contribution to her demise. Grady describes this deep dive into demented levels of dearth, stating, "If the dystopian narrative was pessimistic, the suicide narrative is downright nihilistic. It wallows in feelings of despair and self-loathing. It cannot imagine the world getting any better."[18] If one does not have a settled philosophical base in which to process life, it can quickly become unraveled. And if one's world is only about what matters to oneself, or if one accepts the nihilistic view that nothing matters, when life gets hard, some choose not to get up, but rather to check out. It should be no surprise that the "most recent data

---

[17] Anthony Gockowski, " 'Abolition of Whiteness' Course Offered at Hunter College," May 25, 2017, http://www.campusreform.org/?ID=9231.

[18] Constance Grady, "The YA dystopia boom is over. It's been replaced by stories of teen suicide," *Vox*, October 18, 2017, https://www.vox.com/207,10/18/15881100/ya-dystopia-teen-suicide-13-reasons-why-hunger-games.

from the Centers of Disease Control indicates that, between 1999 and 2014, suicide in the U.S. rose dramatically for both men and women in every age bracket up to age seventy-five."[19] As such, philosophy matters, and it has critical consequences.

The troubling lack of recognition of the importance of philosophy means that we initially ignore it and then learn the hard way that it matters. Theologian and philosopher Francis Schaeffer said, "One reason it is ignored is that in many of the chairs of philosophy there is a radical denial of the possibility of drawing a circle that will encompass all … Philosophies of today are anti-philosophies … They have given up hope of a rational circle to give an answer to life, and are left with only the anti-rational … This new unifying concept is the concept of a divided field of knowledge."[20] This is profoundly ironic since, as previously stated, the word *university* carries with it the idea of searching for unity amid a diversity of subject matters. When we see things for what they are, we are individually sane and collectively cognizant that we are all in this together.

I believe that Schaeffer was right when he said that society cannot function without integration and coherence. As evidence, human minds involuntarily search for patterns and structures to explain whatever we are viewing. This search for rationality may be put on hold, but it never really stops until we find an adequate answer. Our choice is whether we commit to the search for reality or for arbitrary "absolutes" to placate the void. The good news, according to C. S. Lewis, "is that the laws of logic are not human conventions created differently from culture to culture … I conclude … that logic is a real insight into the way in which real things have to exist. In other words, the laws of thought are also the laws of things: of things in the remotest space and the remotest time."[21]

Another beef against philosophy occurs when it is compared to the knowledge gained by science. Today, many speak of the "scientific method" as the only appropriate basis of knowledge. And while science is an excellent and necessary tool, it is only one way of knowing things. Science can't prove or tell us why we love someone; why we have accurate, life-saving intuitions at just the right moment; or if a disabled fetus being considered

---

[19] Aaron Kheriaty, "Dying of Despair," *First Things*, August 2017, 3, https://www.firstthings.com/article/2017/08/dying-of-despair.

[20] Francis Schaeffer, *Trilogy* (Wheaton, IL: Crossway Books, 1990), 17.

[21] C. S. Lewis in *Seeing Beauty and Saying Beautifully* by John Piper (Wheaton, IL: Crossway Books, 2014), Kindle edition, 129.

for abortion will discover the cure for cancer. As Professor Dallas Willard stated, "Everything that really matters in life falls outside the boundary of science. Can any of these sciences tell you how to become a truly good person? Science can't deal with that, because some questions can't be quantified. Science turns out to be only a portion of the much broader field of knowledge."[22]

An additional impediment to getting philosophical is that humankind has a love/hate relationship with the truth. We love it when it tells us what we want to hear; we hate it when it gets in the way of our desires. As Augustine said, "Why does truth call forth hatred? … Simply because truth is loved in such a way that those who love some other thing want it to be the truth, and precisely because they do not wish to be deceived, are unwilling to be convinced that they are indeed being deceived. Thus, they hate the truth for the sake of that other thing which they love, because they take it for the truth. They love truth when it enlightens them, they hate it when it accuses them."[23] A significant issue for those who hate the truth, as noted in James Sire's book *Habits of the Mind*, is that "the turning away of truth … does not mean the mind will stop functioning; it only means the mind will not perceive the truth. Worse, I would add: not only will the mind not perceive the truth, it will succumb to falsehood masquerading as the truth."[24] These falsehoods are often related to our philosophies about ourselves and others. One such falsehood is that we are defined and controlled by whatever longings and aspirations (positive or negative) come out of our hearts. In actuality, however, we can choose our philosophical allegiances.

The Philosophy of Me

Focusing on oneself necessarily deals with the issues of one's identity, ego, and self-esteem. I think we can generally agree that in our current world, "me" is generally given more noodle time than "we." In fact, autonomy has been the primary personal goal for many Americans over the past several decades. The root of the word *autonomy* comes from *autos* (self) and *nomos* (custom or law), thus the idea that one is subject to his or her own

---

[22] Dallas Willard, *The Allure of Gentleness* (New York: HarperOne, 2015), Kindle edition, 13.

[23] Augustine, *Confessions* 10.23.

[24] James W. Sire, *Habits of the Mind* (Downers Grove, IL: InterVarsity Press, 2000), 93.

law. The concept of autonomy is not a hard sell. Who doesn't want to care about oneself and see to it that one gets everything one wants? Number one, right? And modern advertising has fueled the beast. Buy something, anything, for yourself. You deserve it. Buy it, use it, and when you are tired of it, throw it away and get something new. Newer, better, faster, younger. Everyone else is doing it. You can pay for it later. Or you can figure out a way to make someone else pay for it.

In this mean, less-than-brave, new world, the fulfillment of individual desires is viewed as our greatest good and a legitimate goal. Ours is a feel-good society. How I feel is the most important question and securing what I desire the most important goal ("I'll have more of happiness, if you please"). A 2015 study by the Barna Group "reveals the degree to which Americans pledge allegiance to the 'morality of 'self-fulfillment.'"[25] According to the study, this new morality can be summed up in six guiding principles, with those surveyed indicating they "completely" or "somewhat" agreed by the following percentage scores:

- The best way to find yourself is by looking within yourself (91 percent).
- People should not criticize someone else's life choices (89 percent).
- To be fulfilled in life, you should pursue the things you desire most (86 percent).
- The highest goal of life is to enjoy it as much as possible (84 percent)
- People can believe whatever they want, as long as those beliefs don't affect society (79 percent).
- Any kind of sexual expression between two consenting adults is acceptable (69 percent).[26]

But how I feel doesn't really help me if it doesn't match up with the way things really are. I may feel like I am a good singer, but I shouldn't ignore or misinterpret groans for applause. Having wrong or illegitimate views about ourselves can cause us to stub our individual and collective toes in an unending number of painful ways.

One painful way is when we base our self-worth on unstable sources,

---

[25] Barna Group, "The End of Absolutes: America's New Moral Code," May 25, 2016, https://www.barna.com/research/the-end-of-absolutes-americas-new-moral-code/.
[26] Barna Group, "The End of Absolutes."

such as the opinions of others, the pursuit of causes, or the acquisition of things. As author Timothy Keller informs, "If we get our very identity, our sense of worth, from our political position then politics is not really about politics, it is about us. Through our cause, we are getting a self, our worth. That means that we must despise and demonize the opposition."[27]

Another painful outcome from a persistent personal focus is that it often results in having extreme views about oneself. One extreme is self-aggrandizement that breeds a sense of false value and a corresponding sense of entitlement. Inaccurate self-perception creates problems in our interpersonal relationships. When it is primarily about me, I am not satisfied until my needs have been met. These unfulfilled entitlements often give motivation to inappropriate means of achievement. As Dallas Willard observed, "Surely, we need something less unstable than human desire on which to build either our lives or our societies."[28]

The other extreme is the problem of self-loathing. For instance, when someone does not like who he/she is physically (race, gender, appearance), rather than working to accept oneself, some opt to change it. This is a rebellion of the clay attempting to become an unapprenticed potter. Attempting to make modifications to a hard-wired design often results in more noticeable and problematic issues. This includes the lingering disillusionment from not being able to accept oneself for who one is. This typically becomes a compound problem, because when someone cannot accept him/herself, it becomes particularly hard for that person to believe that others can accept them as well.

Another painful toe stubbing produced by the "me-first" platform is that it often results in the pursuit of choices that are detrimental to the community. Self-focus, for example, typically discourages acts of charity. This situation was aptly described by Professor Allan Bloom in his classic 1987 book, *The Closing of the American Mind,* in which he stated, "Survivalism takes the place of heroism as the admired quality. If it's truly all about me, then the self-sacrifice necessary to save you becomes foolish and counterproductive."[29] His predictions have unfortunately materialized.

---

[27] Timothy Keller, *The Reason for God: Belief in an Age of Skepticism* (New York: Riverhead Books, 2008), 175.
[28] Dallas Willard, *The Divine Conspiracy Continued* (New York: HarperOne, 2015), Kindle edition, 175.
[29] Allan Bloom, *The Closing of the American Mind* (New York: Simon & Schuster, Inc., 1987), 84.

Take for instance Planned Parenthood's current advertising campaign on its website entitled MyAbortionMyLife.org.[30] Additionally, the 2016 Barna survey on America's new moral code demonstrates that "the highest good, according to our society, is 'finding yourself,' and then living by what's right for you."[31] In this environment, it's hard not to see the negative impact this has on motivating people to help others. As a case in point, an October 2017 study released by the Chronicle of Philanthropy shows that only 24 percent of taxpayers reported a charitable gift on their tax returns in 2015, down from 30 percent a decade earlier.[32] In addition, in 2016, UCLA published a study demonstrating a significant decline in charitable giving in the Los Angeles area, from $7.6 billion in 2006 to $6.03 billion in 2013.[33]

A second collective example is that democracy predictably suffers in a self-absorbed culture. The supreme law of the United States, the US Constitution, states, "*We* the People of the United States, in Order to form a more perfect *Union*," not "*Me* the Person of (my address), in Order to form a more perfect *Division*." America is built upon the necessity of a collective us. Our democratic-capitalistic system was built to run on the fuel of collective objectives, not on protective subjectives. As President John F. Kennedy famously insisted, "Ask not what your country can do for you, ask what you can do for your country." When the me is prioritized in government, it materializes in the following ways: The "Fat Leonard" corruption scandal currently has rocked navy personnel from stem (admirals) to stern (enlisted), with Malaysian defense contractor Leonard Francis pleading guilty to bribery for providing cash, prostitutes, trips, and other gifts in exchange for defense contracts, fraudulent payments, and inside information on ship schedules.[34] Hillary Clinton took over the Democratic National Convention operations during the 2016 Democratic

[30] "My Abortion, My Life: Ending the Stigma Around Abortion," https://www.myabortionmylife.org/.
[31] Barna Group, "The End of Absolutes."
[32] Drew Lindsay, "Fewer Americans Find Room in Their Budgets for Charity, Chronicle Data Shows," *Chronicle of Philanthropy*, October 3, 2017, https://philanthropy.com/article/Share-of-Americans-Who-Give-to/241345.
[33] Larry Kaplan, "Charitable Giving in Los Angeles Declines Considerably as Big Dollars Go Elsewhere," *Nonprofit Quarterly*, June 6, 2016, https://www.nonprofitquarterly.org/2016/06/06/charitable-giving-in-los-angeles-declines-considerably-as-big-dollars-go-elsewhere.
[34] Craig Witlock, "Fat Leonard' scandal expands to ensnare more than 60 admirals," *Washington Post*, November 6, 2017.

primary election in which she was a candidate. And only 19 percent of the public says, "they can trust the government always or most of the time," according to a 2015 Pew Research Center study.[35]

A fourth painful outcome from a persistent personal focus is that narcissism discourages personal responsibility. The me-first concept is part and parcel of the pursuit for an autonomous world, where humans are at the center of the universe and entitled to the unfettered pursuit and acquisition of his/her personal desires. To justify the legitimacy of individual desires, one adopts a worldview that conveniently claims that desires are innate rather than artificial. In other words, one's behavior is legitimized because it is the fulfillment of an innate desire that cannot be denied without physically, psychologically, or economically damaging the individual. In a Darwinian worldview, creation is the chance collision of atoms with no overarching purpose, and survival of the fittest is the highest ethical good where might makes right. In a Freudian worldview, the ultimate goal is to become happy and remain so, thereby necessitating the removal of any repressive barriers to that happiness. In a Marxist worldview, socioeconomic conflict between economic classes is the persistent antagonism of human history, so a classless society must be created whereby everyone receives the same income regardless of their contribution.

A fifth example of how the me-first philosophy negatively impacts society is that it encourages an "ends justifies the means" ethic. If it is all about getting what one wants, then one must do what one must do to get it. Consider, the current sexual harassment scandals and the #MeToo claims of previous harassment incidents. A me-first secular philosophy contributes to the sexual and psychological robbing of Pamela to pay Paul. Consider pertinent comments made by Washington Post opinion writer Christine Emba in her article "Let's Rethink Sex": "At the bottom of all this confusion sits a fundamental misframing: that there's some baseline amount of sex that we should be getting or at least allowed to pursue. Following from that is the assumption that the ability to pursue and satisfy our sexual desires … is paramount."[36] Alongside the terror related to this line of thinking, there is another hazard worth noting. It is a necessary precondition that before

---

[35] "Beyond Distrust: How Americans View Their Government," Pew Research Center, November 23, 2015, http://people-press.org/2015/11/23/beyond-distrust-how-americans-view-their-government.

[36] Christine Emba, "Let's Rethink Sex," *Washington Post*, November 26, 2017, https://washingtonpost.com/opinions/lets-rethink-sex/2017/11/26/d8546a86-d2d5.

anything goes, everything else must go, including virtue, because it stands as a psychological barrier to self-fulfillment. In our intellectual helplessness, we discard our virtue furniture (e.g., "prudence, temperance, respect and even love")[37] to make room for the new "modern" furnishings.

One last toe plow into the "me table" is that it is counterproductive and futile, unable to provide a basis for achieving the good society. For one thing, it doesn't match reality. Consider that despite all the diversity present in life (in people, attitudes, preferences, etc.), life continually pushes for these differences to come together. It is because we need each other. Our differences are like the pieces of a puzzle. Each piece is needed to complete the picture. If all the pieces were the same, we wouldn't need one another, as we would only be one more of the same thing. In a profound way, our differences were designed to bring us together, not keep us apart. For another thing, the me is exclusionary and therefore lonely. As Francis Schaeffer noted, the "ultimate in autonomous freedom is being crazy."[38] If one is completely free from anyone or anything, then one is in perpetual solitary confinement. This realization puts an exclamation point on just how insidious the addiction of self can be.

The Philosophy of Us

Political scientist James Q. Wilson said the "central problem for social science is to explain social order. How do people manage to get along?"[39] How do we subdue our personal desires for the common good? Whose values will ultimately be chosen to govern society? Individually, can we live with the compromises reached? I believe the long-term impact of the prevailing philosophy of me has unfortunately also trickled down and is polluting the philosophy of us.

One way that intellectual helplessness appears in a group setting is when segments of society work against America's pluralistic framework and try to assert the will of the few (usually the self-identified "elite") on the many. Take for instance the content of sex education and contraceptives provided to minor students without the knowledge or approval of parents. Or some universities requiring that students be addressed by their gender

---

[37] Emba.
[38] Francis Schaeffer, *Trilogy*, 254.
[39] James Q. Wilson, *On Character*, 191.

pronoun preference: he or she, or even they or "ze."[40] Or potential jail time for health care workers in California who repeatedly use the wrong pronoun for elderly transgender patients.[41]

Pluralism allows each of us to contend for our values, and out of that contention emerges a consensus we can agree to live by. That's the beauty of pluralism. It doesn't mean extinguishing ideas; it means contending for them and attempting to find a practical truth out of the consensus. Pluralism looks for unity on the basis of compromise and consensus. You can keep your beliefs; you just can't claim all of them, all the time.

In contrast, today the entrenched elitist minority is "looking for unity on the basis of uniformity."[42] This is the polite way to put it. The more direct and factual description is this mobilized minority demonizes those they disagree with, so they can "justifiably" destroy them. I presume they don't want the competition because they are afraid they would lose in the marketplace of ideas. It appears that large segments of the media (e.g., network and cable news, national newspapers) are a part of this devolution and are using their informational monopoly to falsely claim majority support for the relativistic viewpoint that all ideas are considered equal, valid, and justified, except, of course, those who disagree with their autonomous viewpoint. This minority seeks unity based on acquiescence and subjugation. You can't keep your beliefs and you can't claim them if they conflict with the elitist agenda.

Part of this crisis may have come about because we have forgotten that life is a story with multiple characters, not a competition to see which one group or person can win. Our stories are told in our sacred scripture; in our history; in our movies, plays, and operas; in our books; in our videos; in our comedy; and in our yarns. As author Daniel Levitin has said, "We are a storytelling species, and a social species, easily swayed by the opinions of others ... Our brains are built to make stories as they take in the vastness

[40] Lindsey Bever, "Students were told to select gender pronouns. One chose 'His Majesty' to protest 'absurdity,'" *Washington Post*, October 7, 2017, https://www.washingtonpost.com/news/education/wp/2016/10/07/a-university-told-students-to-select-their-gender-prounouns-one-chose-his-majesty/?utm_term=.40f34ffdec7fa.

[41] Brooke Singman, "New California law allows jail time for using wrong gender pronoun, sponsor denies that would happen," Fox News, October 9, 2017, http://www.foxnews.com/politics/2017/10/09/new-california-law -allows-jail-time-for-using-wrong-transgender,pronoun-sponsor-denied-that-would-happen.html.

[42] Francis Schaeffer, *Trilogy*, 230.

of the world with billions of events happening every second."[43] Stories require an audience. Indeed, they are not fully real or enjoyed until we are able to share them with others. Stories let us in on what we all know but seldom admit: that we play multiple parts in our personal dramas before we our released from this life. We become intellectually helpless when we predominately focus on ourselves and stop experiencing, creating, and sharing our stories. As Allan Bloom commented some thirty years ago, "Country, religion, family, ideas of civilization, all the sentimental and historical forces that stood between cosmic infinity and the individual, providing some notion of a place within the whole, have been rationalized and have lost their compelling force. America is experienced not as a common project but as a framework within which people are only individuals, where they are left alone."[44]

Intellectual helplessness is also created in a community setting when we see ourselves primarily as individuals rather than a whole. Take, for instance, the Black Lives Matter movement. Of course, black lives matter. It is not because any one race of people is special but because we are all children of God and therefore everyone matters. When I smell and taste a freshly baked cookie, I don't say, "Wow, the brown or white sugar is fantastic." I say, "This cookie is incredible." Deconstructing the cookie is unnecessary. Similarly, deconstructing humanity by race is inane, exhausting, counterproductive, and potentially dangerous. It's a demand for a separate and distinct identity, not universal rights for all races. It insists on respect for a specific race of people, not simply for a person. Separating out individual races only opens the door for arguments of preference, competition, and exclusion, where none was intended or helpful. Martin Luther King famously proclaimed, "I have a dream that my four little children will one day live in a nation where they will not be judged by the color of their skin but by the content of their character."

Intellectual helplessness in a group setting also comes about when mobs are formed. Mob psychology encourages anarchical behavior as it falsely projects the notion that the mob's sentiments are widely shared and presents opportunities for its participants to avoid individual responsibility. The Founding Fathers were concerned about how easy it was to stir up a group

---

[43] Daniel Levitin, *Weaponized Lies: How to Think Clearly in the Post-Truth Era* (New York: Dutton Publishers, 2016), 123.

[44] Bloom, *The Closing of the American Mind*, 85.

of intellectually helpless people, so they chose a republic governed by elected representatives rather than a pure democracy governed by the masses. Today we need to be concerned about the flash mobs of mediocre elites expunging free speech and debate on college campuses; cavalierly calling for impeachment of sitting presidents; and trying, convicting, and punishing people by media rather than by due process in a boardroom or courthouse.

Given the potential abuses of the collective, out of necessity, we must lovingly check each other. This is institutionalized in America through the concept of checks and balances in our three branches of government: executive, legislative, and judiciary. The trick is not to do it in a heavy-handed, better-than-thou approach, but rather as a fellow pilgrim trying to help another voyager become a better person. As C. S. Lewis said, "It is hard enough, even with the best will in the world, to be just. It is hard, under the pressure of haste, uneasiness, ill-temper, self-complacency, and conceit, even to continue intending justice. Power corrupts; the 'insolence of office' will creep in. We see it so clearly in our superiors; is it unlikely that our inferiors see it in us?"[45]

The Philosophy of Religion

Practically, one's philosophy of religion (i.e., faith, creed, belief, conviction) boils down to a decision regarding the previous two sections: the choice of a philosophy of us or a philosophy of me. It is the proverbial fork in the road in which everything else rests. If one chooses a philosophy of us, one is open to certain kinds of ideological and religious frameworks to cast allegiance, and to guide one's thoughts and actions in a collective setting. If one chooses a philosophy of me, it takes one down a narrower path where thoughts, decisions, and affiliations are motivated by what one personally gets out of relationships.

It shouldn't take long to discern that a stout self-religion can quickly lead to all kinds of situations where intellectual helplessness is revealed in the petri dishes of our flowering selves. Eyes directed inward miss all the joys and obstacles outward. It results in riding the bumper cars of life all the day long. Here are some examples of taking the "self-fork" creates significant intellectual obstacles:

---

[45] C. S. Lewis, *Christian Reflections* (Grand Rapids, MI: William B. Eerdmans Publishing Company, 1967), Kindle edition, 120.

- excluding other, potentially better points of view
- retrofitting thoughts and communication modalities (words, research, history) to align with one's personal desires
- bringing about one's desires by unrestrained license, which brings not freedom but repression of others and slavery to those desires
- conflicting desires between individuals results in continuous turmoil and polarization
- inability to see a reason and thus the motivation to help others
- believing the narcissistic magic that just saying something makes it so
- viewing other people as servants to one's ends
- relegating oneself to finding happiness and meaning without a known location, map, or compass
- needing constant personal reaffirmation
- dismissing the need for self-examination and exacerbating one's infinite capacity for self-rationalization and self-delusion
- believing that one can handle complete power and authority wisely and competently amid corrupting influences
- reaching conclusions without the prerequisite humility or caution required to offset human nature
- resenting things and people that stand in the way of self-aggrandizement (e.g., sacrifice, virtue)
- punishing those who disagree

The contrasting philosophy of us also has its own brushes with intellectual helplessness, but in a different way. It originates from the issue of having choices. Choices require differentiating between options. And the differences matter. Many people today take the "us" turnoff on the freeway and believe they have done their part. At that point they stop thinking, believing they are home free, as all future choices at that point are equally as good. However, in the supermarket of religious or community organizations, not all brands taste the same or are filled with the same nutrients. One must squeeze each tomato in the bin to find the best one. Logically, all religions and community organizations can be wrong, but they cannot all be right. Intellectual helplessness pushes us to believe that exclusiveness is wrong, that anyone or anything that claims to have the truth is arrogant and separatist. But that view is limiting and false, not to mention ironically exclusive. One plus one is two, not three, four, or five. Is it bad for the answer "two" to claim exclusivity? The issue is not really with the claim but with its accuracy and enforcement. I offer you the answer "two" for your sake; but you can choose "four" and find out the hard way that it is not the way to go. Then when you come back, you will be more open to rediscussing the answer "two." In a free country, we can choose, learn, and get back on the right road. In an authoritative structure, you get lima beans and must lima-like it.

Intellectual helplessness is also created within a philosophy of us when the government takes actions and the media takes positions that contradict America's national motto, thereby chipping away at meta-narratives that bind us as a people. In 1954, Congress added the words "under God" to the oath or pledge of allegiance to the United States.[46] In 1956, Congress passed by joint resolution, and President Eisenhower signed into law, the declaration that the official motto of the United States is: "In God We Trust."[47] Yet, in 2017, a high school district in Georgia issued an edict banning all athletic coaches from participating in *student-initiated* prayer.[48] And some media outlets have taken to "prayer shaming,"[49] mocking people of faith for praying for those who were slain during the San Bernardino, California, and Texas Sutherland Church shootings.[50]

Fortunately, our country's Declaration of Independence helps keep us mission-centric. Job one for every US citizen is to protect our Creator-given unalienable rights through the ordered institutions of liberty. Making philosophy-of-us choices based on freedom (not license) keeps us on a solid foundation.

---

[46] Wikipedia, https://en.wikipedia.org/wiki/Pledge_of_Allegiance.

[47] Wikipedia, https://en.wikipedia.org/wiki/In_God_We_Trust.

[48] Todd Starnes, "School District Orders Coaches to Stop Bowing Heads in Prayer," November 7, 2017, https://www.toddstarnes.com/column/school-districts-orders-coaches-to-stop-bowing-heads-in-prayer.

[49] Emma Green, "Prayer Shaming After a Mass Shooting in San Bernardino," *The Atlantic*, December 2, 2015, https:///www.theatlantic.com/politics/archive/2015/12/prayer-gun-mass-shootings-san-bernardino-4185631/.

[50] Tammy Bruce, "Mocking people who pray in response to shock and suffering is obscene and corrupt," Fox News, November 8, 2017, http://www.foxnews.com/opinion/2017/11/08/tammy-bruce-people-who-pray-in-response-to-shock-and-suffering-is-obscene-and-corrupt.

The Philosophies of Evil and Suffering

I include a brief discussion of the philosophy of evil and suffering because it is such an everyday part of life, and one that we all struggle with. It is an area rife for outbreaks of intellectual helplessness.

Evil

Let me jump right in and emphatically state that there is evil in this world, and we all experience pain and suffering. Evil can be viewed as the intentional carrying out of acts that directly violate the peaceful design of life. It is rebellion against a created order. It is hate instead of love, exploitation instead of stewardship, dishonesty instead of truthfulness, murder instead of nurturing, sabotage instead of encouragement, ugliness instead of beauty, manipulation instead of persuasion, disloyalty instead of fidelity, and corruption instead of decency. When we deny the existence of evil, we become intellectually helpless, and help it metastasize. Consider the following examples.

Let's start with the existence of evil as it relates to mass murder. Anyone who has lived through the twentieth century has learned of evil up close and personal. It was by far the deadliest century per the numbers of people slaughtered for genocidal, ideological, and other irrational reasons. These are *some* of the century's most deadly atrocities:

- Chinese "Great Leap Forward" under Mao Zedong: estimates are between 18 to 55 million were slaughtered
- Soviet Union "forced famine" under Joseph Stalin: 7 million slaughtered
- Nazi Holocaust under Adolph Hitler: 6 million slaughtered
- Cambodian genocide under Pol Pot: 2 million slaughtered
- North Korea under Kim Il Sung: 1.6 million slaughtered or imprisoned
- Armenian genocide under Turkish Ottoman Empire: 1.5 million slaughtered
- Bangladesh genocide by Pakistan: 1.5 million slaughtered
- Rwanda genocide by Hutu government: 800,000 slaughtered
- Bosnia-Herzegovina: 200,000 slaughtered

Let the impact of these numbers (that correspond to human beings) sink in for a bit, and realize that it doesn't include our recent twenty-first century tragedies in Sudan, Afghanistan, Syria, North Korea, New York (9/11), San Bernardino, Orlando, Boston, Paris, Manchester, Nice, Barcelona, Brussels, and others being actively planned as I write. It is catastrophically ironic that these mind-numbing atrocities occurred during a period in which humankind was at the height of its intellectual hubris. For some time now, the collective world has well been on its way from theism to naturalism as the dominant worldview. Intellectuals have been espousing humans as being the center of the universe, declaring that we are smart enough and virtuous enough to create our own common good. Humanism, secularism, and relativism were the vehicles used to bus us toward this desired autonomy. The artificial delusion of the sufficiency of humankind was peddled while the above mass slaughters were being committed over and over on every continent, making the current outbreak of fake news look trivial. N. T. Wright has a great deal to say about our intellectual helplessness connected to evil in his novel *Evil and the Justice of God*.[51] Some of his conclusions are the following:

- Evil is not just a philosophical problem but a practical one.
- Politicians and the media have tried to live as though evil wasn't so much of a problem after all, and they are having to wake up after the fact to admit that evil is a four-letter word.
- This state of affairs has led to three things in particular that I see as characterizing the new problem of evil. First, we ignore evil when it doesn't hit us in the face. Second, we are surprised by evil when it does. Third, we react in immature and dangerous ways as a result.

Second, let's briefly discuss evil as it relates to efforts to destroy freedom. Freedom is an unalienable right and a primary goal of humankind. America has three written charters of freedom: its Declaration of Independence, US Constitution, and Bill of Rights. In the Declaration of Independence, it is the second of three unalienable rights: life, liberty, and the pursuit of happiness; in the Constitution, the preamble states that one of the primary reasons it was created was to "secure the blessings of liberty

---

[51] N. T. Wright, *Evil and the Justice of God* (Downers Grove, IL: IVP Books, 2011), Kindle edition, chapters 1, 2.

to ourselves and our posterity"; and the Bill of Rights provides the specific freedoms franchised to each citizen. The first freedom listed in the Bill of Rights is one of religious freedom of conscience: "Congress shall make no law respecting an establishment of religion, or prohibiting the free exercise thereof." It is the first right because it is foundational. Without the right of conscience to think, act, and speak as one chooses, no other rights are possible. Given the unalienable nature of liberty and its enshrinement in all three of our charters, efforts to remove it from our culture can be legitimately considered an act of evil because it is a deliberate attempt to remove from a person what a "Creator" has bestowed.

An interesting twist on evil as it relates to freedom is the context in which freedom must exist. Freedom is the responsibility of the people and its government. As Thomas Jefferson famously stated, "The price of freedom is eternal vigilance." Democratic government recognizes each person's right to freedom and is entrusted with enforcing its equal application. But, as cultural observer Os Guinness points out, "Freedom faces a fundamental moral challenge. Freedom requires order and therefore restraint, yet the only restraint that does not contradict freedom is self-restraint ..."[52] Therefore, in order for freedom to be sustained from generation to generation, the people and their government must collaborate. It is evil when either the government takes actions that unjustifiably deny freedom to its citizens, or the people do not keep their commitment of consenting to be governed in an orderly fashion by giving up some of these predesignated freedoms.

Pain and Suffering

Now let's briefly examine our intellectual helplessness regarding pain and suffering. First, "the impulse to avoid suffering and spare loved ones the pain of watching is more than understandable. It's human. But the idea that we can and should go to any lengths to avoid pain and suffering, at all costs, assumes that nothing good can come from pain and suffering. And that just isn't true."[53] Although we wouldn't wish for it, or order up a side of pain for ourselves, most people realize there are several benefits that come

---

[52] Os Guinness, *A Free People's Suicide: Sustainable Freedom and the American Future* (Downers Grove, IL: IVP Press, 2012), 20.

[53] Warren Cole Smith and John Stonestreet, *Restoring All Things* (Grand Rapids, MI: Baker Books, 2015), 150.

from pain and suffering that we might not otherwise experience. Some of these are as follows:

C. S. Lewis:
- "The perception of ourselves which we have in moments of shame must be the only true one ... In trying to extirpate shame we have broken down one of the ramparts of the human spirit."[54]
- "Pain is God's megaphone to rouse a deaf world ... troubling them by warning them in advance of an insufficiency that one day will undo them."[55]

Benjamin Franklin:
- "Nothing brings more pain than too much pleasure; nothing brings more bondage than too much liberty."

Dallas Willard:
- "Moral development of personality is possible only in a world of genuine freedom."[56]

Michael Novak:
- "Suffering is testing whether humans can remain faithful to God's purposes in creating them—whether we will show grace under pressure ... The drama of their [Founding Fathers] lives can be simply stated: will they exemplify under pressure a noble use of liberty, as their forebears did?"[57]

Second, our intellectual helplessness in this area is multiplied by the false but commonly held belief that humans are basically good and just need the right social institutions to make the good society. The purging statistics of tens of millions of people should suffice as solid rebuttal against this age-old claim. Famed journalist Malcolm Muggeridge has lamented, "We have forgotten that most empirically verifiable (though most denied)

---

[54] C. S. Lewis, *The Problem of Pain* (New York: HarperOne, 1940).
[55] Lewis, 91.
[56] Dallas Willard, *Renewing the Christian Mind: Essays, Interviews, and Talks* (New York: HarperOne, 2016), Kindle edition, chapter 30.
[57] Novak, *On Two Wings*, 11.

part of human experience—the depravity of man."[58] The human condition is not an "either/or" but an "and" condition. The struggle between good and evil is basic to human nature both on an individual and collective basis. Take for instance, the history of the Nobel prizes. Swede Alfred Noble made his fortune inventing dynamite, believing it would end all wars. As a way of making amends for the many negative outcomes of this false presumption, he funded annual awards to "those who, during the preceding year, shall have conferred the greatest benefit to mankind" in five categories: physics, chemistry, physiology or medicine, literature, and peace.[59]

Third is the false idea that we can stop the dysfunctional behavior that causes pain and suffering anytime we want to, solely on our own power. Again, there is far too much evidence to say otherwise. Humankind isn't smart enough, good enough, or willing enough, on a consistent basis, to make this happen. We need help. We need a concerted effort in moving toward kindness on a consistent enough basis to make it a habit, rather than a periodic write-off on our annual "good-come" taxes.

Fourth, intellectual helplessness related to pain and suffering is increased when we unsuccessfully try to snuff out any feelings of legitimate guilt. In a recent *New York Times* editorial entitled "The Strange Persistence of Guilt," columnist David Brooks discusses the paradox in the pursuit of a guilt-free existence through easygoing relativism. "This 'strange persistence' of guilt leaves contemporary Westerners living in the worst of all possible worlds. Secularism and relativism have not liberated them from the need to 'feel morally justified,' nor has it freed them from feelings of guilt. What it has done is to deprive people of the means to do anything meaningful about their sense of guilt … We have no clear framework or set of rituals to guide us in our quest for goodness."[60] The reason? Author Eric Metaxas postulates, "because if there were true forgiveness and redemption, there would have to be an acknowledgment that there was something that needed to be forgiven and something about us that needs to be redeemed."[61] And that would debunk the notion that humankind is good enough and smart enough to create a utopian society.

---

[58] Malcolm Muggeridge, as paraphrased in *Can Man Live Without God* by Ravi Zacharias (Dallas, TX: Word Publishing, 1994), 40.

[59] Nobel Prize, https://www.nobelprize.org.

[60] David Brooks, "The Strange Persistence of Guilt," *New York Times*, March 31, 2107.

[61] Eric Metaxas, "No Sin, No Forgiveness Either," BreakPoint, April 20, 2107, http://breakping.org./2017/04/breakpoint-no-sin-no-forgiveness-either/.

Fifth, our difficulty with offering legitimate forgiveness makes it difficult to stop the hurt cycle. Most often we deal with forgiveness from extreme positions. One extreme is to adopt the approach of never forgiving. That approach ironically keeps the victim in a state of constant mental torment on multiple levels: the continual rehashing of the pain, the exhausting and convicting planning for revenge, and anxiety over the possible consequences from implementing any planned retaliatory actions. The other extreme is to give the perpetrator a pass on accountability, in which he/she does not have to acknowledge their wrong, or suffer any consequences that would extinguish the behavior in the future. Both extremes are counterproductive. A better way, according to N. T. Wright, is to have "a settled determination to name evil and shame it; without that there is, after all, nothing to forgive. To follow that, forgiveness means that we are equally determined to do everything within our power to resume an appropriate relationship with the offender after the evil has been dealt with. Finally, forgiveness means that we have settled it in our minds that we shall not allow this evil to determine the sort of people we shall then become … Forgiveness doesn't mean 'I really don't mind,' or 'it didn't really matter.' I did mind and it did matter, otherwise there wouldn't be anything to forgive at all, merely something to adjust my attitude about."[62]

Intellectual Helplessness in Family

> *My complaint of the anti-domestic drift is that it is unintelligent. People do not know what they are doing; because they do not know what they are undoing.*
> —G. K. CHESTERTON

So how is your extended family? Nobody has a perfect one, right? Is Uncle Bubba still hiding from space invaders? Is Aunt Ruth still gossiping about family secrets? Is Roger still chasing ants with a magnifying glass? Does Willamette still think she's a Flintstone? Fortunately, this section is not about family peccadillos. But it is about a more precarious topic: how some of our views on the institution of the family are contributing to our intellectual helplessness.

As identified at the beginning of this chapter, for many people, the primacy of family has been nudged to a lower rung on the moral-cultural

---

[62] Wright, *Evil and the Justice of God*, chapter 5.

ladder. This is a consequential mistake for several practical reasons. One such reason is the critical roles or mission assigned specifically to the traditional family:

- procreation to ensure the future of civilization
- training to civilize, socialize, and educate children on the moral-cultural fundamentals of life
- community development to work with other families to develop a civil and productive community structure and activities
- stability and public safety to take young men and women off the street, domesticating them with family, vocational, and civic responsibilities

Since the beginning of human history, these roles have been assigned to families for a reason: it works. In a family, parents share a deep emotional, mental, and physical bond that allows them to journey through life's ups and downs together. In that environment, they procreate for both the continuation of the species and for a further opportunity to share and bind themselves together through a joint creation. They participate in creating the future. In a sense, they form an ongoing (family) corporation. The children are civilized and socialized by the two people who love them most and want the best for them. In this training environment, families provide the original organizational structure where children learn about authority, how to deal with individual idiosyncrasies, and their respective roles and responsibilities for their adult lives. As they journey out of the nest, they take with them an inculcated moral-cultural DNA to productively manage themselves within the context of a larger community where they must fit in and survive.

This is the original and best model. To be sure, there are other models that work in varying degrees, and each of us in a democratic society is entirely free to choose an alternative to the traditional model. But just as with most things in life, the imitation usually is not as good as the original. Study after study and common sense tell us this is true. There is no better model for raising a well-adjusted child than having a mom and dad in a stable environment. There are known special and complementary roles that a mother and a father play with a child. Kids need both. There are other ways to raise a family, but there are not better ways. Consider the conclusive research of Mexican sociologist Fernando Pliego who has studied the sociological evidence of whether the current multiple "family" structures produce the same level of well-being. Pliego accumulated data from 351 studies in thirteen democratic countries on five different continents and found the results to be remarkably consistent. In an article detailing study results, author Steven W. Mosher noted, "Nearly all demonstrate that where a father and a mother are living together with their natural or adopted children, there are tremendous benefits. The members of these traditional families enjoy better physical health, less mental illness, higher incomes, and steadier employment. They and their children live in better housing, enjoy more loving and cooperative relationships, and report less physical and/ or sexual violence. Moreover, when the bonds between parents and children are more positive, drug, alcohol, and tobacco use is lower, children are better socialized and cooperative, they commit fewer crimes, and they perform better in school ... Professor Pliego concluded that the natural family was far superior to other forms. He found that 89.4 percent of the studies concluded that intact families produced a higher level of well-being that other family types."[63] This truth often freaks out some people, but the anger and emotion of the traditional formula being contrary to what one desires does not change the reality of it. And it is not hateful to recognize the truth for what it is. We become intellectually helpless as a nation when we "pretend, as many governments do, that all family structures are created equal."[64]

I'm wading into this controversial pool not because I have a death wish from the elitist minority, but because it is absolutely essential that we respectfully debate the issue of family on sagacious grounds to determine if our biases contribute to our intellectual helplessness. If "the heart wants what the heart wants" because it makes sense from an economic (business), political (government), and social (moral-cultural) perspective, then, by all means, let's open the floodgates of public institutions and the public purse. If it doesn't, however, for democracy's sake, while we allow for and do not discriminate against people for making their own choices, let's not divert scarce public resources from essential needs to parochial wants. I do not love my neighbor less if I say no when he asks to use my water spigot to fill his pool.

From an *economic* perspective, it is important to acknowledge that

---

[63] Steven W. Mosher, "351 Studies from 13 Nations Prove Benefits of Households with a Dad, Mom and Their Kids," Aleteia, January 20, 2015, https://aleteia.org/2015/01/20/351-studies-from-13-nations-prove-benefits-of-households-with-a-dad-mom-and-their-kids.
[64] Mosher.

there is a finite amount of public resources available for an unlimited number of requests. This means that unavoidable choices must be made on what gets funded with public dollars. Tough decisions must be made on what distribution will provide the most positive, tangible impact to the most people. Analogously, that means public laws should reflect, and public money should be spent on, the best and most effective alternatives. In the past, special rights and privileges were given exclusively to the institution of traditional marriage because it is the most effective means of procreation, the most effective way to rear children, and the most effective way to ensure domestic stability. We short-circuit the prudent use of scarce public resources when we divert them to lesser alternatives. Take, for instance, the federal government's funding of $554 million to Planned Parenthood in 2016,[65] an organization that engages in sex-selective abortions in which parents can choose to abort female babies. *Newsweek* reported last year that sex-selective abortions are on the rise in United States.[66] "So-called 'family planning' clinics like those affiliated with Planned Parenthood are helping women kill their unborn daughters ... Last year, after the state of Indiana passed a law banning sex-selective abortion, a federal judge granted a permanent injunction against the law at the request of ... Planned Parenthood."[67]

Again, I am not proposing taking away anyone's right to choose an alternative, or making a moral judgment about that alternative. I'm simply suggesting that alternatives to traditional marriage do not provide a more productive outcome. Since opening Pandora's box on what constitutes a family, we have created a seemingly unlimited number of possible options that cannot all be funded. When the government says yes to one suboptimal alternative, on what basis would it say no to others? So, economically, it is prudent to fund the alternative(s) that historically produces the best outcomes.

From a *political* perspective, democratic government operates most efficiently when it allows the most effective alternative of the traditional family to fulfill its millennium-old role. If multiple, competing models of

---

[65] *Planned Parenthood 2015-2016 Annual Report*, 28.

[66] Kelsey Harkness, "Sex Selection Abortions Are Rife in the U.S.," *Newsweek*, April 14, 2016, http://www.newsweek.com/sex-selection-abortion-rife-us-447403.

[67] John Stonestreet and G. Shane Morris, "Planned Parenthood vs. Little Girls," BreakPoint, October 26, 2017, http://breakpoint.org/2017/10/breakpoint-planned-parenthood-vs-little-girls/.

the family are artificially recognized as equivalent, it creates inefficient, subsidized competition. The competition and dividing of resources invariably weakens the gold standard and invites other influences to try to fill the voids created. One such influence is the state. When a family is unable, or abdicates its role, to civilize, socialize, and educate in the moral-cultural arena, which is happening in many places in our country, tragic consequences become more frequent and cannot be ignored for public health and safety reasons. In response, the state either enters the picture as an ill-suited savior attempting to bring order to chaos, or cheerfully to expand its power base and ideological philosophies.

The strong family is a natural check and balance to the power of the state. Without the diverse nature of individual families built around unifying traditional values, the state can attempt to legislate and enforce each political administration's idea of morals and cultural values under the force of law. It is not an exaggeration to suggest that this is already happening. The state—through legislation, public education, and the media—has attempted to make certain former familial taboos sacrosanct and certain former staples anathema. Take, for example, the Illinois Department of Children and Family Services (DCFS). It has appointed a LGBTQ czar who enforces new "enhanced" policies that encourage children under their care toward LGBTQ identities. According to Mary Hasson of the Federalist, "The State of Illinois will not tolerate 'exposing' the vulnerable children in its care to people who believe human beings are either male or female and cannot 'become' the other ... The new DCFS policies are less about safety and well-being and more about using state power to 'overrule' basic, empirical (and common sense) truths about human beings and replace them with ideological assertions that validate adult feelings rather than benefit children ... The state's LGBTQ czar oversees the sexual orientation and gender identity of *all* children and youth under the state's care. Every child in the system is given 'LGBTQ appropriate' sexual health resources and put through LGBTQ-orientated sexual health education ... DCFS says that the child's right to privacy prevents disclosing the child's sexual orientation or gender identity to *anyone*, including family members and other staff, unless the child gives permission."[68] The state is the wrong parent for this task

---

[68] Mary Hasson, "Illinois Purges Social Workers and Foster Families Who Don't 'Facilitate' Transgenderism," the Federalist, May 30, 2017. http://thefederalist.com/2017/05/30/illinois-purges-social-workers-foster-families-dont-facilitate-transgenderism.

and is vocationally out of its depth. Such roles were meant for philosophy and for family who know and love those they raise, not for a distant and less-than-caring government that rules over those it monitors.

From a *social* perspective, the modern mantra of unlimited choice to meet any of one's desires appeals to the ego and as a fix for the addictive habits of self-indulgence. However, it does not pass the smell test of what's best regarding the family. Alternatives to the traditional family are not equivalent. First, no model other than a man and a woman can "provide for procreation except through a petri dish."[69] Take for instance a 2010 study by the Institute for American Values in which 485 adult offspring of sperm donors were surveyed. The study cites several troubling findings among donor offspring compared to those raised by biological parents:

- They are twice as likely to struggle with substance abuse and delinquency.
- They are 1.5 times more likely to have battled depression.
- On average, donor offspring hurt more, were more confused, felt more isolated from their families, and wondered who their families really were.
- Nearly half were disturbed that their sperm donor was involved in a commercial transaction without any thought of them personally.
- About half confessed trust issues after being lied to about their origins.
- More than half said they wonder if they are related to people who resemble them.
- Almost as many feared being attracted to or having sexual relations with someone to whom they were unknowingly related.[70]

Second, what public good do the alternatives to traditional marriage provide other than saying yes to a personal desire? Is it better for children to have two moms or two dads? Is it more efficient for continuation of the species to have alternative models? Is it more cost effective for society? Does it promote needed unity in the culture, or does it add to an

[69] Charles Colson, *My Final Word: Holding Tight to the Issues that Matter Most* (Grand Rapids, MI: Zondervan, 2015), 140.
[70] Sonja Corbitt, "My Daddy's Name Is Donor: New Study on Children of 'Reproductive Technologies,'" Catholic Online, June 24, 2010, http://www.catholic.org/news/national/story/.php?id=37096.

already polarized society? Do those who espouse change allow those who disagree to keep and live out their beliefs? Working the political system to ineffectively and inefficiently support an endless number of fractional personal-preference experiments does not fulfill the goals of the common or the good. It just makes it harder for the tried-and-true model to be supported and administered.

Thus, the assault on the traditional family is unintelligent. I once heard a story about a new homeowner in a rural area who decided, upon moving in, that he would remove the old, short stone wall that appeared randomly placed on his property. As the heavy equipment came onto the property to begin removal of the wall, an elderly man came by and asked the owner what was going on. The owner said he wanted to get rid of the unsightly wall. The neighbor asked the new owner if he knew why the wall was built in the first place. The owner said he didn't; he just knew he didn't like how it looked. The neighbor politely suggested to the new owner that perhaps he should learn why the fence was built before he tore it down, and then he walked away. Perhaps we should saturate ourselves with the reasons for the traditional family—and its importance to society and a stable democratic governance—before we go tearing or watering it down. And we should certainly analyze the potential/actual consequences of any proposed/implemented changes to any foundational institution. The record is disturbing.[71] This is another example of extreme hubris in which the desires of a current generation irrationally presume an advanced level of wisdom over and above that of millennial wisdom and practicality.

We should also consider the possibility that because the arguments for the alternatives to the traditional family are tenuous and difficult to make on logical and practical grounds, perhaps the only way an elitist minority can succeed is to (1) encourage mad rushes toward autonomous behaviors that intentionally do not provide sufficient time for deliberation and reflection, or (2) become the malicious minority and falsely claim that any arguments against their position are based solely on hate. Part of becoming a competent parent is being able to say no, even when your kids hate you for it. If under intense pressure, society collectively succumbs

[71] David Sergeant, "What's changed in Britain since same-sex marriage?", *Spectator Australia*, September 7, 2017, https://www.spectator.com.au/2017/09/whats-changed-in-britain-since-same-sex-marriage/.

to lesser positions because of the fear of being labeled hateful people, we render ourselves intellectually helpless in pursuing and maintaining better alternatives.

Intellectual Helplessness in Education

The whole purpose of education is to turn mirrors into windows.
—Sydney J. Harris

Among rational people, there is almost no need to debate the existence of intellectual helplessness in today's educational climate. Current events are the best apologetics.

The traditional mission of education is to:

*   Discover true knowledge.

    The key to discovering knowledge is identifying those things that conform to reality. The next part of the quest is to seek coherence by identifying where diverse individual subjects fit together as a whole (*unity* amid *diversity*). These discoveries apply to both the mental (*thinking*) and emotional (*feeling*) realms. Without a clear *why,* it is difficult to present a compelling *what* or an effective *how.* True knowledge explains both the cold reality of what is tangibly there (head knowledge) and satisfies and accurately explains the soul's intangible deepest longings (heart knowledge).

*   Develop the whole person.

    The word *integrity* comes from the Latin adjective *integer,* meaning whole or complete. In this context, a person of integrity is a whole and complete person. True knowledge is the fuel that feeds the development of the whole person. In this process, a person learns to think clearly about the world and engage it deeply when and where he/she can. A whole person discovers what is good in a culture so he/she can promote, protect, and celebrate it, and what is detrimental in a culture so it can be discontinued. The whole person also learns how to appropriately address an issue: how to research, interview, separate fact from fiction, consider all sources, and provide an objective, comprehensive, balanced, and qualified analysis.

• Prepare for a vocation.

Love is charity in action. Service is education in action. Put them together and we really have something: good works from a grateful heart. As quoted at the outset of this section, "The whole purpose of education is to turn mirrors into windows." While we are being educated, we look inward; when we graduate, we look outward. When we are young, we take food out of our parent's refrigerator; when we are older, we put food into it.

Our intellectual helplessness in education results from mission failure. Take, for instance, fulfilling the role of *discovering true knowledge.* People naturally search for coherence in life, and education is the primary way society provides it. But on many college campuses, discovering true knowledge is like trying to find Waldo.[72] Instead of encouraging the treasure hunt for knowledge in all locations, many universities wall off opportunities for the search in precisely those areas that might make the most difference. It's like the dad who says to his teenage daughter's potential suitor, "Sure, you can date my daughter. You just will have to do it between the hours of noon and two in the afternoon, only on Sundays after church, and with me tagging along." Many of today's universities are not trying to encourage discovery and testing, but acceptance of a status quo they create. This approach does not produce a customized cadre of clear and rational thinkers, but an assembly line of one make and model of thought. Take, for example, the following accounts:

• Princeton Theological Seminary announced Presbyterian pastor Timothy Keller as the recipient of its 2017 Abraham Kuyper award for excellence in Reformed Theology, and then the seminary rescinded its award after people complained that Keller did not agree with Presbyterian orthodoxy on such subjects as women's

---

[72] Where's Wally?, published in the United States as Where's Waldo?, is a British series of children's books created by English illustrator Martin Handford. The object of the game is to find Waldo hidden among dozens of illustrated people doing a variety of amusing things in a given location.

ordination and LGBT issues. In response, Princeton's conservative professor Robert George and Harvard's liberal professor Cornel West came together to support Keller and freedom of thought and expression, stating, "It is all too common these days for people to try to immunize from criticism opinions that happen to be dominant in their particular communities," and might it "not be better to listen respectfully and try to learn from a speaker with whom I disagree? Might it better serve the cause of truth-seeking to engage the speaker in frank civil discussion?"[73]

- A University of Washington Tacoma's Writing Center issued a press release telling students that expecting Americans to use proper grammar perpetuates racism.[74]

- Litigation has been filed against Cal State University San Marcos for allegedly violating its First Amendment obligations by using mandatory student activity fees in a discriminatory manner, allowing $296,000 in funding for two student community centers administered by the university (i.e., Gender Equity Center, LGBTQA Pride Center), and only $38,629 for one hundred other student groups, many of which promote differing points of view.[75]

There are many reasons for the reluctance by some in academia to meet their obligation to doggedly pursue true knowledge. One of the reasons, according to Professor Phillip Johnson, is that "What went wrong in science is that influential scientists became so devoted to ideological causes, including those that expanded the power and prestige of science, that they neglected their primary duty to test all theories impartially, including those from which they derive wealth and prestige."[76] In 2011, Professor John Ioannidis, director of the Prevention Research Center at Stanford

---

[73] John Stonestreet and Roberto Rivera, "Free Speech on College Campuses—and Seminaries," BreakPoint, March 29, 2017, http://www.breakpoint.org/2017/03/free-speech-on-college-campuses-and-seminaries.
[74] Walter E. Williams, "College Campus Disgrace," Townhall, March 8, 2017, https://townhall.com/columnists/walterwilliams/2017/03/08/college-campus-disgrace-n2294631.
[75] Mike Adams, "Welcome to CSU-S&M," Townhall, May 22, 2017, https://www.townhall.com/columnists/mikeadams/2017/05/22/welcome-to-csusm-n2330051/.
[76] Phillip E. Johnson, *The Right Questions: Truth, Meaning & Public Debate* (Downers Grove, IL: InterVarsity Press, 2002), 190–191.

University School of Medicine, wrote about the epidemic of false claims in academia motivated by competition and conflicts of interest in economics, social sciences, natural sciences, and particularly in biomedicine. Ioannidis stated, "The problem begins with the public's rising expectations of science. Being human, scientists are tempted to show that they know more than they do" and "adequate safeguards against bias are lacking. Research is fragmented, competition is fierce and emphasis is often given to single studies instead of the big picture. Much research is conducted for reasons other than the pursuit of truth. Conflicts of interest abound, and they influence outcomes. In health care, research is often performed at the behest of companies that have a large financial stake in the results. Even for academics, success often hinges on publishing positive findings. The oligopoly of high-impact journals also has a distorting effect on funding, academic careers and market shares."[77]

Francis Schaeffer prophetically projected this calamity decades ago: "I do not believe for a moment that if the men back at that point of history had had the philosophy, epistemology of the modern man, there would ever have been modern science. I also think science as we have known it is going to die. I think it is going to be reduced to two things: mere technology, and another form of sociological manipulation. I do not believe for a moment that science is going to be able to continue with its objectivity once the base that brought forth science has been totally destroyed."[78]

Regarding education's second role, many educational institutions cannot *develop the whole person* because they are not a whole organization. Hypocrisy abounds at multiple levels. In several institutions, many of the positive attributes claimed by the university are knowingly false. Take these statements, for instance:

- "We value diversity and are non-discriminatory in our hiring practices." Then why are liberal professors the overwhelming majority of staff?[79]

---

[77] John P.A. Ioannidis, "An Epidemic of False Claims: Competition and conflicts of interest distort too many medical findings," *Scientific American*, June 1, 2011, https://www.scientificamerican.com/article/an-epidemic-of-false-claims/?print=true.
[78] Schaeffer, *Trilogy*, 326.
[79] Bradford Richardson, "Liberal Professors Outnumber Conservatives Nearly 12 to 1, Study Finds," *Washington Times*, October 6, 2016.

- "We value tolerance." Then why do universities create safe zones for only certain races or genders of people?[80] Why was "post-election self-care" provided to students following the election of President Trump?[81] Why do we forbid teachers from participating in student-initiated prayer?

- "We value free speech." Then why are conservative speakers not allowed to speak on some campuses? How is it an acceptable strategy for a university to exclude other points of view from students, curtailing the self-correcting process of free debate and discussion?[82]

- "We insist upon academic honesty." Then why is student cheating on the rise, less stigma being attached to it, and discipline seldom administered?[83]

- "We have high academic standards." Then why do many universities have minimum average grade requirements for students that professors must adhere to (e.g., the average grade for students in class must be a B-plus)? And why do we treat students more like customers to please, rather than students to educate?

- "We are serious about research." Then why are there several instances where researchers take liberties with the truth in the pursuit of fame, wealth, and cultural dominance?[84]

[80] Williams, "College Campus Disgrace."

[81] Armstrong Williams, "Harvard's Season of Digesting," Townhall, April 17, 2017, https://www.townhall.com/columnists/armstrongwilliams/2017/04/17/harvards-season-of-digesting.

[82] Theodore Bunker, "UC Berkeley Faculty Urge Boycott of Conservative Speakers," Newsmax, September 18, 2017, https://www.newsmax.com/PrintTemplate.aspx/"nodeid=814263.

[83] "Academic Cheating Fact Sheet," Stanford University, https://web.stanford.edu/class/engr110/cheating.html.

[84] Wikipedia, "Notable individual cases of scientific misconduct in the United States," https://en.wikipedia.org/wiki/Scientific misconduct.

- "We are here to educate our students." Then why are many universities indoctrinating rather than educating?[85]

A significant reason for the existence of hypocrisies in education is the belief by some intellectuals that they do not have to play by the rules. In this regard, nuclear scientist and professor Vinoth Ramachandra observed that "intellectuals are especially prone to self-deception, seeing themselves as the standard-bearers of the cult of originality, having emancipated themselves from all the constraints of tradition, community and obligation."[86] The grand hypocrisy of this is that some intellectuals use the rules when it suits them and ignore them when they are inconvenient. The "standards" are helpful when intellectuals need to raise money and recruit students. They are also handy for dealing with any conservative who becomes a campus nuisance. They are expendable when it causes too much work, threatens to render an unwanted conclusion, or simply gets in the way of what one wants.

Another example of failing to develop the whole person comes in the frantic pursuit of acquiring "victim" status to gain specious moral authority for one's position. Take, for example, the term *microaggression* and its proposed University of California definition, which overflows with tones of victimhood: "everyday verbal, nonverbal, and environmental slights, snubs, or insults, whether intentional or unintentional, that communicate hostile, derogatory, or negative messages to target persons based solely upon their marginalized group membership."[87] Or consider the case of professors and students at the University of Virginia who wrote their school president "to demand that she stop quoting Thomas Jefferson," the founder of the university, "because he no longer satisfied the dictates of identity politics."[88]

---

[85] Anemona Hartocollis, "College Students Protest, Alumni's Fondness Fades and Checks Shrink," *New York Times*, August 4, 2016, https://www.nytimes.com/2016/08/05/us/college-protests-alumni-donations-.html?

[86] Vinoth Ramachandra, *Subverting Global Myths* (Downers Grove, IL: InterVarsity Press, 2008), 154–155.

[87] Fred Barbash, "The war on 'microaggressions:' Has it created a 'victimhood culture' on campuses?", *Washington Post*, October 28, 2015, https://www.washingtonpost.com/news/morning-mix/wp/2015/10/28/the-war-over-words-literally-on-some-american-campuses-where-asking-where-you-are-from-is-a-microaggression/?utm_term=.3b7038f0d1a8.

[88] Toni Airaksinen, "'Victimhood culture' has taken over college campuses, alleges new book," *USA Today College*, January 23, 2017, http://college.usatoday.com/2017/01/23/no-campus-for-white-men/.

In an article entitled "Microaggression and Moral Cultures," published in the journal *Comparative Sociology,* university professors Bradley Campbell and Jason Manning believe the motive of the microaggression movement is not so much to create awareness among the offenders as to elevate the status of the offended. "When the victims publicize microaggressions, they call attention to what they see as the deviant behavior of the offenders … and call attention to their own victimization."[89] Professor Phillip Johnson agrees, observing that "the goal of political activity is to disempower the oppressors and empower the victims, often so they do some oppressing of their own. Anyone who has spent much time in one of our great universities will know what I mean. Rules that were formerly thought to be absolute, such as freedom of thought and expression, are discarded whenever the victim's interests so demand. An oppressor who says something that offends a designated victim is sentenced to sensitivity training, but the victims may abuse the oppressors all they like."[90]

Whole people mean what they say, and say what they mean, and they do not seek victimhood for the sake of using it to their advantage. To break free from this cycle, education needs to go beyond its current concentration on grades, graduation rates, forced ideology, and making universities "happy campuses" where students feel psychologically protected from perceived intolerant or offensive ideas. They must return to a traditional mission of developing people of integrity. Students should be *better,* not just more educated or information filled. The best universities used to do this. Take for instance the content of the seals of the big three Ivy League schools: Harvard (Veritas), Princeton (Vet and Nov Testamentum), and Yale (an open book with Hebrew words). It is interesting to note that many elementary schools still give a grade for citizenship while at the university level, this would be considered passé in most institutions.

When we examine education's role of *preparing students for a vocation*, many students today are conditioned in a manner that makes it more difficult for their success in the workplace, not easier. Take, for instance, the following common educational rituals and compare them to their applicability in the workplace:

---

[89] Barbash, *Washington Post.*
[90] Johnson, *The Right Questions*, 122.

- You don't have to go to class if you don't want to. There will be no consequences to your grade if you are still able to produce by reading the books and getting class notes.
- If you don't agree with the professor's viewpoint, you can ignore it.
- It's okay to be inadequately prepared for class.
- You can have a certain amount of poor grammar and punctuation in your reports; it won't be held against you.
- Students do not recognize the coherence among academic disciplines and thereby miss important discoveries that would profit the university.
- Texting and using the internet during class are tolerated.

Additionally, students' focus during their educational experience is typically on obtaining a degree.[91] Many strive to get the grade, not the life lesson(s). When that happens, we oftentimes produce smart idiots. They become polished book covers without meaningful content.

Intellectual Helplessness in the News Media

> *Journalism largely today consists of saying "Lord Jones is dead," to people who have never heard that Lord Jones was alive.*
> —G. K. CHESTERTON

The news media is an institution in which truth should be *stronger* than fiction. Unfortunately, for many media outlets today, the truth is on indefinite holiday. And the American public agrees. America's trust in the media has remained at historic lows for the past several years. A 2015 Gallup poll showed that only four in ten Americans trusted the mass media. In 2016, that number dropped 8 percentage points to 32 percent.[92]

Let's get back to basics: Why is there media? Because of human curiosity about the world and our anxiety about knowing about events that impact our lives. And how much, and in what ways, do we depend on media in everyday lives? To measure this question, ask yourself another question: What if, suddenly, there was no media? What impact would it have on you?

---

[91] "Academic Cheating Fact Sheet," Stanford University.
[92] Rebecca Riffkin, "America's Trust in Media Remains at Historic Low," Gallup, September 28, 2015. http://www.gallup.com/poll/185927/americans-trust-media-remain-historical-low.aspx.

Functionally? Psychologically? That's why the topic of the media has been included in the discussion of moral-cultural (social) issues.

There are at least four basic roles for media: to *inform, persuade, entertain*, or *sell*. In my university course, over the past decade, I've asked each class to list what the priority order of these roles should be versus what it currently is.

What the Roles of the News Media Should Be

Every class over the past fifteen years has agreed that the first priority of the media should be to *inform*. To properly inform the public, the news needs to be a true representation of the facts. In adequately fulfilling its role to inform the public, the media provides a critical check and balance for society. It allows citizens to make informed decisions according to their individual conscience based on factual information.

The classes then typically list *persuade* as the next priority of the media. In that pursuit, the boundaries of persuasion include identifying opinions as opinion, presenting truthful facts, placing things in their proper context, and developing reasoned arguments, all in an effort to provide an intellectually honest and persuasive case.

To *entertain* is typically the third priority chosen for the media, to provide right-brained balance to the daily grind of left-brained activities.

Lastly, the classes generally agreed that to *sell* should be the last priority of the media. While it is recognized that the media has become a business, making money is seen as a lesser priority. And this comes from business students.

The Actual Current Roles of the News Media

Unfortunately, when my classes were asked to identify the actual roles currently displayed by the news media, the priority order of the roles was entirely reversed: sell, entertain, persuade, inform. That's like a baseball player going up to the plate to hit with his glove. The results aren't pretty. The following activities serve as a guide to determining what the media considers its highest priorities:

Steven A. Danley

Priority given to the role of selling:

- Journalists consistently appear to be more concerned about their individual professional attainment, recognition, speaking time on camera, and monetary reward, rather than ensuring the reader has all the relevant facts of a story.
- Advance promotional trailers sensationalize or overstate new stories to hook the audience.
- Decisions about which stories are covered in the news are made primarily by conglomerate executives and lawyers rather than news executives.
- Advertisers have an inordinate say in what news is covered and who delivers it.
- Advertising segments appear to overshadow news content.
- Noncommittal words, such as *expect, anticipate, assume,* and *news alert,* are consistently used to lure an audience to an unbaited hook.
- There is an overaggressive focus on the assignment of blame for the occurrence of negative events.

Priority given to the role of entertaining:

- Gratuitous sex, violence, and extreme behaviors are consistently presented in the news of the day.
- The news being presented consistently appeals more to one's emotions rather than intellect.
- The newscasters and guests are more news readers and entertainers than committed and knowledgeable about their subject matter.
- News show guests typically argue, name-call, interrupt, and display emotional outbursts with the interviewers and other guests, with whom they disagree.
- Every moment of the newscast is choreographed to achieve a predetermined outcome.
- Issues appear to be manufactured, with little relevance and meaning to everyday life.
- News media personalities consistently push to appear on late-night entertainment shows to gain celebrity status.

Priority given to the role of persuading:

- News media personalities belittle those who disagree with their viewpoints rather than asking more in-depth questions to understand the rationale of the dissenter.
- News media personalities appear to manipulate their readers/viewership into certain points of view by providing more speculation than fact, and consistently providing only one side of a story.
- The topics of personal interest to news media personalities are consistently covered over and above the important news events of the day.
- Sidestepping and avoiding the answering of questions maintains audience focus only on one's talking points.
- News media personalities monopolize time by asking long, drawn-out questions filled with opinions, thus limiting the response time of invited guests to provide their points of view.
- Clearly debatable points are falsely presented as widely accepted facts.
- There's a failure to probe generic answers to questions that are technically accurate but meant to deceive the viewer/reader into believing that the responder agrees or is compliant with a concern when, they are not. For example, a US senator is asked if he/she had ever been guilty of sexual harassment and responds, "I have never sullied my *political office* with any claim of sexual harassment," even though the senator previously had been accused of sexual harassment while working in the *private* sector.

Priority given to the role of informing:

- Reports from various outlets on important issues or events are consistent.
- The information being presented is comprehensive, relevant, in context, and truthful.
- Opinion is clearly stated as such.
- The presentation of facts is sufficiently neutral and objective, even when the facts are different from what a reporter would like them to be.

- Interviewees are pushed to truthfully answer the questions posed and asked to clarify any "weasel" words.
- Reporters admit when they make a mistake.
- Reporters are hired who have the skill set and experience to understand and articulate important new stories.

The transposed reality of news media priorities is creating anarchical havoc in America. Large segments of the news media are not only missing the mark, but they are also shooting at a different target altogether. They are competitively advocating for personal points of view without an ethical structure, which results in a no-holds-barred gladiatorial tour de *farce*. As a result, the public is often force-fed empty news calories. In this environment, fiction is intentionally presented as fact to achieve ideological, political, and economic goals. Unfortunately, this is not hard to do. Nobel Laureate (in economic science), psychologist, and writer Daniel Kahneman notes that "a reliable way to make people believe in falsehoods is frequent repetition, because familiarity is not easily distinguished from truth."[93] Many in the media know this and use it to their advantage.

If missing the mark were not enough, the mainstream media doubles and triples down on their disingenuousness by (1) falsely claiming/implying that the majority of Americans agree with their views and (2) punishing those who disagree by belittlement or demonization. The average American, company, or institution is terrified of being inappropriately labeled by the media as racist, homophobic, intolerant, environmentally insensitive, or anything other than pristine. Indeed, such damage to the average person or organization can mean the difference between being able to financially support oneself. In addition, it substantially increases the risk of physical, economic, and reputational violence against those falsely labeled. In many instances, the media has declared war, using weapons of ideological mass destruction, against those who might have a different viewpoint on social issues. Take for instance the following comments made by CNN anchor Anderson Cooper. In May 2017, Cooper railed against conservative commentator Jeffrey Lord on Cooper's television show when Lord disagreed with Cooper's assessment of the importance of President Trump's calling FBI Director James Comey a "nut job" to Russian officials.

---

[93] Daniel Kahneman, *Thinking Fast and Slow* (New York: Farrar, Straus and Giroux, 2011), Kindle edition, chapter 5.

Cooper said, "If he [Trump] took a dump on his desk, you would defend it."[94] Cooper later apologized for the comment. In June of 2016, after the Orlando nightclub shooting spree, Cooper blindsided Florida Attorney General Pam Bondi on live television outside the hospital where victims were being treated, saying to Bondi, "Do you really think you're a champion of the gay community? … Is it hypocritical for you to portray yourself as a champion of the gay community? I'm just reflecting what a lot of gay people have told me; they don't see you as that." Bondi replied, "I'm not portraying myself as anything other than trying to help human beings."[95]

Today, people are literally being accused, tried, and found guilty or innocent in a "court of media" rather than in a court of law. The usurpation of the determination of guilt or innocence to a "media court" environment bastardizes our democracy and should terrify each of us. This condition has become so routine and so negatively impactful that it would now make sense for each newscast to begin with a disclaimer: "the Surgeon General has determined that the news media may be hazardous to your health." The low standard of culpability regarding the unethical use of fiction represented as fact, the public demonization of people with differing viewpoints, and the wanton stirring of emotion to mute rationality, greatly contribute to making us a nation of the intellectually helpless.

Many social commentators agree. Today, "what is becoming more predominant in our information age is the lack of ability to discern wisdom and truth in the avalanche of opinion dressed up as fact."[96] We have "round-the-clock" media coverage, "but we have mistaken the compression of space and time for the conquest of space and time … Necessary automation … undermines the possibility of human deliberation and decision, thus hallowing out serious journalism, responsible politics and the very possibility of statesmanship … The more speed increases, the faster

---

[94] Nicole Bitette, "Anderson Cooper apologizes for 'crude' remark directed at Trump supporter Jeffrey Lord," *New York Daily News*, May 20, 2017, http://www.nydailynews.com/entertainment/tv/anderson-cooper-apologizes-crude-remark-directed-at-trump-supporter-jeffrey-lord.

[95] Nicole Bitette, "WATCH: Anderson Cooper slams Florida Attorney General Pam Bondi for her hypocritical LGBTQ stance: 'You've basically gone after gay people,'" *New York Daily News*, June 14, 2016, http://www.nydailynews.com/news/national/anderson-cooper-slams-floria-ag-hypocritical-lgbt-stance-article-1.2.673861.

[96] Dallas Willard and Gary Black, Jr., *The Divine Conspiracy Continued: Fulfilling God's Kingdom on Earth* (New York: HarperOne, 2014), Kindle edition, 78.

freedom decreases."[97] Perhaps today it is more apt to describe the speed of type as the speed of hype.

The News Media Caste

In general, members of the mainstream media do not resemble most Americans. Most are writing at, not for, the masses. According to newspaper columnist Joel Kotkin, "This shift in the media role has roots in both class and geography. Journalism used to be a 'craft,' rather than a credentialed profession. You learned the business by covering local news and working at small papers. Reporters often owned homes in the suburbs, had families, and maintained connections with people outside the intelligentsia. Today's mainstream news media seem to reflect increasingly the values of our increasingly doctrinally progressive academic institutions … Increasingly, top journalists, as Obama speechwriter Ben Rhodes noted, are often young, highly educated ingenues who 'literally know nothing' and can be easily misled by attractive figures."[98] They write and converse in non sequiturs because many have no hands-on experience with their subject matter and can make a mediocre living off the babble from their bubble of ideological fantasy. They advertise intellectual wheat but sell their product from a gluten-free store.

In their article, "The Media Bubble Is Worse Than You Think," Jack Shafer and Tucker Doherty offer potential reasons for this predicament, describing it "not just as embarrassment for the press but as an indictment. In some profound way, the [2016 presidential] election made clear, the national media just doesn't get the nation it purportedly covers."[99] Shafer and Doherty examined the physical location of where most journalists work as a major factor in their homogeneous thought: "The national media really does work in a bubble, something that wasn't true as recently as 2008. And the bubble is growing more extreme. Concentrated heavily along the coasts, the bubble is both geographical and political."[100] Their article

---

[97] Guinness, *A Free People's Suicide*, 82–83.
[98] Joel Kotkin, "Media Losing Search for Truth," *Orange County Register*, May 7, 2017 Opinion section.
[99] Jack Shafer and Tucker Doherty, "The Media Bubble Is Worse Than You Think," *Politico*, May/June 2017, https://www.politico.com/magazine/story/2017/04/25/medi-bubble-real-journalism-jobs-east-coast-215048.
[100] Shafer and Doherty, "The Media Bubble."

pointed out that in the past, this coastal influence was balanced out by the number of newspaper jobs spread throughout the United States. Presently, however, this is no longer the case as "newspapers have jettisoned hundreds of thousands of jobs due to falling advertising revenues,"[101] having been replaced by internet publishing jobs that are again concentrated along the liberal coasts. "The people who report, edit, produce and publish news can't help being affected—deeply affected—by the environment around them … Journalism tends toward the autobiographical unless reporters and editors make determined efforts to separate themselves from the frame of their own experiences."[102]

Death by the News Media

It is profoundly ironic and disturbingly noteworthy that an institution whose primary mission is to inform the masses in order to hold its moral-cultural, government, and business institutions accountable is entirely unaccountable. Prophetically, the Bible states, "My people are destroyed from lack of knowledge."[103] This is the terrifying impact of the media today. It is no longer a settled disposition among our citizens that we are being told the truth by those whose job it is to do so. But this is only part of the catastrophe.

Today the mainstream media is negatively impacting the ability of our nation to function at every level. It is bad enough to withhold the truth. It is worse to misrepresent it to pursue an agenda. Consider these examples:

- Reports that Fusion GPS, the communications firm that was hired by the Democratic National Convention and the Clinton campaign to produce and see to the distribution of the unproven *Steele* dossier on Russian collusion in the 2016 presidential campaign, *paid* several reporters to print stories on the topic. Fusion GPS founders, former *Wall Street Journal* reporters, appear to have established a network of other former *Wall Street Journal* reporters in their various new positions (i.e., CNN, *New Yorker*, *New York Times*, *Washington Post*, NBC News), whom they allegedly pay to have

---

[101] Shafer and Doherty, "The Media Bubble."
[102] Shafer and Doherty, "The Media Bubble."
[103] Hosea 4:6, Bible, New International Version.

information from various dossiers published by their current news outlet employers. The House Intelligence Committee subpoenaed Fusion GPS records that confirmed Fusion GPS paid journalists, whose names and their news organizations have yet to be released. In addition, two Fusion GPS founders who testified before the House Intelligence Committee pleaded the Fifth Amendment to every question they were asked on the subject. Fusion GPS's niche, as a liberal opposition research firm, is to have opposition research turned into news stories. It previously has been accused of producing "fictional misinformation," such as—the compilation of "a dossier for a UAE sheik who toppled his uncle for the throne"; the spreading of "propaganda in support of the Maduro regime in Venezuela"; and "Fusion's work for Planned Parenthood to discredit David Daleiden and his Center for Medical Progress (CMP)—in every case, little of what Fusion GPS proffered was accurate or based on fact, but all of it was used by pliant media, more often than not friends from Simpson & Co.'s [Fusion GPS founders] days in legitimate journalism."[104]

- Similarly themed personal attacks against President Trump by several media outlets using identical negative verbiage, strongly suggests coordination and prediscussed/distributed talking points (e.g., "lack of empathy" in regard to victims of Hurricane Harvey, "racist" in regard to immigration issues, "white supremacist" in reference to Charlottesville, and "mentally unfit for office").

- In his acceptance speech for the International Center for Journalists Founders Award for Excellence in Journalism, Chris Wallace stated that he believes the president "may have a point" when he complains about media bias and unfairness. "I believe that some of

---

[104] Ned Ryun, "There is nothing normal about Fusion GPS dossier," The Hill, November 5, 2017, http://thehill.com/opinion/white-house/358828-there-is-nothing-new-about-the-fusion-gps-dossier; Rowan Scarborough, "Firm behind dubious Trump-Russia dossier paid multiple journalists for work," *Washington Times*, November 24, 2017,/https://www.washingtontimes.com/news/2017/nov/24/fusion-gps-russian-dossier-firm-paid-multiple-journalists-for-work; and Lee Smith, "Fusion GPS Scandal Implicates Media in Possible Pay-to-Publish Scheme," the Federalist, December 4, 2017, http://thefederalist.com/2017/12/04/fusion-gps-scandal-implicates-media-possible-pay-publish-scheme.

our colleagues—many of our colleagues—think this president has gone so far over the line to bash the media, it has given them an excuse to cross the line themselves, to push back … We don't need to offer opinions or put our thumb on the scale. Be as straight and accurate and dispassionate as we first learned to be as reporters."[105]

- In his testimony to a Senate intelligence committee on June 8, 2017, regarding media stories on Russian collusion, former FBI Director James Comey stated, "There have been many, many stories partly based on classified information about lots of stuff but especially about Russia that are just dead wrong. The challenge, and I am not picking on reporters, about writing stories about classified information is the people talking about it often don't really know what's going on."[106]

- During the sustained national media attention in 2014 on Ferguson, Missouri, media outlets were actively searching for evidence to confirm the (false) allegation that the shooting was a race-motivated murder of a black man by a white police officer.

Littering the national landscape of minds with falsehoods or innuendo has several negative consequences. One, it results in those being falsely accused having to spend their time fighting falsehoods rather than doing their jobs. This is especially distressing for the national government. There are so many problems on so many levels that need to be addressed to work toward the good society. Every illegitimate moment taken away from national security, health care, immigration, infrastructure, law enforcement, and economic development weakens our country and continues the suffering of people who need a solution. How many people are killed because resources are diverted from securing the country to addressing falsehoods? How many people go bankrupt because economic and health care cost issues are not addressed in a timely manner due to defending false claims?

[105] "Chris Wallace: Trump 'May Have a Point' About Media Bias," *Fox News Insider*, November 10, 2017, http://insider.foxnews.com/2017/11/10/chris-wallace-receives-icfj-founders-award-excellence-journalism-speaks-about-media-bias.
[106] Jeff Poor, "Hannity: 'James Comey Humiliated the Mainstream Press' with His Testimony," Breitbart, June 10, 2017, http://www.breitbart.com/video/2017/06/10/hannity-james-comey-humiliated-mainstream-media.

How many people lose their lives due to public infrastructure deficiencies not implemented because of time spent in political quagmires between parties? How many people are killed by illegal aliens who are not deported? The list goes on and on. The news media has contributed to our intellectual helplessness by diverting resources away from productive service provision to the unproductive disproving of false accusations.

Second, people and organizations choose not to pursue their unalienable rights of freedom of conscience and speech because in doing so, they have a real chance of being publicly demonized by the news media and losing their ability to make a living or potentially jeopardizing their personal safety. As a result, the media has become a weapon for the mass destruction of individual and corporate liberties through blackmail.

- Dennis Prager wrote for the website Townhall that Americans who hold conservative views or who voted for Trump "rationally fear ostracism by their peers, public humiliation, ruined reputations, broken families, job loss and the inability to work in their field."[107] Prager cited several examples of retaliation, including attempts by some left-wing members of the Santa Monica Symphony Orchestra and Santa Monica city government to prevent him from conducting a Haydn symphony at the Walt Disney Concert Hall because of his conservative viewpoints.

- The media publicizes the Southern Poverty Law Center's list of hate groups,[108] even though it dubiously lumps in principled conservative groups (e.g., Family Research Council) with bigots. In 2012, this practice resulted in Floyd Corkins showing up at the Family Research Council headquarters with a gun, later telling the FBI he got the idea from seeing the group on Poverty Law Center's hate group list.[109]

---

[107] Dennis Prager, "Conservatives in America—Like Marranos in Medieval Spain," Townhall, September 5, 2017, https://www.townhall.com/columnists/dennisprager/2017/09/05/conservatives-in-america--like-marranos-in-medieval-spain/n2377054.

[108] Dakin Andone, "The Southern Poverty Law Center's list of hate groups," CNN, August 18, 2017, http://www.cnn.com/2017/08/17/us/hate-groups-us-map-trnd/index.html.

[109] Megan McArdle, "Southern Poverty Law Center Gets Creative to Label 'Hate Groups,'" Bloomberg, September 7, 2017, https://www.bloomberg.com/view/articles/2017-9-07/southern-poverty-law-center-gets-creative-to-label-hate-groups.

- Media outlets and other groups misrepresented the facts and hate-labeled Jack Phillips, a cake artist in Colorado.[110] Phillips is accused of refusing to serve a same-sex couple in his store. In 2012, he was asked to design a cake for a gay couple's upcoming wedding. Phillips stated that he would sell them any cake in the store (i.e., serve them) "but that he could not, due to his religious convictions, use his cake-design talents to participate in the celebration of their ceremony."[111] Phillips was later fined by the Colorado Civil Rights Commission and ordered to attend, along with his employees, a "re-education" program and provide quarterly compliance reports. He also received death threats. In June 2018, the US Supreme Court ruled, 7 to 2, in favor of Phllips.

Third, it encourages the media to be a power broker rather than a conduit for the sharing of accurate information to the real owners of the country, its citizens. Although the pen is supposed to be mightier than the sword, the current mainstream media have stolen both the arrows and the olive branches from the great seal of the United States and are simultaneously wielding both. When the media seek power instead of sharing information, they are out of their depth and expertise. And it shows in their tactics. Power should only be granted to those who have the character and proper motivation for the common good. It is a fascinating and frightful observation that while autocratic governments co-opt their media, in America, the mainstream media is attempting to co-opt its government.

Fourth, much of the media has become lousy tutors for communication. Neil Postman commented, "TV news shows an anticommunication, featuring a type of discourse that abandons logic, reason, sequence, and rules of contradiction."[112] A precondition of effective communication is forthrightness, yet many mainstream media activities today are not communication but conjecture. At times, this is the result of wanting to "scoop" the field with exclusive news, where one does not take sufficient

[110] Zack Ford, "Gay couple to anti-gay baker: This is how nondiscrimination laws are supposed to work," ThinkProgress, October 25, 2017, https://thinkprogress.org/baker-lgbt-aclu-commission-briefs-f2f041b4b807/.

[111] John Stonestreet and David Carlson, "Get the Facts Right about Jack (Phillips, That Is), BreakPoint, November 9, 2017, http://www.breakpoint.org/2017/11/breakpoint-get-facts-jack-phillips/.

[112] Neil Postman, *Amusing Ourselves to Death* (New York: Penguin Books, 1985), 105.

time to properly vet the information received. At other times, conjecture is rampant when the media covers a crisis or breaking news event. In these situations, it is common to have nonstop, continuous coverage of an event, even when there is nothing new or worthwhile to report. News channels and their broadcasters struggle to fill the airtime, becoming news stocking stuffers with fill-the-gap crap. The same information is repeated, and the video gets put on an endless loop; guesses are made as to the what, why, and when of the event; and experts are brought in to discuss unknown or unclear circumstances of the events or to psychologically evaluate a perpetrator whom no one adequately knows.

Fifth, much of the mainstream media today operates like a cult. It requires your conscience, your soul, your money, your preferences, your devotion, and your allegiance. Differing opinions are anathema. In his article, "The Mass Media Cult Goes Pathological," James Lewis details the perceived obsessive-compulsive and morbid habits of the mainstream media related to Donald Trump being elected president. He postulates that the election has placed the American ruling class in "a kind of death anxiety … which is also why they constantly fantasize about killing Donald Trump."[113] Lewis laments that the current liberalized concentration of the media "has the same effect as cult indoctrination," and he expresses his concern that "for a *mental* mass monopoly, you don't need to violate anti-trust law. All you need is mass media that make up the 'news' by consensus, not by empirical reality … The bottom line is that *any ideological monopoly creates cults.*"[114] Lewis, for affirmation, pointed to the JournoList scandal. In 2007, a private Google Group forum was established to have confidential electronic discussions of politics and the news. Membership was limited to "several hundred left-leaning bloggers, political reporters, magazine writers, policy wonks and academics."[115] Eventually, examples of the email conversations among members were published, which raised ethical concerns about the membership's objectivity as members of the news media. Here are some examples of concerns:[116]

---

[113] James Lewis, "The Mass Media Cult Goes Pathological," American Thinker, May 15, 2017, http://www.americanthinker.com/articles/2017/05/the_mass_media_cult_goes_pathological.

[114] Lewis, "The Mass Media Cult."

[115] Michael Calderone, "JournoList: Inside the echo chamber," *Politico*, March 17, 2009, http://www.politico.com/news/stories/0309/2006.html.

[116] Wikipedia, https://en.wikipedia.org/wiki/JournoList.

- On July 20, 2010, the Daily Caller published the dialogue of a JournoList conversation concerning minister Jeremiah Wright. The contributor discussed killing the Wright story, because it reflected negatively on Barack Obama.

- In reference to an ABC News-sponsored debate between Obama and Hillary Clinton, a JournoList member tried to rally his fellow members by stating, "Listen folks—in my opinion, we all have to do what we can to kill ABC and this idiocy in whatever venues we have. This isn't about defending Obama. This is about how the [mainstream media] kills any chance of discourse that actually serve the people."[117]

- Another JournoList member stated, "If the right forces us all to either defend Wright or tear him down, no matter what we choose, we lose the game they've put upon us. Instead, take one of them—Fred Barnes, Karl Rove, who cares—and call them racists."[118]

- Another JournoList member wrote that she would laugh if she saw conservative radio talk show host Rush Limbaugh have a heart attack in front of her.

Tucker Carlson, who back in 2010 edited many of the stories in the Daily Caller about JournoList, wrote in a July 22, 2010, article, "Again and again, we discovered members of Journolist working to coordinate talking points on behalf of Democratic politicians, principally Barak Obama. This is not journalism, and those who engage in it are not journalists … I've been in journalism my entire adult life, and have often defended it against fellow conservatives who claim the news business is fundamentally corrupt. It's harder to make that defense now."[119]

The excuses from JournoList members to soften the culpability of their intentions, actions, and impacts (e.g., most people didn't participate in the conversations; these were supposed to be private conversations; for the

---

[117] Wikipedia, https://en.wikipedia.org/wiki/JournoList.
[118] Wikipedia, https://en.wikipedia.org/wiki/JournoList.
[119] Tucker Carlson, "Letter from Editor-In-Chief Tucker Carlson on the Daily Caller's Journolist coverage," Daily Caller, July 2, 2010, http://thedailycaller.com/2010/07/22/letter-from-editor-in-chief-tucker-carlson-on-the-daily-callers-journolist-coverage/.

most part the media has no significant power; this was simply talking with no intent of coordinated action)[120] ring hollow and are typical of shadow groups. In today's world, few people have extra, unclaimed time. People generally do not join and participate in something that they consider insignificant or meaningless. Rather, as discussed in chapter 1, ideas are important. They evolve into worldviews that shape our values, determine our actions, and have consequences for the roles of business and government. People act based upon what they think!

This troubling information details the thought patterns of an entire subset of a profession whose role in a democracy is to objectively report the facts to the American public. It appears clear that many of them actually wish for their proclaimed "enemies" to implode and, therefore, are at a minimum contemplating and at worst plotting or taking action against any person or ideology that is contrary to their point of view. This is antithetical to our democracy. We become intellectually helpless as a nation when critical segments of society wish for its elected leaders to fail and are willing to accept the awful consequences of failed economic, social, and political systems and policies, just so they can have their way. In this environment, intellectual hospitality is placed on indefinite leave and cyanide-laced Kool-Aid is passed out by members of an ideological cult to spike the drinks of the "deplorables."[121] Is it not more democratic to wait for an election year, to run an effective candidate for office, administer an aboveboard primary campaign, and ethically compete for the highest office in the land?

Intellectual Helplessness in the Arts Media

You use a glass mirror to see your face; you use works of art to see your soul.
—GEORGE BERNARD SHAW

The arts media includes such things as the performing, painting, sculpting, and writing arts. These are culturally imperative areas because they fulfill several human needs and societal functions. One need is the creation and enjoyment of beauty. The human soul needs creative aesthetics to serve as a salve for the trials of living, and as motivation to continue the journey.

---

[120] Wikipedia, htps:en.wikipedia.org/wiki/JournoList.
[121] Dan Merica and Sophie Tatum, "Clinton expresses regret for saying 'half' of Trump supporters are 'deplorables,'" CNN, September 12, 2016, http://www.cnn.com/2016/09/09/politics/hillary-clinton-donald-trump-basket-of-deplorables/index.html.

Another helpful function of the arts is that they can give us a preview of where culture is heading. It allows us to see what is hidden in the depths of the mind by what is produced from our imagination onto the canvas, page, screen, and stage.

Modern attempts to debeautify the arts (e.g., placing a urinal on a wall and calling it a fountain of urine, littering song lyrics with F-bombs, and planting gratuitous sex and violence in movies) has been a tremendous blow. This is perplexing to me since I have little creative ability in most of these areas. Perhaps this has intensified my desire for artists to produce legitimate and beautiful expressions of what is good, possible, and worth pursuing.

The degrading of the good has filtered its way from our minds into our souls into the outward expression of our art. This has contributed to our intellectual helplessness by diminishing our ability to see and reflect the good in ourselves, or to provide worthy modeling for future generations, thereby blunting the necessary emotion of hope. Poor art (e.g., indiscernible, uninspiring, unstimulating) also demonstrates that our minds are valuing the wrong things. Beauty is intrinsic, and every soul knows true beauty when it sees it. There are no arguments over the beauty of a sunrise, a mountain pasture, or a pristine beach; the warmth of a marriage ceremony, bar mitzvah, or quinceanera; and the power of an injustice accurately portrayed on canvas, on stage/screen, or on a sculptor's block. These examples need no critique, only gratitude. When we recognize, promote, and reward quality art, it produces more of it. When we take individualism to an extreme and applaud the crude and degrading parts of our nature for diversity's sake, we begin constructing our own gallows. Vulgar art is no art at all; it is only flatulence in the church of beauty and wisdom. As C. S. Lewis so aptly said, "An author should never conceive of himself as bringing into existence beauty or wisdom which did not exist before, but simply and solely as trying to embody in terms of his own art some reflection of eternal Beauty and Wisdom."[122]

Showcasing illiterate art also lets the unqualified into the mix. When the criteria for admission into the academy of arts are watered down, it allows mediocrity to appear and procreate. Soon there is less cream and more crap. Hucksters know they don't have the chops to survive on the merits of their work, so they seek ownership of the profession to ensure

---

[122] Lewis, *Christian Reflections*, 7.

their survival. Once power is secured, merit becomes secondary and incompetent loyalty primary. Over time, out of necessity, the definition of art must expand to include the absurd and incomprehensibly abstract because that's all that many of the new so-called artists can produce.

These abstractions put us on a path toward meaninglessness and hopelessness. Meaningful art uplifts the soul and produces hope. Undefined abstractions go too far, giving a false impression of a world of nondesign that mocks reality and cheapens human dignity. Abstraction is progressive in nature. It starts from the abstract individual X to a vague depiction of all Xs, to finally a representation of anything one wants it to be. Then, as Francis Schaeffer pointed out, "the difficulty is that when you get to that point the viewer has no clue what he is looking at. You have succeeded in making your world on your canvas, and in this sense, you have become god. But at the same time, you have lost contact with the person who views your painting. We have come to the position where we cannot communicate … Thus, art and science themselves soon become meaningless."[123]

The arts media also becomes intellectually helpless when large segments of its leadership are morally bankrupt. The recent Hollywood allegations of sexual harassment and assault highlight this condition. First, it is pathetically ironic that an industry whose mission is to provide beautifully crafted examples of the human spirit is controlled by some who impose sexual subservience on its artists as a condition of employment. Second, it is hypocritical and obtuse when the industry that allowed this to occur then proudly campaigns against the thing it allowed. Third, many of the proposed solutions will not result in real change because they do not include advocating for the internalization of better personal or institutional moral values, or for upholding standards by imposing administrative or legal consequences for bad behavior. Rather, the main thrust for change is through a mystical marketing campaign using hip slogans, such as MeToo and Time's Up that "virtue-signal" but never actually turn the car in the direction of the indicator light. Unsurprisingly, true and lasting beauty cannot be recognized or gifted to others by those with marginalized souls.

---

[123] Schaeffer, *Trilogy*, 30.

Chapter 3

Intellectual Helplessness in the Government (Political) Arena

*Government involves questions about the good of man, and
justice, and what things are worth having at what price.*
—C. S. Lewis

*One of the penalties for refusing to participate in politics is
that you end up being governed by your inferiors.*
—Plato

The mission statement of the United States government is found in the preamble of its Constitution: "We the people of the United States, in order to form a more perfect union, establish *justice*, insure *domestic tranquility*, provide for the *common defense*, promote the *general welfare*, and secure *the blessings of liberty* to ourselves and our posterity." (Emphasis was added.)

So how are we doing? Is there more or less justice? Is there more or less domestic tranquility? Is there more or less common defense? Is there more or less promotion of the general welfare? Is there more or less securing of the blessings of liberty to ourselves and our posterity? I think it is evident that we still have a long way to go in reaching our elusive "more perfect union."

Unfortunately, based on the current condition of our culture, it appears that a great many Americans have lost the history and thus the significance and meaning of our origins, which would make achievement of our mission possible. One of the things that makes America great in the eyes of others is the freedoms offered on the basis of voluntary obligation. This holistic ignorance has made us vulnerable to the manipulations of the self-serving who unabashedly push a false, revisionist narrative of our heritage that benefits them.

To illustrate, let's examine the roles of government named in our mission statement, and identify the evidence of intellectual helplessness found in each one.

Justice

Far too often these days, lady justice is peeking. It's not of her own accord, as her hands are occupied balancing her scales and holding her sword. It's the unscrupulous who are raising her blindfold. For instance, as Dallas Willard questioned, "How can we allow something to be morally and ethically indefensible yet legally acceptable? … That something could be legal (just) and at the same time highly immoral (unjust) on the basis of some legalese directly contradicts the moral gravity the law must maintain in order to command any respect or authority to govern human behavior."[124] Take for instance Hillary Clinton's takeover of the Democratic National Convention (DNC), by paying off its debt in exchange for securing control of its operations, to ensure she was nominated as the Democratic candidate for the 2016 presidential election. This behavior is demonstrably unethical and emphatically consequential, yet it unconscionably appears that the inner workings of political campaigns are currently outside the purview of the law.

Also consider the false notion that you can't legislate morality. As Chuck Colson astutely observed, "All law implicitly involves morality … Morality is legislated every day from the vantage point of one value system over another. The question is not whether we will legislate morality, but whose morality will be legislated. Law is but a body of rules regulating human behavior; it establishes, from the view of the state, the rightness or wrongness of human behavior."[125] The loss of the traditional morality of the Founding Fathers is an area of significant concern today. James Q. Wilson observed, "In some circles, it has become a mark of unsophistication to use the language of morality in discussing the problems of mankind. When we have lost our ability to speak of morality, our habits of the heart have been

---

[124] Willard, *The Divine Conspiracy Continued*, 266.
[125] Charles Colson, *God & Government: An Insider's View on the Boundaries Between Faith and Politics* (Grand Rapids, MI: Zondervan, 2007), 315.

subverted by the ambitions of the mind."[126] As a result of many denying the importance of traditional morality on the health of a nation, we have become hog-tied by our blindness. The obvious dilemma is that while we know there are problems, often we can't suggest that someone might be doing something wrong, or talk about any solutions that might make people uncomfortable. We desperately need to use the moral framework adopted by our Founding Fathers to justly address our social and political issues. Without it, we do not have a sufficient basis for judging whether things are good or bad, right or wrong, and thereby make wise choices for our future. While it might be easier to suggest we don't have a collective morality, life never works that way, and our souls, as well as our founding documents, tell us it is just not true. That's why it is imperative that politicians and bureaucrats remain faithful to achieving a balanced mission of limited government *and* the rule of law. Justice is facilitated when the freedoms of conscience and expression don't violate the common good, or when human rights are upheld. Government has no written mandate to be the "thought police" who coerce us into certain points of view, but it does have a duty to be the "action police" against those activities that violate just laws.

In addition, justice only becomes real when we faithfully apply the law when called for (accountability of the sword) and on an equal basis (fairness of the scales). Disregarding the law or applying it discriminatorily makes the law impotent and unjust. Our democratic- capitalistic system, like a fine piano, must have all its keys properly tuned to make beautiful music. One key is the judicial branch of government. When the note of the judiciary is sharp or flat, the chord of democracy is weakened. The court is sharp when it overreaches its authority due to hubris; it is flat when it abdicates its responsibility due to fear. Today it is demonstrably evident that the sharpness of the judicial branch has encroached on the legislative branch's mission to make laws based on the will of the people. Take for instance the court's intrusion into issues of social significance, such as the definition of marriage, abortion, and immigration. For better or worse, "the people" should determine the rules of society they live under, as they must live with the consequences of the choices that are made. This encroachment has been encouraged by the subservient gerrymandering of the courts by some in the executive branch. When judicial appointments are not made based on a jurist's experience and expertise in knowing and following the spirit and

---

[126] Wilson, 112.

intent of law, but rather on the willingness to usurp and rewrite it, the judiciary climbs over the fence of its constitutional boundaries and trespasses onto the property of the people to govern themselves through their elected representatives. In these cases, we become intellectually helpless as we allow the undemocratic will of the few to overthrow the will of the many.

Another slap to the face of justice occurs when law enforcement fails to uphold the laws of the land. Consider these examples:

- For all the chicanery involved in and around the 2016 presidential election (e.g., Wikileaks evidence, DNC rigging of Democratic primary, FBI impact), no one has been held accountable.

- For the Benghazi tragedy, no one has been held accountable.

- For former president Bill Clinton's secret rendezvous with then attorney general Loretta Lynch on an airport tarmac in Phoenix while wife Hillary Clinton was under investigation by the Federal Bureau of Investigation, no one has been held accountable.

- For the illegal releasing of confidential government information to the public, or the illegal unmasking of the names of American citizens, no one has been held accountable.

- For the collection by the FBI of "substantial evidence that Russian nuclear industry officials were engaged in bribery, kickbacks, extortion, and money laundering designed to grow Vladimir Putin's atomic energy business inside the United States," and eyewitness accounts and documents "… indicating Russian nuclear officials had routed millions of dollars to the US designed to benefit former president Bill Clinton's charitable foundation during the time Secretary of State Hillary Clinton served on a government body that provided a favorable decision to Moscow," no one has been held accountable.[127]

[127] Dan McLaughlin, "New Russian Nuclear Scandal Raises New Questions About Clinton Foundation," *National Review*, October 1, 2017, http://www.nationalreview.com/node/452776/print; and Katie Pavlich, "With Bribery, Russian Nuclear Officials Made Bill and Hillary Clinton Richer," Townhall, October 17, 2017, https://townhall.com/tipsheet/katiepavlich/2017/10/17/russianclinton-hill-story-n2396220/print.

- For the unauthorized use of a private server by then secretary of state Hillary Clinton, which sent and received unsecure confidential and classified information, no one has been held accountable.

- For the meticulous deletion of tens of thousands of emails on that server after receiving a federal subpoena for the information, no one has been held accountable.

- For Hillary Clinton spending significant portions of her working day as the secretary of state meeting with and currying favors for donors to the Clinton Foundation, no one has been held accountable.

- For the refusals to follow federal immigration law and the resulting tragic deaths of several US citizens by illegal aliens, no one has been held accountable.

- For elected officials who have publicly admitted that their families entered the country illegally and obtained false identification, no one has been held accountable.

- For those who ordered and carried out the IRS's admitted illegal targeting of conservative nonprofit groups by revoking their tax-exempt status for being irritants to the Obama administration, no one has been held accountable.

- For the Obama Justice Department's manipulation of economic settlement agreements with investigated firms to funnel settlement payments to the administration's political friends (organizations) that had nothing to do with the case, while intentionally excluding conservative groups for the same consideration, no one has been held accountable.[128]

---

[128] Alex Pappas, " 'Smoking gun' email reveals Obama DOJ blocked conservative groups from settlement funds, GOP lawmaker says," Fox News, October 25, 2017, htpp://www.foxnews.com/politics/2017/10/25/smoking-gun-reveals-obama-doj-conseravtive-groups-from-settlement-funds-gop-lawmaker-says.html.

- For those in the Veterans Administration who mismanaged and worsened the misery of injured military veterans, no one has been held accountable.

- For the raping of a fourteen-year-old girl by illegal aliens in Maryland, no one has been held accountable.

When our country cannot count on its law enforcement community to enforce or abide by the laws of the land, intellectual helplessness becomes manifest in several different ways. First, it results in there being no legitimate place to turn to right wrongs. In some cases, it appears likely that federal law enforcement agencies have been complicit in not only failing to adequately investigate and justly address the evidence of potential crimes committed by its former political masters, but also in opening and pursuing nonevidence-based investigations into its current, unwanted masters. Consider the following examples:

- In regard to the Bill Clinton / Loretta Lynch tarmac meeting, recently released emails from the FBI "show the FBI more concerned about a whistle-blower who told the truth about the infamous Clinton-Lynch tarmac meeting than the scandalous meeting itself." The FBI had originally claimed that these emails could not be located, but later produced them after a Freedom of Information Act lawsuit was filed.[129]

- Former Obama-appointed inspector general for the intelligence community, William McCullough III, has claimed in national television interviews that when he identified that Hillary Clinton had "beyond classified" materials on her private email server, he was marginalized and repeatedly threatened that he would lose his job once Ms. Clinton became president, inaccurately accused of politicizing the situation, and inappropriately criticized for not taking into consideration the political consequences of his actions

[129] Jeff Crouere, "Lying to FBI Is Illegal; How About the FBI Lying to Us?" Townhall, December 2, 2017, https://www.townhall.com/columnists/jeffcrouere/2017/2017/12/02/lying-to-fbi-is-illegal-how-about-fbi-lying-to-us-n2417029.

(i.e., doing his job).[130] McCullough was a former FBI agent and worked for the National Security Agency (NSA).

- In early December 2017, the media inexplicably learned that the former FBI deputy director of counterintelligence, Peter Strzok, was quietly fired from Special Counsel Robert Mueller's Russian collusion probe in July 2017 for allegedly sending anti-Trump, pro-Hillary texts to an FBI lawyer with whom he was romantically involved. An examination of Strzok's FBI work résumé also disturbingly showed that he led the investigation of Hillary Clinton's private email server; conducted the untaped FBI interview of Clinton without her being under oath; and was the catalyst for changing then FBI Director Comey's draft language describing Ms. Clinton's actions from "grossly negligent" to "extremely careless," which was crucial in the FBI not recommending that she be charged with a crime. In addition, Strzok was the FBI official who signed the document opening the Russian collusion investigation against Trump; was involved in pushing forward the questionable Steele dossier on Trump prepared by Fusion GPS for the Clinton campaign opposition research; and oversaw the FBI's interview of fired National Security Adviser Michael Flynn.[131]

- The FBI and Department of Justice's (DOJ) handling of the Hillary Clinton email investigation is rife with demonstrable examples of injustice, and exhibits a lack of courage by its leadership.

---

[130] Charles McCullough as interviewed by Tucker Carlson on November 28, 2017, Fox News, http://video.foxnews.com/5661657855001/?#sp=show-clips; and Catherine Herridge on November 27, 2017, Fox News, http://video.foxnews.com/v/5660687058001/?# sp=show-clips.
[131] Laura Jarrett and Evan Perez, "FBI agent dismissed from Mueller probe changed Comey's description of Clinton to 'extremely careless,'" CNN, December 4, 2017, http://www.cnn.com/2017/12/04/politics/peter-srzok-james-comey/index.html; Pamela K. Browne, "Fired FBI official at center of Flynn, Clinton, dossier controversies revealed," Fox News, December 5, 2017, http://www.foxnews.com/politics/2017/12/05/fired-fbi-official-at-center-flynn-clinton-dossier; and Gregg Jarrett, "How an FBI official with a political agenda corrupted both Mueller, Comey investigations," Fox News, December 5, 2017, http://www.foxnews.com/opinion/2017,12/05/gregg-jarrett-how-fbi-offical-with-political-agenda-corrupted-both-Meuller-Comey-investigations.

First, the FBI assigned nonneutral, nonobjective FBI agents to conduct the investigation. The June 2018 DOJ Inspector General report details numerous instances of FBI agent animus against Donald Trump (e.g., "loathsome human," "enormous douche"), support for Hillary Clinton (e.g., "God Hillary should win 1,000,000—0," "[Clinton] just has win now"), and the intent to influence the 2106 presidential election if necessary (e.g., Lisa Page: "[Trump's] not ever going to become President, right? Right?!", Peter Strzok: "No. No, he won't. We'll stop him.").[132] An important question to consider is just who the "we" includes in the word *we'll*.

Second, then FBI director Comey and DOJ Inspector General (IG) Michael Horowitz delineated an overwhelming number of violations of law and policy by Ms. Clinton and/or DOJ/FBI officials in their respective (July 5, 2016) public announcement and (June 2018) IG report. For example, Comey described then secretary of state Clinton's email management practices as "extremely careless," and stated that it was possible that foreign intelligence services gained access to her private email server. In the IG report, numerous examples of misconduct were documented: DOJ and FBI employees improperly disclosed non-public information during the course of an investigation, failed to examine all sources of information, failed to recuse employees with conflicts of interest, inappropriately allowed potential witnesses (i.e., Cheryl Mills, Heather Samuelson) in the room during the Hillary Clinton interview, and that Comey usurped the authority of the Attorney General and inadequately and incorrectly described the legal position of the DOJ during his July 5, 2016 public announcement. Furthermore, the IG report's executive summary states that the text messages between Lisa Page and Peter Strzok are "not only indicative of a biased state of mind but, even more seriously, implies a willingness to take official action to impact the presidential candidate's electoral prospects. This is antithetical to the core values of the FBI and Department of Justice."[133]

Third, Comey drafted an exoneration letter of Hillary Clinton

---

[132] *A Review of the Various Actions by the Federal Bureau of Investigation and the Department of Justice in Advance of the 2016 Election,* US Department of Justice/Office of the Inspector General, June 2018, 399, 402, https://www.justice.gov/file/1071991/download.
[133] *A Review of Various Actions...,* xi-xii.

months before critical written and verbal testimony were obtained and analyzed.

Fourth, despite these widespread examples of violations of law and policy, neither the DOJ (including the IG) or FBI leadership were willing to officially conclude and state the obvious: yes, crimes were committed, and investigator bias impacted the Clinton email investigation. DOJ/FBI leadership simply would not complete the simple equation: one plus one equals (I won't say).

- The collusion investigation into Russia's alleged tampering in the 2016 presidential campaign, involving the Trump campaign, was initiated based on unverified information and then staffed by individuals who have either obvious conflicts of interest or the appearance of conflicts of interest. The justification for the investigation was driven, in large part, by a suspect dossier created as opposition research at the request of Republican challengers to candidate Trump during the primary and then later picked up, paid for, and pushed by Ms. Clinton during the general election. A list of purported staffing conflicts of interest within the Mueller team and the DOJ include the following:

  - Robert Mueller, special counsel for conducting the Russian collusion investigation, was chosen by and reports to Deputy Attorney General Rod Rosenstein, even though Rosenstein is a material witness in the case. One issue that Mueller is examining is whether President Trump fired FBI Director Comey for his work on the Russia probe, thereby obstructing justice. However, it was Rosenstein who wrote the memo recommending that Comey be fired for reasons other than the Russian collusion investigation.[134]

  - Special Counsel Mueller was the FBI director during two uranium scandals involving Russia. In the first scandal, Russian firm Rosatom's American subsidiary, Tenex, was seeking to

---

[134] Gregg Jarrett, "If Sessions leaves, a new DOJ sheriff could rein in or ax Mueller," Fox News, July 26, 2017, http://www.foxnews.com/opinion/2017/07/26/if-sessionleaves-new-doj-sheriff-could-rein-in-or-ax-mueller.

strike an agreement with US nuclear energy providers for their purchase of recycled uranium from dismantled Russian warheads. During negotiations, Tenex engaged in a lucrative racketeering enterprise that was involved in felony extortion, fraud, and money laundering. The FBI utilized a US consultant as its informant to gather evidence and ultimately prosecuted and jailed some of those involved. Tenex's American arm, Tenam USA, is based in Maryland. In the second scandal, Russian president Vladimir Putin, through Rosatom, was seeking to secure US government approval to purchase Uranium One, a Canadian firm, and obtain control of 20 percent of America's uranium supply. Due to its national security significance, the sale of US uranium to a foreign government must be approved by the US Committee on Foreign Investment in the United States (CFIUS). CFIUS is composed of leaders from fourteen US government agencies involved in national security and commerce, with voting members that include the secretary of state (Hillary Clinton at the time) and the attorney general (Eric Holder at the time). Neither Clinton nor Holder informed the members of CFIUS of Rosatom/Tenex/Tenam's illegal activities or the FBI's investigation regarding the selling of recycled uranium to American nuclear energy companies. CFIUS, without the benefit of this critical information, approved the sale of Uranium One to Rosatom. Subsequently, the DOJ agreed to a reduced plea agreement for those involved in Tenam's illegal activities to apparently mute exposure of the events taking place. It was then US Attorney Rod Rosenstein's Maryland DOJ office that administered the plea deal, which was cosigned by attorneys in DOJ's fraud section run by Andrew Weissmann.[135]

---

[135] Andrew C. McCarthy, "The Obama Administration's Uranium One Scandal," *National Review*, October 21, 2017, http://www.nationalreview.com/452972/uranium-one-deal-obama-administration-complicit-not-just; Katie Pavlich, "With Bribery, Russian Nuclear Officials Made Bill and Hillary Clinton Richer," Townhall, October 17, 2017, https://townhall.com/tipsheet/katiepavlich/2017/10/17/russiaclinton-hill-story-n2396220/print; Dan McLaughlin, "New Russian Nuclear Scandal Raises New Questions About Clinton Foundation," *National Review*, October 17, 2017, http://www.nationalreview.com/node/452776/print; John Soloman and Alison Spann, "FBI watched, then acted as Russian spy moved closer to Hillary Clinton," The Hill, October 22, 2017, http://thehill.com/policy/national-security/356630-fbi-watched-then-acted-as-russian-spy-moved-closer-hillary.

- Mueller is a close friend of James Comey who was fired by President Trump.

- Deputy Special Counsel Andrew Weissman, who reports to Mueller, at the time worked for the DOJ's criminal division. He sent an email to then acting attorney general Sally Yates commending her for insubordinately refusing to implement President Trump's travel ban, stating, "I am so proud ... And in awe ... Thank you so much ..."[136]

- Seven of the fifteen attorneys on Mueller's team contributed money to the Obama and Hillary Clinton political campaigns, amounts ranging from $200 to $9,700.[137]

- The Department of Justice demoted Associate Attorney General Bruce Ohr for meeting with Russian dossier author Christopher Steele during the 2016 presidential campaign and with dossier producer Fusion GPS cofounder Glenn Simpson after the election. Days later, it was learned that Ohr's wife, Nellie, was working for Fusion GPS on the anti-Trump Russian dossier.[138]

- The Peter Strzok issues noted earlier.

When law enforcement, at the highest level, does not do its job, or is unethical in the manner it does it, it results in a democratic crisis, because law

---

[136] Catherine Herridge, "Mueller deputy praised DOJ official after she defied Trump travel ban order: 'I am so proud'," Fox News, December 5, 2017, http://www.foxnews.com/politics/2017/12/05/mueller-deputy-praised-doj-official-after-defied-trump-travel-ban-order.

[137] Brooke Singman, "Mueller Probe: Meet the lawyers who gave $$ to Hillary, now investigating team Trump," Fox News, July 24, 2017, http://www.foxnews.com/politics/2017/07/24/mueller-probe-meet-lawyers-who-gave-to-hi...

[138] James Rosen and Jake Gibson, "Top DOJ official demoted amid probe of contacts with Trump dossier firm," Fox News, December 7, 2017, http://www.foxnews.com/politics/2017/12/07/top-doj-official-demoted-amid-probe-conta; and Jake Gibson, "Fusion GPS admits DOJ official's wife Nellie Ohr hired to probe Trump," Fox News, December 13, 2017, http://www.foxnews.com/politics/2017/12/13/fusion-gps-admits-doj-officials-wife-nellie-ohr-hired-to-probe-trump.

enforcement is absurdly asked to investigate itself. And when attempting to investigate the event, no one can be found who was not involved in some way, is objectively neutral without an opinion on the issue and the parties involved, or is not in the chain of command of those they must investigate and is thereby exposed to potential negative career impacts based on the findings of the investigation.

Second, intellectual helplessness is manifest when various groups (e.g., FBI, CIA, Congress, inspector general's office) perform multiple uncoordinated investigations on the same topic (e.g., Russian election collusion and hacking, Debbie Wasserman Shultz, Benghazi, Hillary Clinton private email server, name unmasking). Each agency has its own players, its own agenda, and its own investigators. What happens if they reach differing conclusions? Does each agency have to wait before taking action until all of them have concluded their work? One must consider whether the likely confusion generated by this reality is intentional: an effort to placate immediate concerns, to delay the issue into obscurity, and/or frustrate the masses into inertia.

Third, intellectual helplessness is manifest when there is a widespread flouting of laws/regulations due to a lack of consistent application and enforcement. When it becomes clear that there is a high probability that the only punishment for government mal- and misfeasance is public embarrassment, a readily available supply of unscrupulous individuals pursues illegitimate or illegal attempts to obtain fame, fortune, and power.

Fourth, intellectual helplessness is manifest when circumstances encourage people to consider taking matters into their own hands. Take for instance, homegrown terrorists, police shootings, the shooting of US Congressman Steve Scalise, immigration quagmires, the media's use of fake news, President Trump's beneath-the-dignity-of-the-office tweeting, and so forth.

Fifth, when justice is only intermittently administered, it provides arrestees the defense of unequal treatment under the law if they are charged when others have skated over the pond of criminal behavior without falling in. Consider the respective jail time and guilty pleas for lying to the FBI by Martha Stewart and former NSA Director Michael Flynn, compared with that of Hillary Clinton.

And sixth, it communicates that our democracy is not sacred and thus not worth dying for. Sacrifice is thereby relieved of duty. As Conrad

Black, writing for the *National Review* recently stated, "America deserves a dignified chief and a loyal opposition."[139]

Domestic Tranquility

The primary responsibility of federal, state, and local governments is the security and well-being of its citizenry. A stable environment is necessary for a democratic state to function. Yet, one of the truest and most glaring observations of our times is divisive unrest. Everywhere we turn, there is conflict. Intellectual helplessness has manifested itself into so many nooks and crannies of our society that it is extremely difficult to get out of the paper bag of problems we voluntarily jumped into.

First, we haven't connected the philosophical dots that "ideas have consequences, and bad ideas have victims."[140] Democracy without virtue is not possible. It's a fool's errand. As a result, it matters what you and I think. Again, our thoughts determine and control our actions.

There are only two restraints on behavior: the moral restraint of conscience and the physical restraint of force by the government. We either figure it out on our own (with the help of family and friends) or the government will do it for us, gleefully. Ethics are intended to blunt the need for government intervention. The purpose of ethical systems is to provide a systematic approach for moral judgment based on logic, reason, analysis, and reflection. When we do not establish and enforce ethics, we open the floodgates to mediocrity and eventual subjugation.

Professor Susan Tolchin wrote an insightful book in 1999 entitled *The Angry American*.[141] In it, she identified the first signs leading to a climate of national anger:

- absence of truth and civility
- decline in intelligent dialogue
- the rising decibels of hate

---

[139] Conrad Black, "The Newest Round of Anti-Trumpism," *National Review*, December 5, 2017, http://www.nationalreview.com/article/454347/donald-trump-michael-flynn-obstruction-unlikely.

[140] John Stonestreet as quoted at various seminars and in various publications.

[141] Susan J. Tolchin, *The Angry American: How Voter Rage Is Changing the Nation*, 2nd ed. (Boulder, CO: Westview Press, 1998).

- the proliferation of the media
- the polarization of society

Tolchin stated that the common target for this anger was government, due to the expectation that it is all things to all people, since the establishment of the entitlement era. Tolchin moved on from the symptoms of anger to what she considered its real causes:

- The widespread denial of beliefs or values that have sustained the nation and culture for two hundred years.

  Examples include the increasing disappearance of the staples of our national heritage and citizenship inculcated over centuries, such as the flag salute, Ten Commandments, definition of marriage, legal immigration, and the expectation of a modicum of honesty in government. Tearing down our long-vetted heritage means that it must be replaced by something else. In our microwave society, the "replacement" ideas have been inadequately marinated in intellectual sauce and insufficiently cooked, exposing its partakers to thought poisoning. Predictably, since these replacement ideas are of predominately lesser quality, it inadvertently opens the floodgates to the submission of other bad ideas, given the new risk of discrimination claims if other bad ideas are not adopted. When we knock down or lower the protective wall of better thought, we encourage lesser ideas to climb over it. This results in the replacement of an exclusive wine cellar of the best vintage ideas with a warehouse of mediocre offerings. We exchange quality for quantity and water down our soul and intellectual capacity. To add insult to injury, the daily grind of governing reminds us that democracy can only handle so many critical issues at one time. Without the necessary winnowing for better ideas, we wind up drowning in the quicksand of each grain of loosely packed ideas, rather than standing on the firmly packed ground of classical thought.

- The observation that society would rather take sides and compete with each other than sit down and negotiate for the common good.

Tolchin suggested that the 1999 political climate had "all but swept aside the former preponderance of reasonable discussion ... The take no prisoners bipolar approach to issues has also rendered them easier to manipulate, and nuances become harder and harder to convey in an age given to sound bites and easy answers."[142] As the villain, Fernon, said to the hero, Edmond Dantes, in *The Count of Monte Cristo* before their duel to the death, "I can't live in a world where you have everything, and I have nothing."[143] This dynamic is even more prevalent today.

- The lack of a moral consensus on right and wrong.

This lack of moral consensus personifies the philosophy of us versus the philosophy of me dilemma. In the philosophy of us camp, morality is typically viewed as transcendent, based on time-tested ethics and beliefs, less subject to change. In the philosophy of me, right and wrong is approached as a dynamic proposition. It is typically based on a majority vote of what we collectively feel is good and bad at a certain point in time. This emotion- or desired-based morality, of course, is subject to revision as more personal satisfaction choices are created by changes in technology and other catalysts.

These two distinct views of morality are so radically different that conflict among the parties who hold them is inevitable. Part of the reason for this conflict is that a majority-based morality produces a litany of nuanced situations due to the myriad of considerations and arguments that complicate issues. Take for instance current cultural discussions regarding whether having children has a negative impact on climate change. In his article entitled "Science proves kids are bad for Earth. Morality suggests we stop having them," Travis Rieder argues that having children is unethical because it contributes to the destruction of the earth's environment due to each new person's emission of greenhouse gases. He even compares the birth of his daughter to a murderer: "If I release a murderer from prison, knowing full well that he

---

[142] Tolchin, *The Angry American*, 13.
[143] Alexandre Dumas, *The Count of Monte Cristo*, 1884.

intends to kill innocent people, then I bear some responsibility for those deaths … Something similar is true, I think, when it comes to having children: Once my daughter is an autonomous agent, she will be responsible for her emissions. But that doesn't negate my responsibility."[144] In this worldview, it is assumed that humans are the problem and the environment is more important than humanity. And yet, instructively, it is humans who are asked to think and act (rather than the environment), and to illogically subordinate themselves to a soulless nature. In this and other parochial views like it, people are routinely encouraged to supremely care about, and take action to address, the latest issue de jour—only it is never just one more issue. In this example, we are asked to keep track of our personal "carbon footprint ledger" and to "stop pretending the decision to have children doesn't have environmental and ethical consequences."[145] In contrast, a theistic worldview states that God made the earth and humankind, and commanded humans to "be fruitful and multiply" and to have dominion over and be a good steward of the earth.[146]

A hopeful point worth noting in all of this, is that there may be some rational approaches in closing the distance between these two camps of morality. If we take the time to consider the nuances of various points of view, many times there is some middle ground to be found. Take for instance the idea of transitory or situational ethics. While this idea might sound attractive, with some thought, most people realize that it is not very practical in the real world. This claim can be supported rather quickly when we ask the right question: would I consider something moral if it happened to me? When we make it personal, we make it concrete and practical. For instance, whenever I discuss with my students the concept of the relativity of morality, I simply ask them for their wallet. When they ask why," I firmly reply, "Because I want it. If nothing can be considered right and wrong, then I demand your wallet." This is a real conversation ender. And for those who insist upon more

---

[144] Travis Rieder, "Science proves kids are bad for Earth. Morality suggests we stop having them," NBC News, November 15, 2017, https://www.nbcnews.com/think/opinion/science-proves-kids-are-bad-earth-morality-suggests-we-stop-ncna820781....

[145] Rieder, "Science proves kids are bad for Earth."

[146] Genesis 1:27–28.

discussion, I sometimes trot out the elderly lady analogy. I ask students if they were to witness an elderly lady having difficulty walking across a busy intersection with a bag of groceries in her hand, what choices would be available to them. The three choices typically agreed on are to help the lady, ignore the lady, or push her into oncoming traffic. When I ask if there is any disagreement or confusion as to what the "right" response is, there is a confirming silence.

Another approach is for each party to check the validity of their assumptions on issues. For instance, are there any flaws in data collection, are theories/opinions being presented as fact, have there been repeated experiments that yield the same results, have predictions materialized in the manner expected, and is there sufficient humility and dedication to accept whatever the results are? The ability of those on different sides of an issue to play by the same set of rules and abide by verified outcomes is key to keeping a productive, civil, and sufficiently unified society.

- The diminishing concept of mutual sacrifice for the common good.

This is another outcome of the me-versus-us philosophical choice. By definition, the me philosophy makes decisions based on what an individual gets out of a situation; the us philosophy seeks acceptable compromise for the greater good.

The philosophy of me is straightforward. I will not sacrifice unless there is a significant personal benefit for doing so. As Humphrey Bogart's character, Rick Blaine, said in the movie *Casablanca*, "I stick my neck out for nobody." In his 2011 article, "America in Decline," Bernard Goldberg stated that in America, prior to the Vietnam War, "hardship was accepted as a part of life. Self-sacrifice for the good of others was the order of the day. Cowardice and narcissism were condemned everywhere."[147] Since then, according to Goldberg, many people having been doing their "own thing."

Self-sacrifice for the common good is often viewed in the

---

[147] Bernard Goldberg, "America in Decline," Bernard Goldberg (website), October 27, 2011, https://bernardgoldberg.com/america-in-decline/?print=print.

context of volunteerism or civic participation. Robert Putnam, former dean of the Kennedy School of Government at Harvard University, struck a chord with the public in identifying and discussing causes for the decline of civic life in America. Five years after writing about the worrisome condition of civic participation in his 1995 article "Bowling Alone: America's Declining Social Capital," Putnam believed time had only reinforced his views, noting that the frequency with which Americans went to public meetings to talk about local affairs was down by about 40 percent.[148] Additionally, today fewer Americans are making charitable gifts. A 2017 article in the *Chronicle of Philanthropy* stated, "Only 24 percent of taxpayers reported on their tax returns that they made a charitable gift in 2015, according to the analysis of Internal Revenue Service data. A decade earlier that figure routinely reached 30 or 31 percent."[149] This decreased level of self-sacrifice has directly contributed to our intellectual helplessness, as we choose not to take the medicine that provides measurable community and individual quality of life benefits to those who partake: better schools, decreased crime rates, individual improvements to physical and mental health, and improvements to child welfare.[150]

The philosophy of us is more dynamic. Mutual sacrifice has a higher probability for occurrence when there are fewer options. There are fewer options when there is more consensus. There is more consensus when there are similar values. There are similar values when there are common worldviews. And there are common worldviews when there are shared ideas about the world. When we multiply options by seeking individual satisfaction, rather than achieving the common good, we increase the chances of choosing a bad option and inevitably create more opportunities for disagreement. And when we have trouble reaching an acceptable

---

[148] Robert Leough, "Robert Putnam on the decline of civic life," *CommonWealth Magazine,* August 1, 2000, https://commonwealthmagazine.org?uncategorized/robert-putman-on-the-decline-of-civic-life.

[149] Lindsay, "Fewer Americans Find Room in Their Budgets for Charity," *Chronicle of Philanthropy,* October 3, 2017.

[150] Kenneth Prewitt, Christopher D. Mackie, and Hermann Haberman, eds., "Civic Engagement and Social Cohesion: Measuring Dimensions of Social Capital to Inform Policy," *National Academies Press,* 2014, https://www.nap.edu/read/18831/chapter/1.

compromise, the tendency is to retreat, become entrenched, and fight it out for individual positions. When we retreat to our extreme positions, the debate can easily become oversimplified, making it easier for politicians, media, and education to divide the parties and manipulate the issue according to their own interests.

When it becomes clear that compromise is not possible, and self-interest is the only avenue for success, it becomes every man and woman for themselves. Suddenly, there is no collective cause worth dying for. And when there is no cause worth dying for, the depressing realization sets in that, alternatively, there may be nothing worth living for.

- The inevitable fragmentation and polarization of society.

In this type of environment, Tolchin accurately predicted the inevitable divisions that would occur. These divisions increasingly move parties toward permanent alienation as each side seeks to "outdo the other in exposing their rival's weaknesses ... In this increasingly autonomous, transient society, voters have come invisible which means they feel virtually powerless ..."[151] For many, this results in an "impotent rage" prompted by desperation. I fear that the fury and impact of this rage is just beginning in our society. For many, disagreement over issues has devolved into hate for the people holding different opinions. Take for instance, a June 23, 2018 rally in Los Angeles, where Congresswoman Maxine Waters encouraged citizens to "personally target" President Trump aides who support his immigrant policy when they go out in public. During her speech she also stated, "I have no sympathy for these people that are in this administration who know it is wrong what they're doing on so many fronts but they tend to not want to confront this President. For these members of his cabinet who remain and try to defend him they're not going to be able to go to a restaurant, they're not going to be able to stop at a gas station, they're not going to be able to shop at a department store, the people are going to turn on them, they're going to protest, they're going to absolutely harass them until they decide they're going to tell the president 'no

---

[151] Tolchin, *The Angry American*, 4.

I can't hang with you, this is wrong this is unconscionable and we can't keep doing this to children."[152] The strong emotion of hate has increased our intellectual helplessness and thus decreased our ability to compromise with those we cannot stand to be around. It appears that for more and more people, their only perceived option is to fight back with violence.

In summary, when citizens disregard their heritage, people take sides. When people take sides, there is a lack of consensus. When there is a lack of consensus, citizens won't sacrifice for the common good. When citizens won't sacrifice for the common good, there is fragmentation and polarization. When there is continued fragmentation and polarization, it results in the failure of democracy and the resulting need for stabilization by force.

Common Defense

It has been painfully accepted by a majority of Americans that there are people who hate the United States and will do anything to destroy it. What has not been universally accepted is the best way to go about defending our country. That is a legitimate and worthy topic for debate.

Unfortunately, in America's most recent past, we have rendered ourselves intellectually helpless as a byproduct of ignorance, appeasement, ransom, and dishonesty. Until recently it has been America's informal policy to adopt a defensive posture, hoping that the fight would remain off our shores. Orlando, San Bernardino, Boston, Riverside, and open FBI investigations of terrorism in every state in the union testify otherwise. When things really got sticky, our government secretly paid off the pesky exuberance of countries like Iran, Syria, and North Korea in return for only their *promise* to cease their destructive impulses against the West and those who do not share their religious affiliation. Then, in a spine-chilling display of arrogance and subterfuge, government officials were braggadocios about ending the nuclear and chemical threats posed by these countries. Now that the truth has been rudely exposed as otherwise, past government officials are now lip-synching the lines from the movie *Casablanca*, "I'm

---

[152] Benjamin Fearnow, "Maxine Waters: 'No Peace, No Sleep,' For Trump Cabinet Members, Applauds Public Shaming," *Newsweek U.S. Edition,* June 24, 2018, http://www.newsweek.com/maxine-waters-trump-harass-kirstjen-nielsen-stephen-miller-sarah-huckabee-993173.

shocked … shocked to find out there is gambling go on in here." Predictably and frightfully, our problems have not gone away using this approach. They have only returned in a more aggravated form, leaving few peaceful options available for dealing effectively with them. As evidence, both Iran and North Korea are still working toward the ability to propel nuclear destruction onto their detractors. Russia is saber rattling in defense of Syria and helping that country move its chemical weapons to Russian air bases in-country for protection. The previous administration's "pinky promises" have placed the United States in real jeopardy.

The General Welfare

As used here, this phrase is defined as the concern of the American government for the domestic health, peace, morality, and safety of its citizens.

Achieving these goals is difficult enough without adding the challenges created by intellectual helplessness into the mix. One such challenge is to define how far the government should involve itself in the affairs of its citizens. In general, a liberal philosophy leans toward the idea that there is a political solution to most problems; a conservative philosophy encourages a much more limited involvement. Going to the extreme in either the liberal or conservative viewpoint is ineffective and inefficient. Salvation or condemnation does not come from either "Air Force One"[153] or the "Invisible Hand."[154] Finding acceptable middle ground based on the unique competencies of the public and private sectors in particular fields, and in the proper defining of essential goods that should necessarily be provided by government is a good start.

A critical factor in this debate is accepting the need to move slow and steady when proposing to increase government involvement. Consider what happens when you prepare a meal. If you are unsure about the quantity of an ingredient, you don't guess and dump in a large quantity at the outset. Rather, you prudently add the ingredient a little at a time, frequently tasting its impact, before adding more. The same is true for government involvement. You can always add more, but it is nearly impossible to remove it from the mix once it has been stirred in.

---

[153] Charles Colson as quoted by John Stonestreet at various seminars.
[154] Adam Smith, *An Inquiry into the Nature and Causes of the Wealth of Nations* (London: W. Strahan and T. Cadell, 1776).

Another challenge created by intellectual helplessness is the government provision of continued entitlements to able-bodied persons. Author Dennis Prager wrote an insightful piece about this situation, discussing the addictive quality of getting something for nothing. He described unqualified recipients as refusing to view the entitlement as an addiction, but rather as a necessary drug to cure a problem. Prager states that this denial is buoyed by the use of the word *entitlement*, as it inaccurately conveys the message that the recipient has a right to the benefits. Additionally, this unsustainable practice has been encouraged by politicians who promise to continue these entitlements in an unspoken quid pro quo for votes. Prager warns that the uniqueness of an entitlement addiction ultimately does more damage to society than any other addiction: "Other addicts can ruin their own lives and those of loved ones, and drunk drivers kill and maim people. But society as a whole can survive their addictions. That is the not the case with entitlement addicts. The more people who receive and ultimately depend on entitlements, the sooner society will collapse economically. Society does not directly pay for drug addicts' drugs, alcoholics' alcohol or gamblers' gambling debts, but it pays every penny for entitlement addicts' addiction."[155]

Another proving ground for intellectual helplessness is in the provision of medical care. This has been an ongoing issue in this country for decades. As a young congressional intern in 1978, I remember reviewing Senator Ted Kennedy's bill for nationalized medical care. Fast-forward to the culmination of the Affordable Care Act or Obamacare. Whether you agree with Obamacare or not, any rational person would have to agree that it was unconscionable for Congress to approve such impactful legislation without first reading the bill. The "just trust me" mantra is like a naked man stepping on a beehive and then pleading, "Don't sting me." We were promised better, less-expensive health care provided by our current doctors. Instead we have been removing the stingers from our personal places. And what's with the political impotence of the Republicans? They've had seven years to craft an alternative.

Another confounding example of intellectual helplessness regarding general welfare has been the recent outbreak of shooting white police officers. There is no doubt our country still has serious issues to resolve in

---

[155] Dennis Prager, "The Most Dangerous Addiction of Them All: Entitlements," *Townhall*, March 21, 2017, htttps://townhall.com/columnists/dennisprager/2017/03/21/the-most-dangerous-addiction-of-them-all-entitlements.

ensuring a universal standard of respect and law enforcement related to all races. But focusing on race as a determiner for anything is dangerous and counterproductive. We all are children of God, and that is the only unifying distinction that really matters. One racial issue is not solved by creating another one in its place.

Another example of intellectual helplessness occurs when government incongruously allows unbridled diversity to become sine qua non, and it stands idly by even when such diversity tramples the constitutional freedoms and rights of its citizens. Any religion, ideology, or cause that seeks to *impose* its tenets onto the social, economic, and political institutions of society and, in the process, deprives individuals of their constitutional freedoms, is untenable. Yet that is precisely what we have witnessed in many American locales. Many of our educational and social institutions have provided access to and supported ideologies/movements whose implementation would result in depriving the rights of free speech, assembly, and life to anyone who disagrees with their tenets. This twisted priority structure poses a clear and present danger to the general welfare. The evidence of this danger is presently manifest in Europe, where laissez-faire governments allow the unvetted diversity of nearly any ideology, which has indirectly encouraged and/or directly contributed to intermittent acts of terrorism and the demographic and social remodeling of societies (a sort of social plastic surgery).

A last example of intellectual helplessness in the area of general welfare is dealing with injustice in an age of secular humanism (humans are sufficient for everything) and postmodernism (rejection of absolutes and objective reality; truth is relative). One problem is consistency. If there are no absolutes, then *injustice* should cease to be a word, because without standards, there is no such thing as the concept of justice. However, since saying the word *unfair* is an involuntary mental reflex whenever one is wronged, we can discard the notion of there being no absolutes.

A second problem is one of approach. If the key question for secular humanists is how to end injustice, the key problem to address is oppression.[156] Since humanists view life as a zero-sum game with only haves and have-nots, the have-nots have fought back by attempting to redefine the game to their advantage, claiming moral authority based on being a "victim" held down by societal oppressors. For example, if whites are at the top

---

[156] Professor Glenn Sunshine, Wilberforce Weekend seminar, Washington, DC, May 2017.

of the food chain, they must have gotten there by oppressing nonwhites; if men are ahead of women, they must have gotten there by oppressing women; if Western civilization is doing better than Eastern civilization, the Westerners must have gotten there by oppressing Easterners. The premise is that the oppressors have lost their moral authority to lead and must step back and provide opportunities for their victims. To facilitate this, building inscriptions must be erased and statutes torn down to decommemorate the oppressors (which illogically also removes the history of the oppression); men must become more feminine, and women more masculine, to create equality; and the West must foot the bill for the security and well-being of the world, ad infi-dumb-nitum.

The Blessings of Liberty

To combat intellectual helplessness connected with liberty, it is helpful to understand the mind-set of the Founding Fathers by identifying why they pursued liberty so diligently, and what they meant and did not mean in their use of the word *liberty* in the US Constitution.

Founding Father Dr. Benjamin Rush confirmed the primary goal of the US Constitution by stating unequivocally, "Liberty is the object of the Republic."[157] This laser-like focus on liberty was born out of hardship and want. As described in the book *Pilgrim's Progress,* "Recollect the civil and religious principles and hopes and expectations which constantly supported and carried them through all hardships with patience and resignation. Let us recollect it was liberty, the hope of liberty for themselves and us and ours, which conquered all discouragements, dangers, and trials."[158] Thomas Jefferson also declared his position on the source and importance of liberty: "The God who gave us life gave us liberty at the same time."[159] That is the reason liberty is described in the Constitution as *unalienable,* something that can neither be given nor taken away by humankind.

Professor Michael Novak has examined and expounded on the profound importance of liberty in and of itself during our founding: "Liberty is the axis of the universe, the ground of the possibility of love, human

---

[157] Benjamin Rush in *On Two* Wings by Michael Novak, 137.
[158] John Bunyan, *Pilgrim's Progress* (Philadelphia, PA: Charles Foster Publishing Co., 1891).
[159] Thomas Jefferson in *On Two Wings* by Michael Novak, 10.

and divine."[160] He continued with his analysis on the logic of liberty and its roots:

> The logic of the founding has its own originality, which is not that of any earlier group of Christian people. It is an amalgam of certain practical strains of Aristotle, Cicero, Seneca, and other writers about natural and civic virtue, mixed with biblical insights and reflections, and fed by many profoundly new reflections of human experience, both ancient and contemporary. Put in its starkest form, this logic moves through seven steps:
>
> 1. The founders saw in the two uniquely human activities *reflection* and *choice* the engines of liberty.
> 2. These activities suggest a highly *moral* concept of the natural right to liberty. This understanding of liberty draws upon both revelation and reason with the result that,
> 3. In matters of liberty, revelation and reason seem to be allies, not foes.
> 4. As experience teaches, without virtue (that is, habits of certain kinds) liberty cannot be sustained; unless you "conform your soul in self-control," you cannot exemplify self-government.
> 5. Given the changeability of human morals over time and the persistent tendency of morals to decline, the free society is inherently precarious.
> 6. Only a source stronger than moral reflection but inwardly linked to it can arrest this remorseless entropy, and that source is religion of a certain kind.
> 7. Trial and error teach that the advantages of liberty and the virtues it inculcates are better secured when religion is *not* established.[161]

---

[160] Novak, *On Two Wings*, 10.
[161] Novak, *On Two Wings*, 86.

Above, Novak provides the philosophical and practical underpinnings of the concept of liberty used by the founders to establish both a foundation (i.e., Declaration of Independence and Constitution) and structure (i.e., three branches of government and their institutions) for the implementation of liberty to a free people. It is an amalgamation of the best aspirations and practical observations of life from both humankind and sacred scripture.

Political science professor Daniel Elazar also specifically addressed the phrase "to secure the blessings of Liberty" found in the Constitution. Elazar writes, "The American founders certainly did not confuse liberty with anarchy. Their writings are peppered with comparisons between the two whose conclusions are unequivocal."[162] Elazar proposed that the founders' understanding of liberty was what he terms *federal liberty*: "the liberty to be a partner in establishing the covenant founding civil society (hence federal, from *foedus* meaning covenant) and then the liberty to live according to the terms of the covenant … True federal liberty requires that humans be partners in making the covenant which defines right and wrong and the rules of the game that flow from that definition before they can be expected to live according to them and that processes be provided for reexamination of the terms of the covenant and, if necessary, to change the rules."[163]

With these understandings, it is apparent that the founders' use of the term *liberty* did not mean *license* to do as one pleases for selfish purposes. It was establishing liberty in order to provide the freedom to participate in the formation of government, and the resulting obligation to live by the rules designed to achieve the common good and build the good society. On a practical note, Novak also stated that "the founders were not primarily metaphysicians; they were nation-builders. They were less concerned to publish precise disquisitions on liberty than to contrive practical institutions of liberty, institutions that would work—and work among people as they were, not some imagined species."[164]

Given this background, how are we doing in "securing the blessings of liberty to ourselves and our posterity?" Are we moving toward more or less freedom, when government institutions or employees do the following:

---

[162] Daniel J. Elazar, "'To Secure the Blessings of Liberty': Liberty and American Federal Democracy," Jerusalem Center for Public Affairs, http://www.jcpa.org/dje/articles2/blesslib.htm, 2.

[163] Elazar, "To Secure the Blessings of Liberty," 4.

[164] Novak, *On Two Wings*, 87.

- Deny the rights of or attempt to economically, politically, or socially destroy people with differing points of view (IRS targeting scandal, Fusion GPS anti-Trump dossier, Colorado Civil Rights Commission fining a baker for refusing to custom design a cake for a gay wedding, US senators illegally attempting to deny federal court judge nominee Amy Coney Barrett a judgeship based on her religious beliefs).

- Intentionally or unintentionally confuse liberty for license and randomly claim all things as morally equivalent (Illinois Department of Child Welfare ensuring children are provided identity training without the permission of their parents; requiring unisex bathrooms).

- Bear false witness by creating and releasing fake news about events or people (Susan Rice stating that Benghazi attack was in response to an inflammatory video; Attorney General Eric Holder claiming he didn't support the surveillance of journalists; Bush administration's claim that Iraq still had weapons of mass destruction; President Clinton stating, "I did not have sexual relations with that woman.")

- Adopt the presumption that liberty should be replaced by regulation. "Citizens used to think that liberty was primary and government had to justify its coercive regulation. Now people assume that government regulations are the neutral starting point and citizens must justify their liberty."[165] This is the mindset behind the bankrupt philosophy of socialism.

- Treat victims like perpetrators in the criminal justice system (sex traffic and domestic violence victims).

- Delay or deny the administration of justice (when the backlog of criminal and civil court cases results in litigants waiting for two years or more for a trial).

---

[165] Ryan T. Anderson, "The Continuing Threat to Religious Liberty," *National Review*, August 3, 2017, http:///www.nationalreview.com/article/450087/religious-liberty-under-attack.

- Institutionalize mediocrity by selecting incompetent leadership in any field.

- Abdicate authority to the malicious minority out of fear of confrontation or malicious and fabricated injury to one's reputation or livelihood (taking on Bill or Hillary Clinton).

- Sexually harass coworkers (congressional payoff fund for sexual harassment cases, Hollywood scandals).

- Cover up illegalities and abuses (Benghazi attack, Watergate, Bill Clinton / Loretta Lynch Phoenix tarmac meeting).

This list obviously can go on and on, which demonstrates our profound intellectual helplessness in securing the blessings of liberty.

Chapter 4

Intellectual Helplessness in the Business (Economic) Arena

*The world is moved along not only by the mighty shove of its heroes, but
also by the aggregate of the tiny pulses of each honest worker.*
—HELEN KELLER

*The object of life is not prosperity as we are made to
believe, but the maturity of the human soul.*
—ALEKSANDR SOLZHENITSYN

As discussed earlier, to fully understand our capitalist economic system, one must become acquainted with the motives of its author, Adam Smith. Smith wanted to discuss what causes wealth (rather than poverty) and present ways to produce that wealth. This was the genesis and motivation for ideas like the invisible hand of competition, free markets, incentives, and private property rights. For Smith, business was a tool to reach a moral objective, the expansion of individual freedom through economics.

Consider that economics is the means of exchange of a given culture. As such, economics is a question of value, and value is an ethical/moral term. As the continuum of corporate scandals emphatically points out, ethically untethered capitalism can have profound moral outcomes. Smith said the fundamental ethical question to be asked of any economic system is whether, taken as a whole over the long term, it will encourage good conduct.[166]

Smith's efforts expanded the discussion of economic justice from one of

---

[166] Wilson, *On Character*, 147.

distributive to *productive* justice. Before capitalism, production was finite. Thus, the ethical question was how best to distribute these limited goods. Smith invented the possibility of economic development when capitalism created the means for ordinary citizens to participate in the production and acquisition of wealth. Once increased production became a reality, the ethical question shifted to one of moral obligation: once you have the tools to produce in quantity, combined with the knowledge that millions are in need, it becomes a clear moral imperative to provide the necessary goods. The rise of commerce and industry precipitated great changes in the moral-cultural order—in morals, in thought, in aesthetics, and in orderly behavior. A new ethos counseled each person to try to better his/her condition.[167] These views were later expanded in the work of Max Weber in the late 1800s and early 1900s. Weber noted that capitalism was formed out of both religious and social factors, which he detailed in his famous work, *The Protestant Work Ethic and the Spirit of Capitalism.* Weber noted the impact of these factors in developing the rationalization and professionalism brought about by the scientific pursuits of mathematics, jurisprudence, bureaucratization of government administration, and effective business management.[168]

Given the magnitude of capitalism's impact on the average person and society at large, it's ironic that many have lost sight of, or have never been instructed about, the fact that capitalism was formed to achieve warm and fuzzy moral-cultural objectives, not cold and abrasive economic conquests. With such a moral imperative, it may surprise some that Smith favored its accomplishment through the freedom of individual choice rather than through the dictates of state control. The *invisible* hand of competition, *free* markets, *positive* incentives, and *private* property all imply at least an opportunity to make initial business decisions free from government intervention.

One of the great comings together in world history was the marriage of democracy and capitalism in forming the political-economic system of the United States. Was it providence or coincidence that *The Wealth of Nations* was written in 1776? In any event, the importance of commerce is one of the great goals of the US Constitution. As Professor Elazar comments, "Commerce is particularly valued because it is an efficient means

---

[167] Novak, *Three In One*, 26, 28.
[168] Wikipedia, "Max Weber," https://en.wikipedia.org/wiki/Max_Weber.

of organizing, harnessing, and diffusing power in light of American values through the marketplace."[169]

With this knowledge of Smith's motives, one can see why capitalism appealed to the Founding Fathers. It was consistent with their objective of liberty and mirrored their choice of a governmental system based on reflection and choice made possible through virtuous behavior. This linking of liberty with business activities concretely expressed itself in the creation of the corporation. The corporation is a legal *entity* granted certain privileges, including limited liability, indefinite life, and special tax treatment. In exchange for these privileges, the corporation has a *responsibility* to the society that granted them. In much the same way as there is a lady named Liberty in the political arena, there are entities named corporations in the economic arena.

Intellectual helplessness in the business arena derives from poor thinking and subsequent bad decision-making by those within business or from those who monitor it.

From Within

When intellectual helplessness is created from within the business community, it is typically through questionable practices. These business practices originate from either personality-based deficiencies of individual managers or from culture- or system-based deficiencies that have become institutionalized over time.[170]

Personality-based deficiencies relate to individual short-circuiting in three areas: one's personal deficiencies (related to identity, ego, or self-esteem); one's interpersonal deficiencies (difficulty establishing and maintaining adequate relationships at work); or one's behavioral deficiencies (based on either fear, self-interest, or lack of an adequate skill set).

Culture- or system-based deficiencies include organizational integrity issues (deficiencies in building and maintaining an ethical work culture); strategic foundation issues (deficiencies in the establishment of effective vision, mission, goal, and value statements for the organization, including deficiencies in building an effective and efficient organizational structure);

---

[169] Elazar, "To Secure the Blessings of Liberty," 10.

[170] Steven A. Danley and Dr. Peter Hughes, *Management Diseases and Disorders: How to Identify and Treat Dysfunctional Managerial Behavior* (Indianapolis, IN: Lulu Publishing Services, 2016).

personnel management issues (deficiencies in the supervision and management of an organization's human resources); process issues (deficiencies in organizational methods for the efficient and effective production of goods and services); or resource management issues (deficiencies in managing an organization's funds, buildings, equipment, etc.).

When businesses and their managers lose sight of the moral and social objectives of business, they analogously attempt to play chess with checker pieces and fail to advance the economic well-being of the communities in which they operate. Contrary to the belief of many practicing corporatists, corporations have multiple constituencies, including shareholders, employees, community, and country. If there is disagreement about constituencies extending beyond shareholders, it demonstrates a forgetfulness from whence one came. These are some well-known recent examples where forgotten business vows have crippled relationships:

- EpiPen pricing scandal—Mylan, the pharmaceutical company that owns the EpiPen product, had significantly raised the price (over 500 percent in a decade) for this lifesaving medication, an auto-injection system that provides a dose of epinephrine to ward off anaphylactic shock that can occur during an allergic reaction. The EpiPen, which costs Mylan about $30 to produce, was going for over $600 before coupons or rebates. The Centers for Medicare and Medicaid Services (CMS) confirmed to lawmakers that Mylan was also overcharging the government for the product. In addition, despite numerous warnings, it appears as if Mylan had continually misclassified EpiPen as a certain kind of drug, which inappropriately increased its price.

- Volkswagen's emissions fraud—the US Environmental Protection Agency (EPA) found that Volkswagen had intentionally programmed its turbocharged direct injection (TDI) diesel engines to activate certain emissions controls only during laboratory emissions testing. This programming caused the vehicles to fraudulently meet US standards for NOx outputs but emit up to forty times more NOx in real-world driving.

- Deepwater Horizon oil rig spill in the Gulf Coast—Owner British Petroleum's management pressured oil rig operations staff with losing their jobs to commence drilling from a deep-sea oil platform without first performing all the standard safety tests and activities because they were behind schedule.

- Wells Fargo—The banking company established phony customer accounts and then charged unwitting customers service fees.

- 2008 subprime mortgage crisis—The housing market was stocked with unstable, high risk subprime loans and banks were colluding with major bond-rating companies to maintain high ratings on bonds that were essentially worthless.

- NFL concussion scandal—The NFL previously failed to acknowledge and satisfactorily address the debilitating effects of concussions on professional football players, resulting in players continuing to play after suffering concussions, and in the league inadequately addressing the players' subsequent medical issues.

From Without

Intellectual helplessness outside the business community is typically the result of government heavy-handedness. One of the ways government creates intellectual helplessness in the business arena is when it fails to understand that businesses enable every other institution to exist. It is the only component of democratic capitalism whose mission is to produce wealth. Business produces products and services the public needs. It provides jobs and paychecks. It provides the infrastructure to get people and products from point A to point B. It tangibly motivates people to invent new and better ways of doing things. When we damage the pump to the economic well, we cannot water the crops and we starve to death. These are specific examples of damaging the business "pump" from the outside:

- large national debt
- high interest rates
- high corporate taxes
- trade policies that unevenly benefit one country over another
- overregulation of corporate activities that cripple a business's ability to provide a product or service at a reasonable price

- poor government oversight of corporate activities that allows illegal, unethical, or uneven competition behaviors in an industry
- different government organizations promulgating regulations and rules that are at cross purposes to each other
- public officials shaking down businesses for personal gain

Another impact of intellectual helplessness in the business arena occurs when government action weakens the ability of the business community to diversify the interests of the republic. Governments can only survive insofar as the material needs of its people are met. Business is both a necessary complement to and a designed check and balance on government. Business diffuses power, wealth, and talent across the nation. It produces a healthy multiplication of interests so no one faction can gain control. Government weakens business's ability to diversify the interests of the republic when it overregulates in extreme pendulum-swing responses to scandals that make the regulatory cure worse than the disease. Examples include poor environmental stewardship that resulted in the highly ambitious National Environmental Quality Act (NEQA); the 2008 subprime mortgage scandal, which vastly complicated the home loan process; and the overzealous Enron-prompted accounting regulations.

PART II

Consequences and Examples of
Our Intellectual Helplessness

Chapter 5

The Consequences of Intellectual Helplessness

Let education and training lapse for one generation, and the whole
grand structure of past achievements falls into ruins.
—RICHARD NIEBUHR

When the moral-cultural, government, and business arenas are saturated with overwhelming evidence of intellectual helplessness, we cannot achieve the good society. There is simply too much poor thinking and subsequent suboptimal choices being made to sufficiently patch the holes in the boat of democratic capitalism. Indeed, our poor thinking has slowly turned up the heat on us frogs in the pot to a point where we can no longer react and jump out of the water before it comes to a boil. Without intervention, we are on track to dehydrate and die in our own saunas. I did not intend to overachieve in identifying the multiple outbreaks of intellectual helplessness; they were just there and could not be ignored. This chapter is concerned with identifying the significant consequences that result from the current epidemic of intellectual helplessness in America.

As noted earlier in chapter 3, the preamble to the US Constitution lists a handful of ends that assist America in pursuing "a more perfect union." Professor Elazar has observed that these ends appear to be listed in a hierarchical order: "forming a more perfect union … will make it possible to establish justice, which will in turn ensure domestic tranquility. Domestic tranquility makes it possible to provide for the common defense, and a country both tranquil and secure by definition promotes the general welfare at one level and can devote itself to further efforts to that end. The highest of these ends is not simply liberty but the blessings of liberty, that encompass justice, tranquility, security, and welfare."[171]

Those ends are *action-orientated*. I would like to suggest that several *thought-orientated* ends precede these action-orientated ends. These thinking (intellectual) ends are also hierarchical. Their presence/absence or proper/improper sequencing can be used to predict our ability to implement efficient and effective decisions that address the needs of the day. Deficiencies in the thought-orientated ends create intellectual helplessness and can impact the taste and, at times, the viability of life. The thought-orientated ends include these:

- reality
- meaning
- identity
- rationality
- choice
- consensus

Reality

Reality is the "state of things as they actually exist."[172] Sanity is the accurate observation, substantial agreement, and integral interaction with reality. Democratic capitalism has heretofore survived untold attempts of ideological assassination because it approximates reality and matches actual life. Each one of us is an economic agent, a citizen (political agent), and each of us seeks meaning, follows conscience, and pursues truth and understanding (moral-cultural agent).[173]

Intellectual helplessness is like wearing the wrong prescription glasses. It keeps us from viewing reality clearly. Here are some of the general consequences of not having 20/20 reality vision:

- We are unable to function effectively in the world. When we don't see things as they really are, and base our actions on what is not there, or miss what is there, we cease to effectively function. We

---

[171] Elazar, "To Secure the Blessings of Liberty,"1.
[172] Oxford English Dictionary, Oxford University Press.
[173] Novak, *Three in One*, 45.

don't celebrate the joys that are right in front of us that would bind us together; we don't react appropriately to the dangers that have the potential for our destruction; and when we do act, we do so incoherently due to false perceptions.

All of us, in our own hubris, at one time or another attempt to create our own definitions of good and bad to fit a desired outcome. The problem is that these definitions are often emotion- rather than fact-based. For many people today, their number one priority is to feel good. Combine this with the philosophy of me, and the priority becomes feeling good about oneself. Thus, anything that makes one feel good is promoted; anything than makes one feel bad is discouraged. When this philosophy is applied to the real word, it looks something like this: I am in favor of unlimited, unvetted immigration because it is who we are; I am in favor of complete religious freedom even when it advocates violence because we shouldn't tell others how to live their lives; I am in favor of mandated universal health care because everyone must be healthy; I am in favor of treating animals as if they were human beings because I love my fur baby; and I am in favor of free university-level education for everyone because they have a right to be educated.

These are all good feelings in the abstract, but they are not balanced with good thinking that would provide for the implementation of an efficient and effective response to each one in real life. For example, unvetted immigration dilutes our American value system by allowing into the country those who may not espouse our values or have no intention of assimilating into our culture (e.g., adoption without becoming family), and increases the danger of allowing terrorist elements into the country; unchecked religious freedom allows for complete freedom to those religions that believe and practice human sacrifice, genital mutilation, the killing of nonbelievers, and subjugation of women; universal health care removes freedom of choice for health care and is unaffordable; insisting on rights for animals removes meat, poultry, and fish from the menu; and universal university education extinguishes initiative and is unaffordable without severe cuts in other critical areas.

When our desires are prioritized over rational thinking, we give away the store, preventing us from acting in a manner that would beneficially address the issues of our day. It relegates us to the porch, drinking beer on a hot summer day, and watching the weeds of the world overtake our gardens.

Functioning effectively also requires that we recognize the existence of both physical and nonphysical realities. The current elite emphasis is that we should only be concerned with physical reality that can be empirically validated by science. This is frighteningly limiting and grossly irresponsible to the obvious. One cannot be serious about obtaining knowledge if one excludes most of what life consists of. How many obvious nonphysical realities are we aware of that dictate our thoughts and behaviors: thinking, truth, logic, time, desires, intentions, intuition, the wind, radio frequencies, spirit, and the like. Not to be morbid, but consider the profound occasion of being present during a person's death. In one moment, there is life: a beating heart, breath, eye contact, warm flesh, and conversation. In the next moment, there is a lifeless body. The body remains, but the spirit is gone. In these moments, there is the profound realization that personhood is nonphysical. When we miss this reality, we irrationally pluck out one of our eyes.

- The death of truth spells the death of civilization. If we cannot agree on what accurately describes reality as it is, we have no basis for a shared perspective, common ground, the common good, or the ability to work as a collective. Socrates realized that "the death of truth would mean the death of virtue, and that the death of virtue would spell the death of civilization. Without truth and virtue, the only possible outcome is barbarism."[174] If we miss the truth of things, we choose convenience and self-benefit over hard work and the common good. In America, that means 324 million people looking out for themselves and scheming to get theirs. If we don't reign in our impulses toward individual satisfaction and create opportunities for common values that illustrate a more beautiful and satisfactory common good, we will destroy the moral and ethical infrastructure required for community.

---

[174] R. C. Sproul, *The Consequences of Ideas: Understanding the Concepts that Shaped Our World* (Wheaton, IL: Crossways Books, 2000), 28.

Meaning

Reality provides a legitimate basis for something to have meaning. Things exist because they have an end, a purpose, or significance. For instance, love exists for the development and maintenance of relationships, shelters are built for protection, air provides oxygen, food provides nutrition, determination motivates activity for achievement, exercise provides health, information provides a basis for knowledge, and the pursuit of truth allows for thinking clearly and acting rationally.

Meaning provides humans with the psychological necessity of purpose, which makes participating in life worthwhile. It gives us guidance, motivation, and hope. When we are intellectually helpless, we become a train wreck of amnesiacs, forgetting our inherent purpose(s). These are some of the consequences that result from a lack of meaning:

- Words lose their significance. If there is no meaning, words are moot. Since there is nothing worth talking about, there is nothing for words to describe. For any words that must be used, if there is no clarity of definition, communication is severely hampered. We become our own burning Tower of Scrabble.

- There are no answers to life's most important questions: Who am I? Where did I come from? Am I significant in any way? Is there life after death? Silence.

- We confuse love with desire. Love seeks and implements the good for others. Desire seeks and implements one's individual wants. If there is a lack of meaning, the obvious default is the pursuit of desire over love in our relationships with others.

- We become consumers rather than creators. With a lack of meaning, our focus becomes ourselves. This focus encourages us to passively receive things for us rather than create something worthy for others to enjoy.

- Incoherence, confusion, dissonance, and separation. If there is no meaning, there is no coherence to life and therefore no reason to bring people together. We lose the ability to interact successfully with reality and each other. If we go too far down this path, our sanity is questioned, and in our self-imposed world of fiction, we may be considered mentally ill.

- The loss of beauty. There is beauty only when there is meaning. I react winsomely to something because it means something to me, deep within my soul.

- Lack of inheritance. Without meaning, there is no ultimate objective and nothing of value to pass on to the next generation. Old age becomes useless.

- Irony is franchised. Irony is created when actual results are the opposite of intended results. Intellectual helplessness franchises a chain of Irony Cafes that serve intellectual fast food, which makes us bloated, overweight, and unhealthy. When too many ironies are in the fire, it produces a menu that includes platters of incongruity, guile, mendacity, farce, sham, pretense, paradox, contrariness, travesty, mockery, satire, sarcasm, sardonicism, and hypocrisy. When there is a lack of meaning, ironic circumstances occur: If there is no meaning, why does everyone want to write a book? Why do people who do not believe in right or wrong try so hard to convince others that their views about right and wrong are right? Why do we want organic in everything except intellectual issues, where we prefer the artificial? Why do we emphasize diversity and then act surprised when there is no unity? Why do people obsess and violently react against past racial slavery and ignore their own enslavement to poor thinking and bad behaviors? Why don't those at the top of terrorism organizations demonstrate leadership by example?

- Subjugation. Power never exists in a vacuum. When life is without purpose, we are easily manipulated and susceptible to intentional distraction by the irrelevant and trivial. We become incapable of ruling or defending ourselves because we see no reason to do so. Inevitably, someone does it for us.

Identity

Meaning makes identity matter. Identity provides the basis for clear and accurate thinking about who we are, what it means to be human, what our skills and abilities are, and what our purpose is (me vs. us). When we are not clear about our identity, it contributes to intellectual helplessness, and can result in the following negative consequences:

- Lostness. Not knowing *who* you are is like not knowing *where* you are. It results in inertia and misalignment. We must get our bearings before we venture out on a productive journey. In the past, for the most part, our bearings were as stable as a compass. North was labeled north, and west was labeled west. We knew and worked on accepting who and what we are. As a result, we accepted and worked with reality to be our best selves. We had a direction and set out toward a logical destination based on reality. Today, we are told that we can make our own fictional compass based on whatever magnetic force we desire. If one is a man and wants to be a woman, just claim one feels more *x* than *y*. If one is a perpetrator and wants to be a victim, just claim that the punishment feels too harsh. If one is an illegal immigrant and wants to be a citizen, just claim that one feels like an American. If one is biracial and wants to identify with only one race, just claim that one feels more black than white. While artificial manipulation may accommodate a desire, it is not better for us psychologically, interpersonally, or behaviorally. For one thing, it's not reality. It's like pretending the traffic light is green rather than red. For another, if we don't know or accept who we are, we will certainly have trouble knowing or caring about other people. Lastly, it encourages us to choose behaviors that satisfy our desires first, rather than the common good. An unclear identity is a maze rather than a map.

- Failure to fulfill our crucial roles. Humans are at the top of Earth's pecking order because we are complex organisms with personalities, aspirations, and the ability to reason, unlike any other creature. When we fall short of fulfilling our stewardship role, we irrationally move down the pecking order, abdicating our authority and our responsibility to rule and care for our planet. To put it succinctly, we are to love people, and positively steward plants, animals, and all other things. When we don't fulfill these roles, the planet suffers.

- Ironic attempts to waive our/others unalienable rights. The word *unalienable* means that certain rights are immutable, and a person cannot be denied them because these rights were not given by humans but by a creator. This idea matches the reality of the human heart's innate desire for freedom. When we miss this truth about ourselves, we become intellectually helpless, allowing others to assert control over us, or we futilely attempt to assert control over others.

- Thinking about our gender based on feelings rather than physical reality. The differences between men and women are obvious, objective, and based on fact and scientific validation. Still, some choose to believe that their gender does not have to be based on physical reality but on how they feel on the inside. This emotion is an intensely personal (identity) matter. It reveals the extreme fragility of human beings in as much as they are sadly unable to accept themselves as they are. The fragility also results from its hypocrisy. The same naturalists who claim reality can only be verified by empirical means abandon that requirement when it comes to their gender identity. In gender identity, what I unempirically feel trumps physical reality. This deep-down, known illusion and hypocrisy create a powder keg of vitriol against anyone who questions it. We are most angry when someone places a mirror in front of our lives. But in the pursuit of truth, we must surrender to the reality that beliefs are relative and facts are not. I may feel like a surgeon, but if I am not one and attempt to operate on someone, chances are it will result in a mess. Today's predominate philosophy of me (vs. us) focuses on feelings over facts, conjuring up a basis on which to validate self-gratification. In this environment, if everything is judged to be relative based on how one feels, one cannot tolerate someone who posits a truth, particularly if it is a truth claim that in some way may impinge upon one's autonomy. Detractors are labeled judgmental at best, evil at worst, for pointing out the obvious. This illusion is the height of intellectual helplessness because if one can redefine one's gender based on how one feels, one can redefine anything at any time because feelings change. And if anything can be anything, nothing can be differentiated, then everything becomes nothing, and hopelessness prevails. Take for instance, professional, scientific findings related to gender confusion:

o   Gender confusion is not a biological problem. It is a psychosocial problem. Psychiatrist Paul McHugh, a leading mental health expert, compassionately warns about the gender-confused becoming falsely "persuaded that seeking a drastic physical change will banish their psycho-social problems."[175]
o   It is biologically impossible to change one's sex. "People who undergo sex-reassignment surgery do not change from men to women or vice versa. Rather they become feminized men or masculinized women."[176]
o   Tracked by Vanderbilt University and London's Portman Clinic, 70 to 80 percent of children with transgender feelings abandon their confusion and grow naturally into adult life. Thus, a better solution is "devoted parenting" rather than "surgically amputating normal organs."[177]
o   A 2011 Swedish study showed that the suicide rate is twenty times higher than the general population for those who have undergone sex reassignment surgery beginning ten years after the surgery.[178]

The problem with all of this is that some are asking society to follow into the darkness of gender confusion and participate in its lostness by acknowledging something that is not objective and true, but rather subjective and false, with dramatic negative consequences.

[175] Paul McHugh, "Transgender Surgery Isn't the Solution," *Wall Street Journal*, May 13, 2016, https://www.wsj.com/articles/paul-mchugh-transgender-surgery-isnt-the-solution-1402615120.
[176] McHugh, "Transgender Surgery."
[177] McHugh.
[178] C. Dhejne P. Lichenstein, M. Borman, Al Johansson, N. Langstrom, M. Landen, "Long-term follow-up of transsexual persons undergoing sex reassignment surgery: cohort study in Sweden," *National Center for Biotechnical Information, US National Library of Medicine*, February 22, 2011, https://www.ncbi.nlm.nih.gov/pubmed/21364939.

- Inability to distinguish friends from enemies. When we don't know who we are, what our purpose is, and what rights we have or don't have, we are necessarily and noticeably fearful, suspicious, and paranoid. We become prime targets for manipulation and are prone to engage in hate and violence as a protective mechanism.

- Seeking victimhood over responsibility. When we miss the lecture on being "endowed by our Creator with certain unalienable rights," we can become unclear about who we are or what our purpose is. The result is insecurity, leading us to believe that someone must be to blame for it. This causes us to see ourselves as victims of a dubious existence. When backed into this nonintellectual corner, we either seek answers or lash out in angry protection. We either determine to aspire to our potential or ask, How low can we go? Unfortunately, today victimhood is rewarded and therefore can be an appealing option. It is like receiving the fictional Willy Wonka gold ticket in hopes of gaining permanent residency at the chocolate factory of entitlement.

Rationality

Identity provides us with knowledge about ourselves, our roles, and our capabilities—the ingredients necessary to practice rationality. Rationality is identifying facts and using a logical process to think, make inferences, and come to conclusions about how things really work, and to use that knowledge for sound deliberation, reasonable choices, and the efficient and effective implementation of our choices. Consider how many intellectual pursuits contain the word *logic*: psychological, sociological, biological, theological, technological. Rationality delivers us from the false or absurd. During the deliberation process, one logically identifies, analyzes, and makes choices between issues and options. When we fail to follow the rules of logic, plug false information into our mental equations, or use the wrong formula to solve a problem, intellectual helplessness results. These are some of the consequences that result from a lack of rationality:

- The replacement of facts, logic, and reason with insufficient or unethical criteria to judge the quality of thoughts and actions. As Dallas Willard observed, there is an ethic to believing the truth

114

and to not believing the truth: (1) we ought to do what is beneficial for human life, (2) our beliefs can cause great good or harm, and (3) we have some degree of control over the beliefs we have, and hence some responsibility to see to it that they are true or at least rational. "To be irrational is to be morally irresponsible, and to be morally admirable we must be rational because of the fundamental importance of true beliefs to human welfare."[179]

Irrationality often occurs when personal desire and appetite prevail and take the place of fact-finding, logic, and reason. Our appetites typically result in rationalization rather than rationality. Rationalization looks for excuses, typically in the form of unreasoned opinions or beliefs, to try to justify what one wants. One unreasoned opinion is believing "the fallacy that once we have analyzed something, we have understood it. Often true understanding … requires participation."[180] Another unreasoned opinion is pragmatism, believing that actions are judged solely on whether they produce successful results, without regard to whether they are consistent with an overarching purpose, or accomplished within moral boundaries. This approach authorizes the utilization of unethical practices to obtain one's desires, such as weaponizing irrationality to intentionally blur an issue, make false accusations against another, avoid responsibility, and confuse and frustrate others into inertia. A final example of an unreasoned opinion is the belief that it is the government's responsibility to provide each citizen will all their needs. Such is the irrationality of socialism, where we essentially attempt to extend childhood and refuse to grow up, transitioning from parental to governmental dependence. In proposing to do so, we irrationally: (1) place the sustainability of our nation in the hands of those who eschew personal responsibility; (2) exterminate the whole point of America (freedom) and its operational platform (democratic capitalism through diversified checks and balances); (3) replace 242 years of democratic success, highlighted by the fact that immigrants are still clamoring for entrance into the US, for a yet-to-be successful system

---

[179] Willard, *Renewing the Christian Mind*, chapter 27.
[180] Andy Crouch, *Culture Making: Recovering Our Creative Calling* (Downers Grove, IL: IVP Books, 2008), 93, 94.

of socialism (e.g., USSR, Cuba, Venezuela, Greece); and (4) preclude our ability to undo any mistakes for a generation—a country can go from democracy to socialism without a fuss, but from socialism to democracy requires a revolution.

- The inability to define or choose better options, or to exclude or winnow poorer options. In our relativistic world, a litany of options abounds for almost any situation. Unfortunately, this has increased the ante in each of the "good, bad, and ugly" option pots. In just one familiar example, advances in technology have delivered more winning hands but also added more places to both wisely and foolishly spend the money. To successfully and efficiently address issues, one must be able to effectively narrow these options to what is practically and ethically best. Author Andy Crouch has stated that "an essential part of the creative process is in fact the work of sorting, separating and even excluding some alternatives in favor of others ... The best creativity involves discarding that which is less than best, making room for the cultural goods that are the very best that we can do with the world that has been given to us."[181] If practical rationality guided by ethical parameters is not used to make these decisions, then illogic, irrationality, and nefarious means take its place, and the sorting process is polluted. Part of that pollution occurs when, as Dallas Willard observed, "a major function of the mind in a broken soul is to find reasons for why what is bad is good ... A man's natural role is to find the right way to act—a way that is just and right, and leads to what is good ... When the person as a whole is doing what is wrong and evil, the mind turns from reason to rationalization. From establishing what is right in order do it, it turns to establishing that *whatever* is done is 'right' and 'good,' or at least 'necessary.' That is the madness."[182] Unfortunately, this has become demonstrably evident in many political elections.

- Not providing sufficient time for deliberation. Another limiting element to rationality is time. In our fast-paced world, we rarely

---

[181] Crouch, 106, 107.
[182] Dallas Willard, *The Great Omission: Reclaiming Jesus's Essential Teachings on Discipleship* (New York: HarperCollins Publishers, 2006), 147.

afford ourselves the necessary time for reflection and analysis due big decisions. We tend to decide quickly and adjust on the fly as necessary. For example: congressional consideration and passage of far-reaching health care legislation without allowing its members to read the legislation; personal impulse purchases of large-ticket items; guilt or innocence being determined by the media; lust fulfillment rather than love commitment; and so on. As Professor Phillip Johnson described, "Trying to get to the answer before one has understood all the right questions is a prime source of error in human affairs … People who start from the wrong foundation don't make just one error, they create a whole tower of errors."[183]

- The dismantling of the foundational legal concept of the "reasonable person." The reasonable person concept describes a hypothetical person in society who "exercises average care, skill, and judgment in conduct and who serves as a comparative standard for determining liability."[184] In order for justice to be considered and administered, there must be a way to determine what a reasonable person would do in similar circumstances. Today, the reasonable person is an endangered species precisely because the entrenched elitist minority has hunted down and tried to maim or kill anyone trying to reason. The use of reason beneficially limits and narrows, separating the wheat from the chaff. This does not play well in an age of unlimited choice and preference. As a result, one consequence is that we are literally in danger of killing off any effective way to reach just decisions that fairly adjudicate complaints or crimes. In many circumstances, we are literally "up a (unreasonable) creek without a paddle.

- Difficulty in recognizing appropriate linkages and updating knowledge bases. Linkages exist throughout reality. Rationality presupposes these connections and takes logistical steps to identify causal relationships before changes are made, and to update multiple databases once changes are implemented. Irrationality and a desire-based approach are ignorant or dismissive of connections

---

[183] Johnson, *The Right Questions*, 28.
[184] Wikipedia, "Reasonable person," en.wikipedia.org/wiki/Reasonable person.

and therefore often fail to look for them or ignore them when inconvenient to one's position. Take for instance "right to life" issues, such as abortion and euthanasia. Few thought to consider that the ability to abort a child to save the life of the mother or terminate a pregnancy due to rape or incest would morph into a nearly unlimited right to abortion, resulting in more than 59 million abortions from 1973 to 2014, or the selling of fetus body parts. And few accurately consider that allowing people the right to die, approved by the government and carried out by medical providers, will likely morph into the "duty to die" when society determines there are too many people requiring too much and too expensive medical care by an insufficient number of providers.

- Deviant opinions and their propagators get more attention than time-tested rationality and reasonable folk. When the gold needle of rationality gets thrown into the haystack of irrationality, it becomes outnumbered and hard to find. The hay fever of brashness and its overamplification sneeze their way into the public eye and drown out the "still small voice" of quiet competence. The loud and the irrelevant soon push aside sanity and obtain a foothold. The volume discount of irrationality becomes the norm over the quiet premium of rationality. Never mind that irrationality is only one-ply and causes mishaps. In this environment, the advantage goes to liars, schemers, cheaters, con artists, empty suits, and egomaniacs. As our culture continues to bombard us with mediocre opinions through manipulative advertising, we come to believe them through repetition and begin to develop a twisted comfort by their presence. As a result, we lose the ability to recognize and choose greatness when we see it. Such is the case when ego-, power- and monetary-driven celebrities drive scripted and staged social agendas; when talented artists can't get their work viewed because they don't have an established media presence to market it; or when those who have the most positive impact on our individual lives (e.g., teachers, coaches, servicemen and servicewomen, ministers, care workers) barely make a livable wage.

- People are more easily led into evil because they have ceased to think clearly. If all opinions are equally valid, then critical thinking is unnecessary, as there is no way to distinguish between reason and unreason, justice or injustice. This pin-your-tail-on-the-donkey approach to one's choice selection results in illegitimate risk-taking, which eventually causes some people to drive the wrong way on a one-way street. As C. S. Lewis commented several decades ago, "Education without values, as useful as it is, seems rather to make man a more clever devil."[185] And as Daniel Levitin said recently, "The unique problem we face today is that misinformation has proliferated and lies can be weaponized to produce social and political ends we would otherwise be safeguarded against."[186]

- The increased use and acceptance of unexamined clichés. Today our language is filled with throwaway lines that sound impressive but fail to yield results. Sounding smart is a sellable attribute as long as one moseys out of town before implementation or controls the analytics group that doctors the results. An unexamined phrase like "celebrate diversity," for instance, takes the positive individual goal of diversity, isolates it from the team goal of unity, repeats it over and over until it is reflexively accepted, and then unilaterally pushes for its unproductive and nonunifying lone achievement. The desire to "Celebrate Sam" is rational when it's his birthday; it is pandering when it's inscribed over the mantel.

- The emotional is more heavily weighted than the intellectual. When logic and rationality are put in a drawer, decisions get made based on emotions, which are fleeting and can be mercurial. Levitin noted, "A big part of the problem here is that the human brain often makes up its mind based on emotional considerations, and then seeks to justify them. People follow their emotional intuition rather than a logical response, oblivious to the increased risk ... An odd feature of human cognition is that once we form a belief or accept a claim, it's very hard for us to let go, even in the face of overwhelming evidence and scientific proof to the contrary."[187] Our resulting

---

[185] C. S. Lewis, "Brainy Quote," https://www.brainyquote.com/quotes/authors/c/c_s_lewis.html.
[186] Levitin, *Weaponized Lies*, xx.
[187] Levitin, *Weaponized Lies*, 124, 205.

impetuousness creates anxiety, fear, instability, and a lack of trust. It also makes it hard to know how to present the disadvantages of a position or a dissenting voice when it is critical that one be given. When one can't appeal to the parking space of rationality, one is forced to deal with the five-story parking structure of emotion.

Choice

Rationality gives us the ability and motivation to make better choices. It encourages the use of liberty to choose the good, rather than license to seek the less-than-good, precisely because it is required to achieve the good society. Intellectual helplessness ensures that poor choices will be made more often than good ones. Some of the consequences resulting from making poor choices are these:

- Establishment of an inadequate strategic foundation. As identified earlier in this book, on a macro level, everyone's initial governing choice is between accepting and cooperating with reality, or trying to cover reality with a façade that aligns with our personal desires. We can choose to be governed by the desire to see that good is done to others and us (i.e., love) or by the desire to achieve personal autonomy (i.e., self-focus). These two different strategic foundations are approximated in the following chart:

Strategic Foundation	Vision	Mission	Goals	Strategies
Love (the philosophy of us)	Relationship	Seek the common good	Justice Freedom Equality Community Maximum joy	Cooperate with reality Obtain moral knowledge Learn servanthood Be sacrificial Maintain balance Exhibit transparency
Self-focus (the philosophy of me)	Happiness	Seek self-satisfaction	Winning License Status Privacy Maximum pleasure	Construct own "reality" Reject moral codes Satisfy one's desires Focus on perception Become member of the elite Promote oneself

We seldom chart out our personal strategic foundations because it is too personal, and doing so requires acknowledging our thought processes and choices.

- Easy ignorance avoids dealing with and fixing problems. In the movie *Scent of a Woman,* Al Pacino's character, Lt. Col. Frank Slade, admits, "Now I've come to the crossroads in my life. I always knew what the right path was. Without exception, I knew. But I never took it. You know why? It was too damn hard."[188] Easy has dominated societal decision-making over the past decade. It is easier to ignore or placate, rather than step into a mess, get one's hands dirty, and be unfairly denigrated for it. It is much easier to disingenuously commit to something one knows he/she won't do, rather than sign on the dotted line. It is easier to hate rather than love somebody who disagrees with us. It is easier to label and call people names, rather than come up with a good alternative or argument for a position. It is easier to incite emotion, than appeal to intellect. It is easier to pay for the problem to go away, rather than toil to correct the behavior. We choose the easy because it is easy. Our moral-cultural, political, and economic systems and consciences would be better served if we chose the difficult because it is the right thing to do.

- Help is refused from legitimate places that can give it. When something does not fit into the flawed ideological boxes of our illegitimate desires, it discourages us from asking for help from reputable sources. We disqualify good philosophies, treatments, products, or people with integrity because it might encourage a change in thinking or behavior that we don't want at any cost—the recognition that we might be fallible, insufficient, and incapable of handling complete autonomy. Examples include attempts to exclude the offering of voluntary service provision or counseling from religious nonprofits, or individuals refusing to give up addictions as a condition of an institution providing them with assistance.

---

[188] IMdb, "Scent of a Woman/quotes," www.IMdb.com quotes.

- People get hurt, particularly the marginalized in society. When bad logic is used and poor choices result, someone always gets hurt. Unjustly, it is usually not the perpetrator but the innocent bystander with limited resources to fight back. Part of the "decisionomics" for choosing bad ideas is to make sure one does not live in the neighborhood where the irrational and impractical are being implemented.

- Ill-gotten gain changes the rules of the game. When wrong choices are rewarded, the rules of the game are unofficially rewritten and displayed in areas trafficked by the ethically challenged. Soon the following pathologies are present:

  - o Unqualified leadership rises to the top, which institutionalizes mediocrity by the survival and propagation of the unfittest.
  - o Good employees are marginalized; bad employees are "opportunized."
  - o There is rampant hypocrisy based on the existence of both official written and unofficial unwritten policies and procedures.
  - o When it is every person for him- or herself, it becomes difficult to see a reason to help the helpless.

- The range of choices is expanded to an unmanageable level. More is not always better. Indeed, good ideas and choices are typically less prevalent than mediocre or bad ones, or everyone would be famous and wealthy. Consistently accepting and implementing bad choices encourages an unlimited number of proposals, making the identification of the Mr./Ms. Right idea more difficult.

- Scarce resources are wasted. In a form of economic, political, and moral-cultural self-mutilation, we allocate our scarce resources to the pyramid schemes of underachievers on an abyss-trek, boldly going where everyone has gone before, having experienced similar failures. There is no originality in mediocrity.

Consensus

Better choices seek the common good and bring us together; poorer choices typically seek personal gratification and necessarily pull us apart. Consensus requires debate and compromise. It is what made the Declaration of Independence and Constitution possible, and their implementation feasible. As identified earlier, Professor Elazar discussed one of the illuminating deliberations in the founders' quest to write an acceptable Constitution, the compromise around the concept of *federal liberty*: "True federal liberty requires that humans be partners in making the covenant which defines right and wrong and the rules of the game that flow from that direction before they can be expected to live according to them and that processes be provided for reexamination of the terms of the covenant and, if necessary, to change the rules."[189] Intellectual helplessness interferes with the ability to create consensus. Deficiencies in this area can result in the following consequences:

- Disagreement is equated with hatred. The mobilized and malicious minority are on a search-and-destroy mission to obliterate anyone who disagrees with them. Their mantra is total autonomy to live life however one chooses. In this worldview, *no* becomes a four-letter word. Yet, in a mind-numbing twist of hypocrisy, total autonomy doesn't include the freedom to choose not to live with an autonomous point of view. In this hyper-personalized environment, disagreement is experienced as hatred: "My choices are me, they are my identity, who I am. If you deny me my choices, you deny me as a person. Therefore, you hate me and are trying to destroy me. As such, I must hate you back before you extinguish my autonomous self." This viewpoint is contrary to human civilization and coexistence. It is a tenet of a civilized society that one can disagree with people without wanting to eradicate them.

- Disorder happens. When there is no acknowledged basis on what is right and wrong, there is no basis for leadership to be exercised. When this is discovered, people start doing whatever they want. Rather than voluntary cooperation, we get competition without

---

[189] Elazar, "To Secure the Blessings of Liberty," 4, 5.

any rules. In response, good people barricade themselves in darkness and mourn their captivity; the hoodlums bask in the sunlight and celebrate their license. Eventually the world gets turned on its head, as the good people must choose to fight to retain their humanity, dignity, and unalienable rights.

- Participation is limited to concurrence. Democracy allows its people a seat at the table to establish the rules in exchange for following those rules once the majority has spoken. When consensus is replaced with obedience to one point of view, it necessarily dilutes the talent pool. Weak-minded and weak-willed sycophants get placed in charge. The tip of the spear becomes Pee Wee Herman, Captain Kangaroo, or Goofy. The insipid can't bring about consensus so they dictate and demand silent obedience to the suboptimal.

- Dictatorship gets invited to the party. Power never exists in a vacuum. And there is always competition among "peace vendors" selling their wares. They know that people are generally willing to relinquish some of their freedom for security. They initially promise balance but inevitably deliver extremes. As a result, civil liberties are denied to conscientious objectors, and different points of view are punished. When there is competition, the winner doesn't walk away without a trophy.

- Affirmation is mandated. In this environment, one's quiet acquiescence to repugnant views is an insufficient level of compliance. There must be a (false) public affirmation of the party line. It is not enough that one silently obeys. The intelligentsia demands that people also publicly *support, facilitate,* and *endorse* that which they vehemently disagree with and enforce sanctions against those who do not assimilate.

The ultimate expression of the above consequences is its manifestation in everyday life. More and more, as we addictively pursue our self-desires over the common good, we are removing the ability of our institutions to achieve their stated missions. It is like disconnecting one's kidneys, preventing the removal of waste products from the body. As a result, it is becoming more and more difficult to get knowledge from education, security and liberty from government, moral authority from religion, civility from family, justice from courts, customer service from business, beauty from art, or accuracy from media.

The next chapter identifies specific examples of the impact of intellectual helplessness in the moral-cultural, government, and business arenas.

Chapter 6

Examples of Intellectual Helplessness

From barbarism to civilization takes a century, from civilization to barbarism takes a day.
—WILL DURANT

The following are examples of intellectual helplessness present and accounted for in American society.

Examples of Intellectual Helplessness in the Moral-Cultural Arena

The examples are listed by the moral-cultural categories of philosophy, family, education, and news/arts media.

Philosophy

*The preservation of the species is a high abstraction which
does not even enter the mind of unreflective people.*
—C. S. LEWIS

*Moral imagination is the strange facility of discerning greatness, justice, and
order, beyond the appetite and self-interest ... It is the combined product of
intuition, instinct, imagination, and long and intricate experience.*
—EDMUND BURKE

Examples of intellectual helplessness emanating from problematic philosophical beliefs include the following:

1. Dismantling of heritage

Today's culture is filled with examples of lack of humility. Somehow, despite all we know about the chaos we have and continue to create, many still irrationally believe we are smart enough to replace or revise the wisdom of our founders who made democratic capitalism possible. Even if one were to develop a better approach, would it be wise to erase our working papers? And who would make those decisions? As noted by Hoover Institution Senior Fellow Victor Davis Hanson, "We are in an age of melodrama, not tragedy, in which we who are living in a leisured and affluent age … pass judgment on prior ages because they lacked our own enlightened and sophisticated views of humanity—as if we lucky few were born fully ethically developed from the head of Zeus … Be careful, 21st-century man. Far more hypercritical generations to come may find our own present moral certitude—late-term and genetically driven abortion, the rise of artificial intelligence in place of human decision-making, the harvesting and selling of aborted fetal organs, ethnic and tribal chauvinism, euthanasia, racially segregated dorms and 'safe places'—as immoral as we find the sins of our own predecessors."[190] Here are a few specific examples:

- Attempts to denigrate and replace the heritage of individual initiative with the acceptance of collective "government day care" (i.e., government entitlement programs that encourage dependence rather than independence).

- Removing moral codes from our public institutions. These codes provide the public with the basis and motivation for our laws and regulations. Take, for example, the Ten Commandments. One does not have to believe in God to recognize the profound contribution these moral codes have made to democratic capitalism. As author T. M. Moore explains, "Wisdom for governing can be discovered in the law of God quite apart from any of its 'religious' import … The law of God is thus a valuable resource for questions of ethics and public policy … The objective … was to bring the good blessings of God—His wisdom, mercy, justice, and love—into the experience of the nations of

---

[190] Victor Davis Hanson, "Our War Against Memory," *National Review*, August 22, 2017, 6, 7.

the world … We disqualify some philosophies not because they don't work but because they encourage a philosophy that we don't want at any cost: of obedience to a higher power rather than autonomous control without any boundaries."[191] Removing these codes provides us with a more perplexing issue: what, if anything, will take its place?

- Removing names and statues of prominent Americans because of the historical issues they were involved with, without considering the context of the situation and the entire character of the person involved. (e.g., Confederate leader Robert E. Lee). By doing so, we also contribute to erasing our past and thereby removing the possibility of learning from our mistakes, or even worse, suggesting that making mistakes (an obvious part of the human condition) is not tolerated. "Let the person among you who is without sin be the first to throw a stone …"[192] Or perhaps more accurately stated today, he who is *with* sin should cast the first stone.[193]

- Being oblivious or noncommittal to the aspirations inscribed on the buildings we occupy (government, schools, media, courthouses, businesses). When this happens, these buildings become false advertisements inscribed on architectural tombs. They become cartons filled with stale milk.

2. Denying objective truth

Remember that truth is the accurate description of reality. If there is no objective reality, there is no truth to guide our path. We become phantoms without an opera. Here are some specific examples of how intellectual helplessness is created when we deny objective truth:

- The necessitation of a new dictionary definition for human deficiencies. Oxford Dictionary's 2016 Word of the Year was *post-truth*: "relating to or denoting circumstances in which objective facts are

---

[191] T. M. Moore, "The Law of God and Public Policy: What Is the Purpose of the Law; A Good Law for All, First Things (Part 1)," http://www.dongtherightthing.com/dtrt-resources/dtrt-blog/entry,45/19645, 2.

[192] John 8:7 as revised from the Bible (Phillips Version).

[193] Hanson, "Our War Against Memory," 6.

less influential in shaping public opinion than appeals to emotion and personal belief."[194] As satirical website Babylon Bee stated, today many believe that the "things that make us feel good are true, right and good, but things that make us feel bad are wrong."[195]

- The utilization of untruth as a weapon to harm people. Examples include gross inaccuracies, such as all ideas are equally valid, Iraqi weapons of mass destruction, safe and guilt-free sex, healthy fast food, and false accusations of sexual assault/harassment. Daniel Levitin astutely observed, "The language we use has begun to obscure the relationship between fact and fiction ... This is a dangerous by-product of a lack of education that has now affected an entire generation of citizens. These two facts have made lies proliferate in our culture to an unprecedented degree. It has made possible the weaponization of lies so that they can all the more sneakily undermine our ability to make good decisions for ourselves and for our fellow citizens."[196]

- The refusal to accept responsibility for one's actions and, even more insidiously, blame the victims for their defensive responses in protecting themselves. This selective amnesia by the perpetrator attempts to deny the fact that one was the cause of one's own misery.

- The subjugation of people by personal fiat. Examples include the master race, "whiteness" as a disability and reason for shame, eugenics, and the removal of parental authority for sex and gender issues regarding their children. As C. S. Lewis aptly observed: "A philosophy which does not accept value as eternal and objective can only lead to ruin. Nor is the matter of merely speculative importance. Many a popular 'planner' on a democratic platform, many a mild-eyed scientist in a democratic laboratory means, in the last resort, just what the Fascist means. He believes that 'good' means whatever men are conditioned to approve. He believes it is the function of him and his kind to condition men; to create

---

[194] Oxford Dictionary, Oxford University Press.
[195] Babylon Bee, October 26, 2016, http://babylonbee.com/news/progressive-evangelical-leaders-meet-affirm-doctrine-sola-feels.
[196] Levitin, *Weaponized Lies*, xiii.

consciences by eugenics, psychological manipulation of infants, state education and mass propaganda. Because he is confused, he does not yet fully realize that those who create conscience cannot be subject to conscience themselves. But he must awake to the logic of his position sooner or later; and when he does, what barrier remains between us and the final division of the race into a few conditioners who stand themselves outside morality and the many conditioned in whom such morality as the experts choose is produced at the experts' pleasure? The very idea of freedom presupposes some objective moral law which overarches rulers and the ruled alike. Subjectivism about values is eternally incompatible with democracy. We and our rulers are one kind only so long as we are subject to one law. But if there is no Law of Nature, the ethos of any society is the creation of its rulers, educators and conditioners; and every creator stands above and outside his own creation."[197]

- Mr. Lewis again enlightens us: "I hold that you are already there whether you recognize it or not: that there are really no new ethical alternatives; that those who urge us to adopt new moralities are only offering us the mutilated or expurgated text of a book which we already possess in the original manuscript. They all wish us to depend on them instead of on that original, and then to deprive us of our full humanity. Their activity in the long run is always directed against our freedom."[198]

- Denying the biological realities of the differences between men and women.

- Denial of liberty for those who refuse to participate in activities that violate one's conscience. (e.g., Seattle florist, Barronelle Stutzman denied her freedom of conscience to not sell her flowers for a gay wedding, which she believes is immoral; pro-life pregnancy centers forced to promote the availability of abortions[199]).

---

[197] Lewis, *Christian Reflections*, 56.

[198] Lewis, 56.

[199] Lauretta Brown, "9th Circuit: State Can Force Pro-Life Pregnancy Centers to Promote Abortion," CNS News, October 18, 2016, https://www.cnsnews.com/news/article/lauretta-brown/appeals-court-uphold-calif-law-forcing-pregnancy-centers-promote.

3. Justifying violence against those who wisely seek boundaries for human autonomy

Today hatred is a primary response against those who claim objective truth that would place boundaries on human autonomy (e.g., limited abortion, enforcement of immigration laws, protecting free speech for all, limiting marriage to between a man and a woman, parental authority for decisions that affect their children, reining in government abuses). It is hatred against filters—hating the air filter for removing the dust, the coffee filter for keeping the grounds out of the liquid. The intensity of this hatred appears to have created a state of temporary insanity, in which rationality has been tossed aside by emotion. It is now common to hear that violence is a justified strategy against those who disagree with complete autonomy to do as one pleases. It is ironically hatred mixed with amnesia. It was not that long ago that the proponents of autonomy were pleading for understanding and tolerance of their proclivities (e.g., homosexuality, transgenderism, abortion on demand, gay marriage). When tolerance was achieved, they sought acceptance. Once majority acceptance was secured, the new demand was for punishment against those who have different thoughts. Déjà vu all over again.

The following are examples of calls for or actual violence against those who advocate for discernment, balance, and prudent boundaries on social issues:

- Assassinations of Abraham Lincoln, Dr. Martin Luther King, John and Robert Kennedy.

- The willingness of some to reluctantly accept the killing of American citizens so we can feel good about accommodating unlimited and illegal immigration.

- University rioting to prevent conservative points of view from being expressed on college campuses.

- The Black Lives Matter movement chants against the police: "What do we want? Dead cops. When do we want it? Right now!" and "Pigs in a blanket, fry 'em like bacon."[200]

- Madonna: "I have thought an awful lot about blowing up the White House."

- Missouri state senator who stated on Facebook that she "hopes Trump gets assassinated."[201]

- Alleged blacklisting (economic violence) of Hollywood actors who confronted Harvey Weinstein regarding allegations of sexual assault and harassment.[202]

4. Human defining of life and one's right to it

The definition of what constitutes human life has been the subject of perpetual debate because people have differing philosophies about it. In contrast, the transcendent view of human life claims an idea outside the intellectual property or invention of humankind. Outside the limitations of human intelligence, ego or ownership, there is a basis for uniformity. In dealing with any issue under debate, it is often helpful to ascertain the motivations of the debaters. Is the debate based on differences between personal and communal interests—that is, what I want versus what is best for the community? Facts can be harsh, but as facts, they must be examined and discussed. Issues that will not go away usually means that intrinsic values are not being satisfactorily addressed, that reality is not being given its proper due. Examples where philosophical differences have resulted in

---

[200] Bill Hudson, "Black Lives Matter Chant Called 'Disgusting' by Police Leader," CBS, Minnesota, August 30, 2015, http://minnesota.cbslocal.com/015/08/30/black-lives-matter-chant-called-disgusting-by-police-leader/; and Ian Tuttle, "Too many protestors choose to escalate tension and increase the likelihood of violence," *National Review*, July 12, 2106, http://nationalreview.com/article/437694/black-lives-matter-hypocrisy-cheering-violence...

[201] Jason Hancock, "'I hope Trump is assassinated,' Missouri lawmaker writes—and quickly regrets," *Kansas City Star*, August 17, 2017, http://www.kansascity.com/news/politics-government/article167755572.html.

[202] Molly Redden, "Peter Jackson: I blacklisted Ashley Judd and Mira Sorvino under pressure from Weinstein," *Guardian--US Edition*, December 16, 2017, https:///www.theguardian.com/fim/2017/dec/15/peter-jackson-harvey-weinstein-ashley-judd-mira-sorvino.

intellectual helplessness and negatively impacted society's ability to effectively deal with the definition of life issues include the following:

- The inability to reach consensus for the starting point of life (e.g., conception, viability, birth) based on objective facts rather than one's desire. This includes downplaying the scientific discoveries of ultrasound, the procedure of partial birth abortion, or the success of adult versus embryonic stem-cell reproduction.

- Attempts to keep life-issue facts concealed or obscured from public view or discussion. Examples include the current nonrequirement to report the number of abortions as a mandatory health statistic, not wanting people to stop and adequately reflect on whether the right to near unlimited abortion is worth the continuing sacrifice being made. It is estimated that approximately 59 million abortions were performed from 1973 to 2014.[203]

- A couple who gave birth to three babies through in vitro fertilization took seven of the unused, still-frozen embryos and turned them into jewelry so the mom could wear her other babies "close to her heart."[204]

- Attempts to extend the pro-choice philosophy beyond abortion to other areas like physician-assisted suicide, or Canada's recent consideration of expanding the current practice of legalized physician-assisted suicide for the terminally ill to the mentally ill as well.[205]

- Requiring kids to get their parents' permission to go on a field trip or take an aspirin at school, but not to get an abortion.

[203] Guttmacher data from the Centers for Disease Control, https://guttmacher.org/united-states/abortion/demographics.
[204] John Stonestreet, "Children Are Not Jewelry," The Point, May 11, 2017.
[205] Elizabeth Llorente, "Assisted suicide for mentally ill? Canada weighs what some European nations already allow," Fox News, April 20, 2017, http://www.foxnews.com/us/2017/04/20/assisted-suicide-for-mentally-ill-canda-weighs-what-some-european-nations-already-know.html.

- Planned Parenthood's alleged sales of fetal tissue and body parts.[206]

- An abortion clinic in Cleveland, Ohio, running a public relations campaign that includes the following messages on billboards: "abortion is a blessing; abortion is sacred; abortion is a family value; abortion is hope; abortion is a second chance; abortion is liberty; abortion is health care; abortion is good medicine."[207]

5. Claiming human rights for animals

Society periodically contends with the issue of whether animals should have the same rights as people. The starting point is to acknowledge that animals are not people and therefore don't have rights; in most states, they are considered property. Now wait, hold on before some of you misunderstand what I am saying. Allow me to add some context. One point is that only people have rights, which are accompanied by responsibilities. One of those responsibilities is the proper stewardship of animals. That includes treating animals properly and looking out for their welfare, with several laws on the books prohibiting cruelty to animals. If animals had rights, a proper conclusion would be that we should not eat any meat, or that we should allow animals to form a union to protest their use as forced labor or entertainment. In a sobering warning regarding the consequences of treating animals like people, G. Shane Morris observes, "When beasts are treated like people, people act like beasts."[208] The following are specific examples where our intellectual helplessness regarding animal rights has impacted our ability to adequately deal with the following situations:

- The intense hostile reaction by some to the shooting at a zoo of a guerilla who had a child in its grasp and was violently jerking the

---

[206] *Select Investigative Panel of the Energy & Commerce Committee Final Report*, Representative Marsha Blackburn, chairman, December 30, 2016, https://archives-energycommerce.house/gov/sites/republicans.energycommerce.house.gov/files/documents/Select_Investigative_Panel_Final)Report.pdf.

[207] Anna Sekulow, "Abortion Is Not a Sacred Blessing," ACLJ, January 10, 2018, https://aclj.org/pro-life/abortion-is-not-a-sacred-blessing.

[208] G. Shane Morris, "Animal Rights Have Driven Us Insane," BreakPoint, June 2, 2016.

child back and forth. In this instance, some called for the child's parents to be shot rather than the gorilla.[209]

- A lawsuit filed in a Manhattan courtroom on behalf of four chimpanzees asking for a writ of habeas corpus, contending that the chimps were being illegally detained.[210]

- Campaigns to confer constitutional rights for pigs.[211]

- Admonitions not to call your pet a "pet" but rather a "companion animal," or not to refer to oneself as a pet "owner" but rather a "human carer."[212]

- In surveys where people were asked who they would save in a fire in their house, the visiting electrician or the family pet, at least half called for saving the family pet.[213]

6. Politicization of insignificant differences for personal gain

There is a litany of differences between people in religion, family origin, gender, race, sexual orientation, income status, food preferences, education, health, and so forth. Some are congenital; some are acquired by preference. The ones discussed here are the less significant differences. These differences don't mean anything outside of what they are: a descriptor of someone or something. They are not indicators of superiority or inferiority. In and of themselves, they make no statement about intelligence, entitlement, personality, position, or status. When we attempt to make something out

---

[209] Sarah Larimer, "Gorilla Killed After Boy Falls Into Cincinnati Zoo Exhibit," NDTV, May 30, 2016, https://www.ndtv.com/world-news/goriila-killed-after-boy-falls-into-cincinnati-zoo-exhibit-1413320.

[210] Krishnadev Calamur, "Research Chimps Get Their Day In Court in New York," National Public Radio (NPR), May 27, 2015, https://www.npr.org/sections/thetwo-way/2015/05/27/410058029/rsearch-chimps-get-their-day-in-court-in-new-york

[211] Kingsley Guy, "Is Florida's Constitution a Sham?" *Sun Sentinel*, February 28, 2014, http://articles.sun-sentinel.com/2014-02-28/news/fl-dgduel-oped0228-20140228.

[212] Chuck Colson, "Of Pigs and People: Speciesism and Rights for Animals," BreakPoint, November 23, 2007, http://52.24/39.89/2017/11/of-pigs-and-people.

[213] Chuck Colson, "In the Name of Rover: Are Animals People Too?" BreakPoint, December 16, 2009, http://breakpoint.org/2009/12/breakpoint-name-rover/.

of what's not there, it's simply a manipulation to benefit the manipulator: whites are better than blacks, tacos are better than enchiladas, Greek is better than Malaysian, bunions are better than warts, women are better than men, dogs are better than cats, etc. When we politicize the nonpolitical, we just plain foul things up. We wind up fighting over the meaningless, unproductively comparing ourselves to other people, trying to make up for the past by transposing victims, and so on. Specific examples that demonstrate intellectual helplessness in this area are as follows:

- claiming that the existence of more male than female doctors automatically results in women's health issues being "disproportionately affected"[214]

- affirmative action to force the selection of certain races of people for employment without consideration of a person's skill set for the position

- students and institutions promoting additional, separate graduation ceremonies for different races as a positive thing[215]

- claiming that the disabled/handicapped are less valuable than able-bodied people

- telling hearing people that they can't clap or cheer at a rally for deaf people because it is insensitive to those who can't hear[216]

- claiming that rich people are smarter than poor people

- claiming that heterosexuals are straight and homosexuals are crooked

---

[214] "Too Many White Men in Charge of Health Care," Fix This Nation.com, May 8, 2017, http://fixthisnation.com/conservative-breaking-news/nbcs-andrea-mitchell-too-many-white-men-in-charge-of-healthcare/

[215] Anemona Hartocollis, "Colleges Celebrate Diversity With Separate Commencements," *New York Times*, June 2, 2017, https://www.nytimes.com/2017/06/02/us/black-commencement-harvard.html.

[216] Carol Brown, "Why clapping is now deemed offensive," American Thinker, May 1, 2017, http://www.americanthinker.com/blog/2017/0/why_clapping_is_now-deemed_offensive.html.

- claiming that any woman should be elected president over a male just because we haven't yet had a woman president

7. Production of despair and hopelessness

The proliferation of the philosophy of radical autonomy into our culture over the past several decades has resulted in devastating consequences. Living out of sync with reality has vastly increased intellectual helplessness in society. The reduced ability of many to see and deal with reality has resulted in dead ends, disappointments, frustration, confusion, isolation, and despair. These bitter pills have impacted the mental stability and behavioral patterns of those afflicted. Three examples help illustrate the magnitude of this issue on society:

- Declining birth rates. The industrial world is facing a demographic crisis from its failure to repopulate at a sustaining rate. George Weigel from Washington, DC's Ethics and Public Policy Center, noted for the European continent, "When an entire continent—deliberately chooses sterility, the most basic cause for that must lie in the realm of the human spirit, in a certain souring about the very mystery of being."[217] As a result, China, Europe, Russia, and Japan are now encouraging their citizens to procreate, some even offering incentives. When selflessness is a fading virtue, the joy of creating the future is reduced, and one of the results is fewer children.

- Increased suicide and drug/alcohol abuse rates. "Angus Deaton, a Princeton economist and Noble Prize winner for his work on measuring human well-being, found that since 1999 there has been an alarming national increase in deaths from drugs, alcohol abuse, and suicide ... Deaton calls these 'deaths of despair.'"[218] Aaron Kheriaty, director of medical ethics at UC Irvine, stated, "Due to this epidemic of premature deaths, the overall life expectancy in the U.S. has begun to decline for the first time since the 1930s ... Rising rates of suicide, drug abuse, and depression can

---

[217] George Weigel, "Catholic Lite and Europe's Demographic Suicide," First Things, May 24, 2017, https://www.firsthings.com/web-exclusives/2017/05/catholic-lite-and-europe-demographic-suicide, 1.

[218] Kheriaty, "Dying of Despair," 2.

all be traced to increased social fragmentation … Social bonds are weakening and the social fabric is fraying. We are at risk of losing a solid identity, a clear orientation, and the coherent narratives that give meaning to our individual and shared lives. In a world stripped of universally binding truths, the sense that we are losing solid foundations leads to free-floating angst."[219]

- Pressure to deny the truth. Today, at nearly every level of society, citizens are intermittently encouraged to deny truth. For instance, education often encourages students to adopt prescribed (usually leftist) points of view; the main-stream media regularly attempts to illegitimately persuade rather than inform (e.g., fake news); business managers often encourage employees to take advantage of customers or look the other way on indiscretions (e.g., Wells Fargo phony account scandal, Volkswagen emissions scandal); governmental entities often fail to hold their own accountable while punishing legitimate whistle-blowers (e.g., NSA surveillance scandals, Veterans Administration scandals, FBI looking for the whistle-blower in Clinton/Lynch tarmac scandal); organized religion is often deafeningly silent on critical moral issues (Catholic priest pedophilia scandals); and families often fail to civilize their children. Asking people to consistently deny the truth is like forcing people to repeat, over and over again, that two plus two equals five. Mental disintegration is the result.

Family

This triangle of truisms, of father, mother and child, cannot be destroyed;
it can only destroy those civilizations which discard it.
—G. K. Chesterton

Family is forever, whether we want it that way or not. As the saying goes, "You can't choose your relatives." But that doesn't stop us from trying. We have taken the desire for unlimited choice and attempted to force it onto every human situation. Having only one choice for something is considered too limiting and boring. We must have choice for choice's sake.

---

[219] Kheriaty, "Dying of Despair," 2, 3, 5.

Unfortunately, we pursue our desire for unlimited preferences as fledgling, unapprenticed social engineers. We will worry about quality later. In the meantime, we toss the waste of failed social experiments in the trash, justifying the process as one more step toward the oxymoron of human divinity. We have forgotten the fundamental objective of change: to make things better. If one can't improve the original, then leave it alone. The rule is that once one realizes that he/she is in a hole, one should stop digging. Here are some examples where our thought processes about the family have compromised our ability to reach reasonable solutions:

8. Denying the supremacy of the traditional family structure (i.e., father, mother, children)

There are several consequences that result from attempting to change a foundational, societal institution that has existed for thousands of years based primarily on our desire to expand our choice palate:

- We ignore the scientific evidence and practical experience of the superior benefits provided to society from the traditional family.[220]

- New laws to change the definition of family are proposed with absolutely no information provided to legislators or citizens on what the specific cultural, economic, or political impacts of the change would entail. It's like not testing a new heart valve before placing it inside a patient.

- Once changes to the definition of family are granted—based solely on personal desire, rather than analysis—there is no justification available to deny any future proposed combination or permutation of other family structures.

- There are insufficient public funds to cover all the alternatives.

- If the family institution can be tampered with on such a trivial basis (human desire), it opens the door for unanalyzed proposed changes in other areas of life.

---

[220] Mosher, "351 Studies."

- The situation where two Australian professors suggested that the root source of inequality in society is the traditional family; therefore, we should consider abolishing it to create a level playing field.[221] In their intellectual helplessness, these professors would rather level the playing field by making all families equally mediocre than helping those with less resources.

- The situation where a public library in Indiana publicized a *Drag Queen* Storytime for children ages two through six, with the advertisement reading, "Learn about someone new! Local drag queens present stories and encourage us all to embrace our uniqueness."[222]

- Another situation at a Long Beach, California, library where "a drag queen wearing five demon-like horns, stark white face paint, and wild auburn hair read to kids at the Michelle Obama Neighborhood Library … as part of LGBTQ History Month."[223]

9. Transposing of the parent-child relationship

Children and young adults are now the de facto leaders in many households. Some of the reasons for this intellectual helplessness include the following:

- parenting principles being determined more by unqualified governmental institutions (Social Services, courts) rather than qualified moral-cultural institutions (family, religious institutions)

- the current environment where there are few accepted standards for behavior so kids feel free to disobey their parents

---

[221] Joe Gelonesi, "Is having a loving family an unfair advantage?" *The Philosopher's Zone*, ABC Radio National, May 1, 2015, http://www.abc.net/au/radionational/programs/philosopherszone/new-family-values/6437; and John Stonestreet, "Families Are Unfair?" BreakPoint, August 21, 2015, http://breakpoint.org/2015/08/familier-are-unfair-2/.

[222] Michael Brown, "Here Come the Drag Queens," Townhall, June 5, 2017, https://www.townhall.com/columnistsmichaelbrown/2017/06/05/here-come-the-drag-queens-n2336298.

[223] Emily Holland, "Horned Drag Queen Reads to Kids at Long Beach Library," Patch, October 17, 2017, https://www.patch.com/california/longbeach-ca/horned-drag-queen-reads-kids/long-beach-library.

- the current environment where unaddressed narcissism and manipulation afford children a mental justification for illegitimately reporting their parents to the police or Social Services to get their way, with the burden of proof being on the parents rather than the child

- adult children being allowed to feed off the hearth teat in perpetuity

- minors being allowed to get an abortion or receive transgender information without parental knowledge or permission

10. Politicization of gender roles

There is no question that men and women can do many things equally as well. To keep it simple, gender doesn't have anything to do with one's innate ability to perform many functions in a quality manner (e.g., drive, parent, think, work, play sports, write, paint, etc.). However, it is also true that men and women are inherently physically, psychologically, and emotionally different from each other, and there are things that women can do better than men and vice versa. When we ignore these differences, or politicize them to create a false narrative for personal gain, we flaunt reality, suboptimize our lives, and contribute to our intellectual helplessness in properly addressing life. Here are some examples of this:

- The intentional exclusion of either a man or woman in raising children.

- The claim that breastfeeding is not "natural" for women.

- Attempts to create new protected classes of people based on inclination and behavior, rather than the biological realities of sex and race.

- Allowing transgender (men to women) persons to compete in women's sporting events. If not properly addressed, this will likely destroy women's athletics.

- Requiring military women to be included in combat.

- Building a society where it becomes a cultural and economic imperative that both men and women work, thus leaving the kids alone during the afternoon hours after school.

- Intentionally denigrating men as a strategy for lifting up women.

- Transgender or multisex bathrooms.

11. Devolution in child and young-adult development

Intellectual helplessness has contributed to the inculcation of poor values and debilitating confusion among our children and youth. Examples are as follows:

- Refusing to identify the gender of one's child at birth because the parent(s) absurdly propose that the child decide its gender when it is older.[224]

- Kids developing their own set of values or dropping out of society when they see a lack of intellectual coherence, or a gap between what they have been taught, and the way things actually are.

- The claim that it isn't important for children to live with both of their parents; they are fine as long as the adults are happy.

- Kids having access to information above their intellectual pay grade: video games filled with killing, horror movies with prolific violence, television commercials filled with sexual topics (e.g., erectile dysfunction, menstrual cycles), cable television laced with extreme and repetitive profanity, internet pornography.

- Enabling perpetual adolescence or "adulting" of adult children in their parent's home.

---

[224] Christine Rousselle, "Canadian Baby Given 'Unknown' as a Gender Identity on ID Card," Townhall, July 4, 2017, https://townhall.com/tipsheet/christinerousselle/2017/07/04/canadian-baby-given-unknown-as-a-gender-on-id-card-n2350426.

- Providing condoms to kids at school. New studies show that such access actually increases teen pregnancies by 10 percent.[225]

- The pursuit of a hookup rather than a dating relationship where kids use each other for sex with no intent of emotionally connecting to each other.

Education

Great Learning and superior abilities, should you ever possess them will be of little and small Estimation, unless Virtue, Honour, Truth and integrety are added to them.
—ABIGAIL ADAMS TO HER SON JOHN QUINCY ADAMS

The traditional purpose of education has always been to learn about reality and pass this knowledge on from one generation to another. It is not knowing for knowing's sake, but knowing for the sake of gaining personal maturity and thus creating a better society and life. The beauty of mission-centric education is that it addresses and improves the individual limitations of humans. Since one person cannot know everything, the pursuit of knowledge is a lifelong journey with new awakenings. One never gets bored. It is an iterative process. It's the law of diminishing intelligence: the more one knows, the more one realizes how much one doesn't know. Every morning becomes a new adventure. When the educational process gets short-circuited by intellectual helplessness, we stand in the wrong line, and only discover our predicament once we make it to the counter. These are examples of how intellectual helplessness in education has impacted our ability to address issues:

12. All hail science

Science is crucial to gaining verified knowledge. It provides us with comfort and confidence. But science is only one symbol in the equation of life. It is not infallible, and it deals in probability, not certainty. Professor Daniel Levitin states, "There are two pervasive myths about how science is done. The first is that science is neat and tidy, that scientists never disagree about

---

[225] Michael J. New, "New Study Shows '90s Era Condom Programs Increased Teen Fertility Rates," *National Review*, June 17, 2016.

anything. The second is that a single experiment tells us all we need to know about a phenomenon ... Real science is replete with controversy, doubts, and debates about what we really know. Real scientific knowledge is gradually established through many replications and converging findings."[226] The following are specific examples of the consequences of intellectual helplessness regarding our misconceptions about science:

- The consistent belief by many that science is the only way to really know something. Science can't adequately explain critical human emotions, re-create historical events, or explain why President Trump insists on tweeting nonpresidential missives.

- The desire for certainty encourages science to be something more than it is and to do more than it can do. Levitin stated that "an unbiased appreciation of uncertainty is a cornerstone of rationality—but it is not what people and organizations want."[227] We are reminded of this every time we see a drug advertisement that says in addition to helping cure a certain ailment, the medication also can harm us in several ways.

- Making the common error of trying to get to the answer before one has understood all the right questions.

- Scientists assuming that there must always be a natural cause because "natural causes are the only kind [science] can address."[228] This encourages the promulgation and improper acceptance of philosophy as science rather than unproven theory, such as with the *theory* of evolution.

- The acceptance of a product after only a single study or experiment has been conducted or when accompanied by phrases such as "organic," or "helps at the molecular level," and so forth.

---

[226] Levitin, *Weaponized Lies*, 182.
[227] Kahneman, *Thinking Fast and Slow*, chapter 24.
[228] Keller, *The Reason for God*, 89.

13. Diversity over unity

People logically look for coherence and knowledge from the institution of education, which was established to provide it. As identified earlier, the word *university* involves trying to find clarifying *unity* amid a *diversity* of knowledge. When that order is reversed, we get a university that counts each bean but doesn't make any coffee. These are some examples:

- Seeing everything in terms of race rather than advocating for a race-blind society. For example, the University of California published a list of "microaggression" statements that students and faculty are to avoid, such as "Where are you from?" or "America is the land of opportunity."[229] Or a Boston University professor who says that the Christmas song "Jingle Bells" is racist.[230]

- Electives, symposiums, or events of questionable value are offered over substantive courses in order to claim one is being diverse, such as a taxpayer-funded Ecosex Walking Tour, where a California public university advertised: "Come experience 25 ways to make love to the Earth, raise awareness of environmental issues, learn ecosexercises, find E-spots, and climax with the planetary clitoris."[231]

- The University of Washington Tacoma Writing Center issued a press release to students stating that expecting Americans to use proper grammar perpetuates racism.[232]

[229] Katherine Timpf, "UC Faculty Training: Saying 'America is the Land of Opportunity' Is a Microaggression," *National Review*, http://www.nationalreview.com/article/419571/uc-faculty-training-saying-america-land-opportunity-microaggression-katherine-timpf.
[230] Caleb Parke, "'Jingle Bells' rooted in racism, Boston University Professor says," Fox News, December 15, 2017, http://www.foxnews.com/2017/12/15/jingle-bells-rooted-in-racism-boston-university-professor-says.
[231] Chelsea Schilling, "'Ecosexual' Professor Wants You to Have Sex with Earth," *Worldnet Daily*, http://www.wnd.com/2017/09/ecosexual-professor-wants-you-to-have-sex-with-the-earth/, September 5, 2017; and Caleb Parke, "Most bizarre college courses 2017: 'Hooking up,' 'Queer Religion,' and 'sexy' vampires," Fox News, December 13, 2017, http://foxnews.com/us/2017/12/13/most-bizzare-college-courses-2017-hooking-up-queer-religion-and-sexy-vampires.html.
[232] Walter Williams, "College Campus Disgrace," Creators Syndicate, March 8, 2017, https://www.creators.com/read/walter-williams/03/17/college-campus-disgrace.

- Training that emphasizes only learning information, to the exclusion of developing character.

- A Boise State University professor under attack from his administration for violating the university's "diversity and civility mantra" by publicizing information about parental rights and the importance of traditional family.[233]

14. The lack of intellectual hospitality

Educational institutions should be intellectual visitor centers. Everyone is welcome to be heard over coffee and cake. Whether you choke or not depends on the quality of the food for thought. In this setting, there is the recognition that we can learn from everyone and every viewpoint—if nothing else, what not to think or do. One does not necessarily have to agree with something to see the virtue or vice in it. Intellectual hospitality states, "When you claim your right to speak, you acknowledge my right to speak. While making your point, you address yourself to my argument and not my personality. You attack my view but not my self-esteem. Character is not the enemy of self-expression, but its necessary pre-condition."[234] When educational institutions forget their mission and goals, they become poor hosts and stunt intellectual growth, as in these examples:

- The lack of intellectual affirmative action in education given that the vast majority of professors have liberal worldviews. In a social climate survey conducted at the University of Colorado, several questions attempted to assess whether students "felt welcomed, respected, discriminated against and/or intimidated due to their race, color, national origin, sex, age, disability, creed, religion, sexual orientation, veteran status, political affiliation, and/or religious affiliation." One question asked was "Specifically, have you felt intimidated to share your ideas, opinions or beliefs in class because of your …?" Of the different social identities named above, "it was political philosophy [23 percent] that was most linked to feelings of

---

[233] Bill Korach, "Professor Under Siege for Supporting Traditional Family," The Report Card.org, November 2017, http://education-curriculum-reform-govenrment-schools.org/2017/11/professor-under-siege-for-supporting-traditional-family.
[234] Wilson, *On Character*, 2.

intimidation, followed by religion or spiritual beliefs [22.1 percent]. In contrast, race/ethnicity [10.9 percent], gender [12.5 percent], sexual orientation [5.5 percent], and gender identity [3.3 percent] scored appreciably lower." When drilled down to those with religious affiliations that were the most likely to feel disrespected, it was Mormon [29.6 percent], Muslim [24.3 percent], and Protestant [23.9 percent], while atheism was 15.8 percent. In regard to political ideology, very conservative students were more than twice as likely as very liberal students to experience disrespect [37.3 percent vs. 16.4 percent], and Republicans were more than three times as likely to feel prejudice or discrimination than Democrats [51.7 percent vs. 14.3 percent].[235]

- Two university professors, who are also members of a local symphony orchestra, led a campaign to disinvite the guest conductor solely because he is a conservative writer and talk show host.[236]

- Students at a Catholic university petitioned against the opening of a Chick-fil-A fast food restaurant on campus based on the owner's conservative religious beliefs.[237]

- Encouraging political correctness by disciplining educators for having nonpolitically correct personal beliefs and celebrating when conservative scholars face discrimination.

- Universities refusing to control protests against conservative speakers, ostensibly using safety as a rationale to cancel their speaking engagements.[238]

[235] George Yancey, "Disrespect, Intimidation and Prejudice at the University of Colorado," Patheos, December 21, 2014, http://www.patheos.com/blogs/blackwhiteandgray/2014/12/disrespect-intimidation-and-prejudice-at-the-university-of-colorado/.
[236] Dennis Prager, "Can a Conservative Conduct an Orchestra?" Townhall, August 1, 2017, https://www.townhall.com/columnists/dennisprager/2017/08/01/can-a-conservative-conduct-an-orchestra.
[237] Eric Metaxas and Stan Guthrie, "Opening Closed Minds the Chick-fil-A Way," BreakPoint, May 3, 2017, http://www.breakpoint.org/2017/05/breakpoint-opening-closed-mnds-the-check-fil-a-way/.
[238] Theodore Bunker, "UC Berkeley Faculty Urge Boycott of Conservative Speakers," Newsmax, September 18, 2017, https:///www.newsmax.com/PrintTemplate.aspx/?nodeid=814263.

15. Indoctrination over philosophical persuasion

A primary goal of education is to provide students with a variety of information and viewpoints for use in the analysis and development of logical and rational conclusions. Philosophy provides the tools for sound evaluation, whereby people are persuaded by facts and experience. It teaches one how to think effectively and efficiently, providing the mental tools to discern between quality and poor ideas. By excluding certain ideas, universities indoctrinate rather than persuade. Indoctrination is the fast food of education and results in couch potatoes. It's bad nutrition and a lack of intellectual exercise. In contrast, philosophical persuasion provides stimulating food for thought and works out of the mind by searching for knowledge, sharing information, debating points of view, and applying critical evaluation skills. Here are some examples of intellectual helplessness made possible by indoctrination:

- Creation of "safe zones" to caudle and protect the intellectually fragile, and "trigger warnings" that advise people that certain topics (e.g., sexual violence, crime, sexism, racism) might be discussed and could trigger bad memories.[239]

- A university English department removing a poster of William Shakespeare because he is a white male.[240]

- In order to help students cope with the perceived traumatic result of Donald Trump becoming president, it was reported that the University of Michigan Law School offered "post-election self-care" with the opportunity to partake in coloring sheets and Lego activities.[241]

---

[239] Emanuella Grinberg, "Trigger Warnings, Safe Spaces: Your Guide to the New School Year," CNN, August 26, 2016, http://www.cnn.com/2016/08/26/us/university-of-chicago-trigger-warnings-safespace.
[240] Stephen Kruiser, "UPenn Students Remove Shakespeare Portrait for Lacking Diversity," *American Spectator*, December 13, 2016, https://spectator.org/upenn-students-remove-shakespeare-portrait-for-lacking-diversity/.
[241] Armstrong Williams, "Harvard's Season of Digesting," Townhall, April 17, 2017, https://www.townhall.com/columnists/armstrongwilliams/2017/04/17/harvards-season-of-digesting.

- Graduate students at Harvard formed a "Resistance School," taught by Harvard lecturers at campus facilities, where for four weeks interested students would participate at no cost in a practical training program that would "sharpen the tools needed to fight back" against President Trump and his agenda.[242]

- A New York college proposing to require a course for its political science majors entitled "Abolition of Whiteness" that examines "how whiteness—and/or white supremacy and violence—is intertwined with conceptions of gender, race, sexuality, class, body ability, nationality, and age."[243]

16. Student worship

Many of today's students are treated more like customers to satisfy than charges to develop. With so many schools to choose from, students become the economic prize of sustainability. This does not contribute to a rigorous high-impact training center but a comfortable low-impact spa. It is getting the robe and champagne before graduation. Examples include the following:

- Professors instructed to meet a minimum average grade objective for their classes.

- Students being encouraged to take class time off if their sensibilities are ruffled by the events of the day.

- Students not thinking twice about requesting that their professors provide them with any and all amenities that will make it easier for them to pass the course: class notes, visual aids, certain speakers, and so on.

---

[242] Williams, "Harvard's Season of Digesting."
[243] J.D. Heyes, "Not Even Kidding: College will require 'Abolition of Whiteness' course for Political Science Majors," National Sentinel, May 29, 2017, https://thenationalsentinel.com/2017/05/29/not-even-kidding-college-will-require-abolition-of-whiteness-course-for-political-science-majors.

- Calling professors by their first name. "Sally, pass me the test answers, please."

- Providing computers, meals, and supplies for graduate students.

17. Fame and fortune

When educational institutions lose their primary focus to educate students, it is often replaced with activities to achieve the individual goals of academicians or administrators. As a result, the mandate of student learning is replaced by the school's pursuit and retention of fame, wealth, and cultural dominance. This primary focus always intentionally or unintentionally encourages unethical behavior. Consider these examples:

- Researchers manipulating findings to their own ideological desires rather than adhering to objectivity standards. Take for instance a British university that revoked grant money from a professor who was studying "detransitioning" transgendered individuals back to their biological sex for those who subsequently regretted their decision because "early results were deemed 'politically incorrect' by the ethics committee." The professor doing the study stated, "The fundamental reason given was that it might cause criticism of the research on social media, and criticism of the research would be criticism of the university. They also added it's better not to offend people … The posting of unpleasant material on blogs or social media may be detrimental to the reputation of the university."[244]

- Dogmatic preference for certain worldviews, driving nonadherents to the margins of education in the age-old practice of once having gained power, ensuring that one retains that power.

- A state audit revealing that its university school system hid $175 million in funds while its leaders requested more money from the state. The audit also revealed that a top school system administrator

---

[244] Timothy Meads, "British Professor Shows 'Sex Change Regret' is Rising, University Takes Away His Funding," Townhall, October 2, 2017, https://townhall.com/tipsheet/timothymeads/2017/10/01/british-professor-shows-sex-change-regret-is-rising-university-takes-away-his-funding-n238930.

improperly screened confidential surveys sent to each campus, deleting or changing any answers that were critical of the university system's president's office.[245]

* School systems working primarily for the benefit of the institution, not the students, in excessive salaries, tenure protections, or roadblocks to nonpublic school options.

News Media

> *Big brother has been replaced by Howdy Doody.*
> —Neil Postman

The news media is the industry designated to transmit the pertinent, factual news of the day in a neutral fashion, using various vehicles of communication. As with any profession, there are good reporters of the news and bad reporters of something less than news. When integrity flourishes in the news industry, it is partly because a majority of the citizenry values knowledge and is committed to the common good. Integrity includes the agreement with, and the commitment to follow, the truth in word and deed. When the public insists upon facts, the media's feet are held to the proverbial fire. The media's primary role is to provide accurate information to a thoughtful citizenry who are properly equipped to analyze and make rational decisions on their own.

As with a soufflé, just a tiny bit of deviation can make the news go flat. Insufficient verification of facts; illegitimate introduction of bias; unapplied logic and reason; fame, fortune, and power over fidelity; and other deficiencies stand in the way of a quality news story. The news competition is fierce. Reporters no longer work for news corporations but for corporate news. Much of the media has changed its focus from neutral informing of the citizenry to partisan advocating of an ideological position. The goal is two-fold: (1) to retain one's customer base, telling it what it wants to hear to keep the lights on, the HVAC working, and the paychecks flowing, and (2) to establish and retain a particular ideological position for the

---

[245] "Napolitano's UC hid $175 million while demanding money, audit says," Fox News, April 26, 2017, http://www.foxnews.com/us/2017/04/26/napolitanos-uc-hid-175-million-while-demanding-money-audit-says.html.

governance of society and the transmission of particular cultural values. In this scenario, the media train has jumped the northbound track of news delivery to the southbound track of news creation. They now have a stake in both the outcome of the news and the income it produces. In such an environment, they see themselves not just as news transmitters, but also as essential purveyors of culture. The actualization of these goals brings power, prestige, wealth, and other accoutrements. Once obtained, there is no relinquishment without a fight. The former miners of fact have wantonly become the moguls of fiction.

The specific examples below illustrate how intellectual helplessness has negatively impacted the ability of the news media to fulfill its mission:

18. Sedition by news edition

Sedition is the "incitement of resistance to or insurrection against lawful authority."[246] At the present time, there is overwhelming evidence to demonstrate the news media's "incitement of *resistance* … against lawful authority." It is painfully and shamefully obvious that these irresponsible actions are not just harming one political figure but all of us, by disrupting the Trump administration's ability to run and protect America. The media appears to believe they are justified in damaging the ability of the country to operate based on their rage over a legitimate election result. Many of the mainstream media's reactions indicate a willingness to pursue revenge over justice, elite privilege over the common good, and autocratic power over democracy. The general public's distrust and despisement of the media appears to be a fact lost or ignored by the mainstream media. They appear to have enough of a customer base for their operations to remain in the black, so they denigrate their opposition, one *pen*-prick at a time, banking on the hope that negative repetition of their dislikes will make a dent in public perception. These same media outlets did not operate in the same manner in their dealings with the Obama administration. And it is not because the previous administration did a better job. We are inexplicably finding out more and more about the former administration's sins of commission and omission.

Examples of media sedition include these:

---

[246] Merriam Webster's Collegiate Dictionary, Merriam-Webster, Inc.

- Polls show that during President Trump's first one hundred days in office, 95 percent of the media's coverage of him was negative. This negativism has been verified by a Harvard study.[247] And, from June through August 2017, a Media Research Center study determined that 91 percent of coverage of President Trump was negative.[248] Whether one likes the president or not, this statistic is over-the-top behavior. Even the proverbial blind squirrel finds an acorn (positive fact) more often.

- The June 2018 Inspector General's report on the Hillary Clinton email investigation stated that "We have profound concerns about the volume and extent of unauthorized media contacts by FBI personnel that we have uncovered during our review." The report further details that members of the media provided gifts (e.g., sporting event tickets, free golf outings, free meals and drinks) to FBI employees in return for their leaking of non-public information.[249]

- Chris Wallace's views that President Trump "may have a point when he complains about media bias and unfairness."[250]

- Intentionally false and/or incompetent reports that Trump didn't have a chance of winning the 2016 presidential election.[251]

- Former president Jimmy Carter stating, "I think the media have been harder on Trump than any other president certainly that I've

---

[247] Thomas E. Patterson, "News Coverage of Donald Trump's First 100 Days," Harvard Kennedy School's Shorenstein Center on Media, Politics and Public Policy, May 18, 2017.

[248] Leah Barkoukis, "Study Finds Media Coverage of Trump During Summer was 91 Percent Negative," Townhall, September 13, 2017.

[249] *A Review of the Various Actions by the Federal Bureau of Investigation and the Department of Justice in Advance of the 2016 Election*, 429-430.

[250] Chris Wallace, Fox News, November 10, 2017.

[251] Tom Westervelt and Raghavan Mayur, "Media Malpractice? Media Bias and the 2016 Election," *Investor's Business Daily*, November 18, 2016, https://www.investors.com/politics/commentary/media-malpractice-media/bias-and-2016-election; and Jim Rutenberg, "A 'Dewey Defeats Truman' Lesson for the Digital Age," *New York Times*, November 9, 2016, https://www.nytimes.com/2016/11/09/buisness/media/media-trump-clinton.html?emc=edit_th_2.

known about … I think they feel free to claim that Trump is mentally deranged and everything else without hesitation."[252]

- Attacking the president's family members, including minor children.[253]

- The readily apparent coordination of media attacks against the Trump administration demonstrated by the use of identical terminology to describe current events.

19. Amusing ourselves to death

Neil Postman's book of this title postulated that America is in danger of amusing itself to death by the distraction of entertainment trivia (what I call "pixel dust") delivered by television. He stated that "the content of our public discourse has become nonsense … that television's conversations promote incoherence and triviality."[254] Here are some specific examples:

- talking heads who have trivial discussions of nothingness 24-7: critiques of what someone is wearing, how one performed at the White House Correspondents Dinner, asking irrelevant questions to fill time gaps

- national political conventions that mimic circus acts

- news show discussions where the participants yell, scream, and interrupt each other rather than civilly debate based on the pursuit of knowledge

---

[252] Maureen Dowd, "Jimmy Carter Lusts for a Trump Posting," *New York Times*, October 21, 2017, https://www.nytimes.com/2017/10/21/opinion/sunday/jimmy-carter-lusts-trump-posting.html?mt.

[253] John Hawkins, "The 7 Worst Liberal Attacks on Donald Trump's Family," Townhall, April 15, 2017, https://www.townhall.com/columnists/johnhawkins/2017/04/15/the-7-worst-liberal-attacks-on-donald-trumps-family-n2313730.

[254] Postman, *Amusing Ourselves to Death*, 16, 80.

- the forced or illogical insertion of topics into media coverage to indoctrinate ideas, such as unlimited and unexamined diversity and tolerance

20. Fake news

Although this is the current term of the day, I don't think it goes far enough. Fake news declares war on the US Constitution. It is a crime against democracy. I much prefer the phrase used by Professor Levitin: "lying weasels."[255] He used this label to match the insidious intentionality of the fabrications, the "weaponizing of lies so that they can more sneakily undermine our ability to make good decisions for ourselves and our fellow citizens."[256] Examples of fake news include the following:

- a fake news story alleging that Hillary Clinton was running a sex slave operation out of a Washington, DC pizzeria led a person to fire an automatic weapon into the store[257]

- editing by NBC of the 911 phone call regarding security guard George Zimmerman's shooting of citizen Trayvon Martin falsely made it appear that he made racist comments[258]

- an erroneous *Newsweek* story falsely claimed military interrogators at Guantanamo Bay had desecrated a Koran which led to several outbreaks of terrorist violence across the globe[259]

---

[255] Levitin, *Weaponized Lies*, 51.

[256] Levitin, xiii.

[257] Cecilia Kang and Adam Goldman, "In Washington Pizzeria Attack, Fake News Brought Real Guns," *New York Times*, December 5, 2016, https://www.nytimes.com/2016/12/05/business/media-comet-ping-pong-pizza-shooting-fake -news.

[258] Michael Brendan Dougherty, "NBC: We're Sorry We Edited the Trayvon Tape to Make George Zimmerman Sound Racist," Business Insider, April 4, 2012, http://www.businessinsider.com/nbc-apoligizes-to-george-zimmerman-for-editing-a-911-call-to-make-him-sound-really-racist.

[259] Paul Marshall, "Deadly Mistake," *National Review*, May 16, 2005, http://www.nationalreview.com/article/214458/deadly-mistake-paul-marshall.

- false reporting of the details of the Ferguson, Missouri, police officer shooting inaccurately claimed that citizen Michael Brown had his arms up and pleaded "don't shoot" before he was killed[260]

- framing the irrelevant and innocuous as news: "The Trump administration met with the Russian ambassador," "Rex Tillerson prefers to talk to the media only when there is something to convey"

- fake news stories created by former New York Times reporter Jason Blair[261]

21. Making the margins the center line

Public opinion polls show that most Americans do not trust the media. One of the reasons is that they often demonstrate poor judgment by taking the fringe elements/ideas of society and presenting them as if they were majority opinion or as a positive. Take these for instance:

- ESPN's decision to remove Asian-American broadcaster Robert Lee from the University of Virginia's football game because he has the same name as Confederate general Robert E. Lee[262]

- labeling brutal dictator Fidel Castro a hero[263]

- CNN publishing the Southern Poverty Law Center's fabricated "hate map" against reputable Christian organizations, damaging

---

[260] Neil Munro, "Holder Admits 'Hands Up, Don't Shoot' Claim Was Bogus," Daily Caller, March 4, 2105, http://dailycaller.com/2015/03/04/holder-admits-hands-up-dont-shoot-claim-was-bogus/.

[261] Ann Coulter, "The Old Gray Liar," Townhall, May 15, 2003, https://townhall.com/columnists/anncoulter/2003,05,15/he-old-gray-liar-n1295851.

[262] Matthew Haag, "ESPN pulls sportscaster Robert Lee from UVA game because of his name," *New York Times*, August 23, 2017, https://www.nytimes.com/2017/08/23/business/media-robert-lee-univerity-virginia-charlottesville.html?mtrref=www.bing.com&gv.

[263] Nicole Russell, "You wouldn't believe whose praising murderous dictator Fidel Castro at his death," the Federalist, November 28, 2016, http://www.thefederalist.com/2016/11/28/wouldnt-believe-whos-praising-murderous-dictator-fidel-castro-death/.

their credibility and increasing the risk of violence against their employees[264]

- claiming that most of the people who vote for conservative candidates are "deplorables"[265]

- taking the camera into sports dugouts, huddles, and locker rooms in an attempt to capture extreme behavior

- televising anything that bleeds, grieves, or fights while ignoring the more common displays of decency between one citizen and another

- creating "reality" television shows that manufacture and script appearances of the seven deadly sins (pride, avarice, envy, wrath, lust, gluttony, sloth) to showcase for entertainment, falsely claiming that it all was spontaneous behavior[266]

Arts Media

Culture is not a territory to be won or lost but a resource we are called to steward with care. Culture is a garden to be cultivated.
—Makoto Fujimura

The arts media includes those involved in creating and presenting the performing, painting, sculpting, and writing arts. The arts are a necessary part of society. They allow for the outward expression of the human creative impulse and the inward consumption of refinement. It is a much-needed antidote for the trials of everyday life. When artists deviate from their intrinsic mission to organically feed the soul, they stray outside their lane

---

[264] Dakin Andone, "The Southern Poverty Law Center's list of hate groups," CNN, August 18, 2017, http://www.cnn.com/2017/08/17/us/hate-groups-us-map-trnd/index.html.

[265] Katie Reilly, "Read Hillary Clinton's 'Basket of Deplorable' Remarks About Donald Trump Supporters," *Time*, September 10, 2016, http://time.com/4486502/hillary-clinto-basket-of-deplorables-transcript/.

[266] Jim Taylor, PhD, "Popular Culture: Reality TV is NOT Reality," *Psychology Today*, January 31, 2011, https://www.psychologytoday.com/blog/the-power-prime/201101/popular-culture-reality-tv-is-not-reality.

and call attention to themselves rather than their art. Below are specific examples of intellectual helplessness created by the arts media:

22. The artists of insurrection

Some artists have moved from Sedition 101 to Sedition 102, with the actual "incitement ... of *insurrection* against lawful authority." When celebrities do this, they encourage others, especially the unbalanced, to consider doing it in the real world. Here are some specific examples:

- singer Madonna's protest rally confession: "Yes, I have thought an awful lot about blowing up the White House"[267]

- rapper Snoop Dogg's video of him pointing a gun at a caricature of President Trump[268]

- unrepentant comedian Kathy Griffin holding up a caricature of the decapitated head of President Trump[269]

- government executive prosecutor Marilyn Mosby in Baltimore allegedly bringing false indictments against six police officers for personal political gain[270]

---

[267] Joi-Marie McKenzie, "Madonna Defends 'Blowing Up the White House' Comment: 'I Am Not a Violent Person'" ABC News, January 22, 2017, http://abcnews.go.com/entertainment/madonna-defends-blowing-white-house-comment-violent-person/story/?id=44972325.

[268] Maeve McDermott, "Snoop Dogg shoots fake-President Trump in new video 'Lavender,'" *USA Today*, March 13, 2017, https://www.usatoday.com/story/life/entertainthis/2017/03/13/snoop-dogg-shoots-fake-president-trump-new-video-lavender/99139774.

[269] Dave Quinn, "Kathy Griffin Is 'Not Sorry' for Infamous Trump Photo: 'I Knew What I Was Doing," *People*, November 8, 2017, http://people.com/tv/kathy-griffin-not-sorry-for-donald-trump-photo/.

[270] Eliot C. McLaughlin and Steve Almasy, "Freddie Gray officers suing prosecutor Marilyn Mosby," CNN, July 28, 2016, http://www.cnn.com/2016/07/27/us/baltimore-marilyn-mosby-officer-lawsuits-freddie-gray/index.html.

- late-night talk show host Stephen Colbert referring to President Trump as Vladimir Putin's "c—— (penis) holster"[271]

- movie director Quentin Tarantino generically calling the police "murderers"[272]

23. Abusing one's forum

For each of us, our occupations provide access to certain resources. If one is a teacher, one has access to classrooms and buildings; if one is a solider, one has access to weapons; a pilot, planes. One's access to these things is limited only for use in the performance of one's professional duties. A teacher doesn't get to take a kid home, a solider doesn't get to put a bazooka in the gun rack of his personal vehicle, and a pilot doesn't get to borrow a Boeing or Airbus for his/her personal vacation. But some celebrities feel they can take their "platform" with them and use it to pursue their personal interests. Consider these examples:

- award shows where celebrities consistently express their viewpoints on issues rather than just saying thank you for an award (e.g., Academy Awards, Grammys, Golden Globes)

- entertainers using their concerts or plays as a venue to express their political viewpoints (e.g., the play *Hamilton* to Vice President-Elect Pence)[273]

- artists taking advantage of the media's need to have access to them for their livelihood, thus "encouraging" them to support celebrity views by presenting them in a positive light

---

[271] Caitlin Yilek, "Stephen Colbert calls Trump's mouth 'Vladimir Putin's c—k holster,'" *Washington Examiner*, November 29, 2017, http://www.washingtonexaminer.com/stephen-colbert-calls-trumps-mouth-vladimir-putins-ck-holster/article/2621850.

[272] Jessica Chasmar, "Quentin Tarantino blasts police as 'murderers' at NYC rally days after cop killing," *Washington Times*, October 26, 2015, https://www.washingtontimes.com/news/2015/oct/26/quentin-tarantino-blasts-police-as-murderers-at=ny/...

[273] Christopher Mele and Patrick Healy, " 'Hamilton' had some unscripted lines for Pence," *New York Times*, November 19, 2016, https://www.nytimes.com/2016/11/19/us/mike-pence-hamilton.html.

- Hollywood movie producers using their positional power to solicit sex from up-and-coming actors (e.g., Harvey Weinstein, et al.)

24. Conflating artistic talent with general intelligence

In our culture, the Greek gods are celebrities or superstars. In the past, this status was based almost entirely on outstanding artistic performance in a certain field. Today, the ability to generate constant media exposure, positive or negative, even with a minimal skill set, can substitute. The life and privilege of a celebrity does not easily facilitate the development of a well-rounded personality. Many a superstar would be more accurately described as a supernova. When we conflate celebrity status with intelligence, it creates intellectual helplessness in evaluating points of view; when we give celebrities accountability waivers for bad behavior, we encourage continuation and proliferation of the behavior. Here are some examples:

- giving unearned merit to the political views of celebrities who have no expertise on an issue

- celebrity encouragement of uncivil disobedience, such as an actress who wants to "take out" Trump supporters with a baseball bat; an actor who contemplates the last time an actor assassinated a president; a Shakespeare in the Park play depicting the assassination of President Trump in New York's Central Park; a movie director stating, "I want a rhino to f— Paul Ryan to death"; a singer depicting his killing of President Trump in his music video; a late-night talk show host saying he would use a pillow to suffocate Trump, just like the one they used to kill deceased Supreme Court justice Antonin Scalia[274]

- unaccountability of celebrities involved in criminal behavior (e.g., guns, drugs, property destruction)

[274] Daniel Nussbaum and Jerome Hudson, "15 Times Celebrities Envisioned Violence Against Trump and the GOP," Breitbart, June 14, 2017, http://www.breitbart.com/big-hollywood/2017/06/15/15-times-celebrities-envisioned-violence-against-trump-and-the-gop/.

- treating celebrity dysfunction as an artistic eccentricity to be admired and imitated, such as unhealthy personality and appearance transformations; offensive sports figure "celebrations" after scoring a touchdown, home run, or winning goal; dangerous exploits with drugs, alcohol, or sex

25. Canonization of the unconventional

Today, real talent often takes a back seat to that which is eccentric, avant-garde, or alternative. We contribute to our intellectual helplessness when we accept or celebrate differences for the sole reason that something is different. Here are some examples:

- rating the quality of a movie or play highly just because it portrays certain cultural issues in a manner consistent with the view of liberal progressives (e.g., issues such as homosexuality, addictions, abortion, climate change, immigration), regardless of its production quality

- movies and books attempting to widen culturally acceptable margins with gratuitous sexuality, profanity, or violence to titillate our base senses for profit

- Hollywood turning a blind eye to the blacklisting of conservatives[275] and those who refuse to trade sex for work[276]

- romanticizing harmful actions or addictions and those who partake (e.g., suicide, sex, drugs, fame)

---

[275] Joseph C. Phillips, "Does Hollywood Blacklist Conservatives?" Joseph C. Phillips (website), September 14, 2015, http://josephcphillips.com/2015/09/does-hollywood-blacklist-coservatives/.
[276] Kira Davis, "The Next Big Hollywood Sex Scandal Is Already Breaking...At Nickelodeon," RedState, October 24, 2017, https://www.redstate.com/kiradavis/2017/10/24/next-big-hollywood-sex -scandal-already-breaking...at-nickelodeon/.

26. Unsporting events

Most professional and some college sporting events are primarily governed by monetary considerations. This is highly ironic since the joy of sports is in large part due to it being a game, a place to escape the seriousness of life. These are specific examples where intellectual helplessness has negatively impacted sports:

- players being asked to participate in political causes that have nothing to do with their sport, such as the USA women's soccer team being requested to wear rainbow jerseys in support of the LGBT movement[277]

- the time of day for holding sporting events is primarily governed by television considerations rather than optimum playing and safety conditions

- paying exorbitant salaries to athletes that increase the ticket and concession prices for the average fan

- the NFL concussion scandal where athletes continued to play despite suffering serious head injuries[278]

- the distribution and use of performance-enhancing drugs that damage an athlete's body over the long term

- it being cheaper and easier to fire a coach rather than hold athletes to behavioral standards

- round-the-clock commentary on future sporting events and their participants, where intense arguments break out over meaningless discussions of unknowable future athlete/team performance

---

[277] Eric Metaxas, "Soccer Player Refuses to Wear Rainbow in Support of LGBT," CNS News, July 10, 2017, https://www.cnsnews.com/eric-metaxas/soccer-player-refuses-wear-rainbow-support.lgbt.

[278] Gary Mihoces, "Documentary: For years, NFL ignored concussion evidence," *USA Today*, October 7, 2013, https://www.usatoday.com/story/sports/nfl/2013/10/07/frontline-documentary-nfl-concussions/2939747/.

- some NFL players hijacking the televised national anthem as the time and place to demonstrate their displeasure with race relations in America[279]

27. Culture of rejection

Emotion is an instinctive reaction of feelings from one's circumstances, mood, or relationships with others. Emotions can be volatile or calming, serving as a powerful catalyst for behavior. Emotions are like electricity—instantaneous, unthinking, powerful—and they can be either good or bad depending on the situation. Used properly, channeled emotions energize positive activity; used carelessly, unchanneled emotions energize negative action or suck the life out of its source. In contrast, thinking takes time and serves as a modulator of one's activities. As such, appealing to one's emotions is the easiest and quickest way to elicit a reaction from someone. The arts first appeal to one's emotions and then to one's intellect. Some of our most powerful emotions are present during an experience of rejection: sadness, anger, anxiety, depression, and resentment. The arts media know this and use it to their advantage. Take reality television for example. Many love to see the emotional responses of people who have been dropped, voted off the island, fired from their apprenticeship, and the like. Intellectual helplessness is generated when we wish for negative things to happen to people for our amusement or entertainment.

Examples of Intellectual Helplessness in the Governmental Arena

If it takes too long, requires too much effort, costs too much money, seems too complicated or causes too much discomfort, then chances are good it won't make the day's agenda.
—RICHARD BARNA

Democratic government has been and will always be a target for critique given that it is the people's institution. Democracy has its family squabbles. When these squabbles escalate into Cain and Abel clashes, however, intellectual helplessness rules the day. Examples include the following:

---

[279] Wikipedia, "US national anthem protests (2016-present), https://en.wikipedia.org/wiki/U.S._national_anthem_protests_(2016%E2%80%93present).

28. Mediocre politicians

Politicians routinely score at the bottom of the opinion poll barrel. An April 2017 Gallup poll showed only a 20 percent approval rating for Congress. The average approval rating for Congress over the past forty-three years, based on 286 Gallup surveys, is only 30 percent.[280] I worked in regional government for over three decades and personally observed both good and bad politicians at all levels. Unfortunately, in my opinion, excellent politicians are in the minority. The bad ones no longer carry with them the obligation, or for some, even the sense of having an obligation to public principles such as justice, democracy, equality, and dignity. For many it is simply a healthy paycheck without a power check. Oaths mean nothing to these types of public officials. They are just words that must be repeated to get the job and begin mining the mountain of self-interest. Unfortunately, people at the top, middle, and bottom of the bureaucratic food chain tend to emulate those who reach the top and control the rewards structure of the organization.

Another critical dysfunction among many a modern-day politician is his/her limited perspective. For many, their field of vision is narrow, their awareness is blunted, their understanding is limited, and their concern is fickle. G. K. Chesterton said it beautifully many decades ago:

> "Whenever we see things done wildly, and taken tamely, then the State is going insane … now things every bit as wield as this are being received in silence every day. All strokes slip on the smoothness of a polished wall. All blows fall soundless on the softness of a padded cell. For madness is a passive as well as an active state: it is a paralysis, a refusal of the nerve to respond to the normal stimuli, as well as an unnatural stimulation. There are commonwealths, plainly to be distinguished here and there in history, which pass from prosperity to squalor, or from glory to insignificance, or from freedom to slavery, not only in silence, but serenity. The face still smiles while the limbs, literally and loathsomely, are dropping from the body. These are people who have lost the power of

---

[280] Jim Norman, "Congress Approval Drops to 20% After February High," Gallup.com, April 11, 2017, www.gallupcom/polll/208472.

astonishment at their own actions. When they give birth to a fantastic fashion or a foolish law, they do not start or stare at the monster they have brought forth. They have grown accustomed to their own unreason; chaos is their cosmos; and the whirlwind is the breath of their nostril. These nations are really in danger of going off their heads in masse; of becoming one vast vision of imbecility, with toppling cities and crazy country sides, all dotted with industrious lunatics."[281]

The following are specific examples of intellectual helplessness demonstrated by politicians:

- inability to reach consensus on the major issues of the day: immigration, health care, military, social services, homelessness, budget, presidential appointments, Supreme Court nominations

- a 2017 Gallup poll showing that Americans continue to have negative views on the performance of government and politicians: only 28 percent say they are satisfied with the way the nation is being governed; Congress engenders the lowest confidence of any institution that tests, and Americans rate the honesty and ethics of members of Congress as the lowest among twenty-two professions; the top problem raised concerning government is the infighting and bickering among politicians; and about six in ten Americans believe that the two major political parties are doing such a poor job representing Americans that a third major party is needed[282]

- judges overreaching their Constitutional boundaries

---

[281] G. K. Chesterton, *In Defense of Sanity* (San Francisco, CA: Ignatius Press, 2011), Kindle edition, 63.

[282] Jeffrey M. Jones, "How Americans Perceive Government in 2017," Gallup News, November 1, 2017, http://news.gallup.com/opinion/polling-matters/221171/americans-perceive-government.

- illegally and discriminatorily basing judicial and other confirmations on a religious litmus test[283]

- approval of unsustainable public employee pensions[284]

- a constant display of public incoherence and irrationality due to the pursuit of private gain over the common good

- the failure to answer questions directly or not at all

- politicians' distrust of each other because they know who they are[285]

- having a well-budgeted slush fund for sexual harassment complaints[286]

29. Perception as deception

It is often stated that perception is reality. This pantomime is not a literal fact but a collateral fiction that causes great damage. It is the proverbial wolf dressed in sheep's clothing. It is incumbent on government leadership to efficiently and effectively run our country by addressing real problems, not the ones conjured up for distraction purposes and personal gain. These are specific examples of intellectual helplessness brought about by creating false perceptions:

---

[283] Alexandra Desanctis, "Feinstein: 'I Have Never and Will Never Apply a Religious Litmus Test to Nominees,'" *National Review*, September 12, 2017, http://www.nationalreview.com/corner/451285/dianne-feinstein-amy-coney-barrett-senate-judiary-hearing-religious-litmus-tests-catholic-faith.

[284] Editorial, "PERB flouts voters' will on pensions," *Orange County Register*, January 4, 2016; and Brad Branan, "California cities get next year's pension bill. 'It's not sustainable,' Sacramento official says," *Sacramento Bee*, October 13, 2017, http://www.sacbee.com/news/investigations/the-public-eye/article178561476.html.

[285] From private conversations with individual politicians.

[286] Jenny Beth Martin, "Congress owes taxpayers answers about its harassment 'shush' fund," The Hill, November 15, 2017, http://thehill.com/opinion/finance/360355-congress-owes-american-taxpayers-answers-about-secret-shush-fund.

- a 2015 Pew Research Center study stated that just 19 percent of the public believes it can trust government always or most of time; 74 percent believe that most elected officials put their own interests ahead of the country's; 76 percent feel that "money has a greater influence on politics and elected officials today than in the past;" only 29 percent say the term "honest" describes elected officials; and 72 percent view elected officials as "selfish"[287]

- the seeming politicization of everything

- characterizing Benghazi as an uncoordinated reaction to a video rather than a coordinated terrorist attack to cover up CIA involvement in Libya[288]

- stating that the money sent to Iran was not a ransom payment for hostages or that all chemical weapons were destroyed in Syria[289]

30. Identity politics

Government has now involved itself in dictating how citizens should think and react regarding sexual/gender identity issues. It is Big Brother on steroids. "Forget the democratic process. Forget free speech, freedom of religion, and the conscience rights of American citizens."[290] Here are some examples of intellectual helplessness in this area:

- The State of Illinois using its power to dictate worker and foster parent thoughts and actions related to sexual/gender issues of *children and youth* under its supervision. According to the website,

---

[287] "Beyond Distrust," Pew Research Center, November 23, 2015, http://www.people-press.org/2015/11/23/beyond-distruct-how-americans-view-their-government.

[288] Kelly Riddell, "Benghazi Report Points out Obama, Clinton Lie," *Washington Times*, June 28, 2106, https://www.washingtontimes.com/news/2016/june/28,behghazi-report-points-out-that-Obama-Clinton-lied.

[289] Ron Allen and Erik Ortiz, "$400M Payment to Iran as Americans Freed Not a Ransom: White House," NBC, August 3, 2016, https://www.nbcnews.com/storyline/iran-nucleartalks/400m-payment-iran-americans-freed-not-ransom-white-house-n622196.

[290] Mary Hasson, "Illinois Purges Social Workers and Foster Families Who Don't 'Facilitate' Transgenderism," the Federalist, https://thefederalist.com/2017/05/30/illinois-purges-social-workers-foster-families-dont-facilitate-transgenderism/.

the Federalist, the state is seeking "to 'overrule' basic, empirical research (and common sense) truths about human beings and to replace them with ideological assertions that validate adult feelings rather than 'benefit' children … The role of adults is simply to 'facilitate exploration of any LGBTQ matters through an affirming approach … The new policies empower the state's LGBTQ czar (officially known as the 'State LGBTQ Coordinator') to oversee the sexual orientation and gender identity of *all* children and youth under the state's care. Every child in the system is given 'LGBTQ appropriate' sexual health resources and put through LGBTQ-orientated sexual health education … The child welfare department says that the child's right to privacy prevents disclosing the child's sexual orientation or gender identity to *anyone*, including family members and other staff, unless the child gives permission."[291]

- When Texas passed a law protecting religious institutions from having to comply with regulations that violate its religious conscience,[292] California prohibited its state employees from traveling to Texas for any "nonessential" official business.[293]

- The ACLU suing Catholic hospitals for declining to perform sex-realignment surgeries.[294]

- Some public jurisdictions determining that any sex can use public bathrooms or school locker rooms.[295]

---

[291] Hasson, "Illinois Purges Social Workers and Foster Families," 4.

[292] Marissa Evans, "Senate passes religious protections for child welfare agencies," *Texas Tribune*, May 21, 2017, https://www.texastribune.org/2017/05/21/senate-passes-religous-protections-child-welfare-agencies/.

[293] Adam Ashton, "Texas, three more states on California's banned trial list," *Sacramento Bee*, June 22, 2017, http://www.sacbee.com/news/politics-government/the-state-worker/article157688724.html.

[294] Andrea Desanctis, "ACLU sues Catholic Hospitals over sex-realignment surgery," *National Review*, April 28, 2017, http://nationalreview.com/corner/447203/aclu-sues-california-catholic-hospital-discrimination.

[295] A.P. Dillon, "Will NC Students Have to Share Bathrooms, Locker Rooms with Other Sex?" Civitas Institute, November 10, 2015, https://www.nccivitas.org/2015/will-nc-students-have-to-share-bathrooms-locker-rooms-with-other-sex/.

31. Lawlessness

Over the past decade, there have been obvious violations or ignoring of the law by those in government, up to and including those at the highest level. Note these examples of intellectual helplessness created by public official lawlessness:

- failing to uphold current immigration laws resulting in US citizens being killed by illegal immigrants who were previously in custody but not forced to leave the country

- illegal releasing of classified information and the illegal unmasking of American names

- targeting of conservative citizen groups by the IRS

- claiming weapons of mass destruction in Iraq as a basis for invading the country

- failing to hold accountable anyone for the pay-to-play activities of the Clinton Foundation

- failing to control violent riots

- retaining convicted felons on voting rolls

- allowing FBI agents with documented political animus and/or bias to conduct investigations on those that are the subject of their animus/bias

- Congress exempting itself from several federal laws, such as the Freedom of Information Act and the Whistleblower Protection Act of 1989[296]

---

[296] Amitai Etzioni, "Congress Acts Like It's Above the Law," *National Interest*, November 28, 2017, http://nationalinterest.org/feature/congress-acts-its-above-the-law-23400.

32. Enactment of bad laws and promulgation of poor regulations

Laws are moral choices that compel or restrict behavior. Regulations are the prescribed rules to be followed in obeying a law. We become intellectually helpless when we (1) make laws and regulations that do not get us closer to our national vision (life, liberty, the pursuit of happiness), or do not work toward the accomplishment of our national mission statement (to establish justice, ensure domestic tranquility, provide for the common defense, and secure the blessings of liberty), and (2) when we enact ineffective laws that unsustainably dilute resources across too many choices. Here are some examples:

- Believing that one can select his/her gender or racial identity rather than it being a set biological or racial reality at birth. Sexual Orientation and Gender Identity (SOGI) "laws have created new protected classes of people based on inclination and behavior, not race, sex, or creed."[297]

- Legal barriers to families assisting mentally ill relatives, such as patient confidentiality, in which relatives are not allowed to receive information, assist in filling out forms, or answer questions of government or medical officials unless their mentally ill family members grant them permission to assist them.

- Passing laws and establishing regulations that don't provide for adequate assistance to the homeless or prevent them from being moved from public areas when they create a public health hazard.

- Excessive and unnecessarily restrictive laws and regulations where the cure is worse than the ailment.[298]

- Poor immigration laws and regulations that do not ensure immigrants are properly vetted before entering the country; giving rights and benefits to immigrants in the country illegally.

[297] John Stonestreet, "Religious Freedom and SOGI Laws," BreakPoint, December 14, 2016, http://www.breakpoint.org/2016/12/religous-freedom-and-sogi-laws/.
[298] "Over-regulated America," *The Economist*, February 18, 2012, http://www.economist.com/node/21547789.

33. Crippling entitlements

There is good aid and there is bad aid. The focus of good aid is to get people back on their feet so they can take care of themselves. Bad aid is doing things for people that they could and should do for themselves, or incentivizing them to find ways to inappropriately remain on aid. This is addicting people to the medicine rather than helping them to change the habits that make them sick. If America is unable to curtail deficit spending, resulting largely from entitlement expenses, we must consider whether we have lost the capacity to self-govern. Examples of intellectual helplessness created by government entitlements include these:

- the federal Governmental Accounting Office (GAO) found $137 billion of improper government payments in entitlement programs for 2015, an increase of $31 billion in two years[299]

- incentivizing women to have more children because it brings in more money than going to work[300]

- significantly increasing the number of protected categories that qualify for entitlement benefits

- having entitlement eligibility decided by lower paid staff

- some government workers fraudulently working the system to see that their relatives or friends receive aid

34. Failing to protect the weak and defenseless

One of the major duties of government is to identify and assist those who can no longer take care of themselves. It is based on the concept that "there

---

[299] Dr. Peter Viechnicki, William D. Eggers, Michael Greene, Jim Guszcza, Brien Lorenze, and Dan Olson, "Shutting down fraud, waste, and abuse," Deloitte Insights, May 11, 2106, https://www2.deloitte.com/insights/us/en/industry/public-sector/fraud-waste-and-abuse-in-entitlement-programs-benefits.html.

[300] Michael D. Tanner, "When Welfare Pays Better than Work," CATO Institute, August 19, 2013, https://www.cato.org/publications/commentary/when-welfare-pays-better-work.

but for the grace of God go I."[301] The following are examples of intellectual helplessness created by government failing to adequately protect the weak and defenseless:

- Treating the mentally ill as if they were sane, and the sane who attempt to help them as if they were mentally ill. For instance, asking the mentally ill to read and respond cogently to legal or financial matters, and disallowing relatives to assist unless they have a power of attorney from their mentally ill relative who often will not agree to do so because of his/her illness.

- Placing roadblocks on private religious nonprofits (e.g., requiring them to provide services that violate their religious beliefs) that are the majority institutions that provide service to the weak and defenseless.[302]

- Providing access to abortion on demand.

- Fertility sterilization or eugenics for the mentally or physical disabled, or inmates. In White County, Tennessee, inmates were given credit for jail time if they voluntarily agreed to have a vasectomy or a birth control implant.[303] In North Carolina, from 1933 to 1977, thousands of people were sterilized based on social workers' evaluations of the individuals' IQ tests and personal history.[304]

- The progression of the idea that an ill person has a "right to die" (assisted suicide) to their having an "obligation to die." This includes

---

[301] John Bradford, *The Oxford Dictionary of National Biography*, vol. 6 (1885), 159.

[302] Eric Metaxas and Stan Guthrie, "Hope for the Homeless," BreakPoint, March 28, 2017, http://breakpointorg/2017/03/breakpoint-hope-homeless/.

[303] Chris Conte, "White County Inmates Given Reduced Jail Time If They Get Vasectomy," NewsChannel5 Network, Nashville, July 19, 2017, https://www.newschannel5.com/news/inmates-given-reduced-jail-if-they-get-a-vasectomy.

[304] Kim Severson, "Eugenics: Thousands Sterilized, a State Weighs Restitution," Constantine Report, January 14, 2012, https://www.constantinereport.com/eugenics-thousands-sterilized-a-sate-weights-restitution-nyt/.

paying doctors a premium for assisting in suicides,[305] and allowing suicides when one feels he/she is no longer useful to society[306] or when it would cut down on health care costs.[307]

35. Leaving troops on the battlefield

A basic pillar of military warrior ethos is never leaving a fellow solider behind. This concept is lost on some politicians and bureaucrats. When a soldier is left behind, all hell breaks loose in morale, and vital character traits are diminished such as sacrifice, commitment, and valor. Examples of intellectual helplessness created by leaving one's troops on the battlefield are as follows:

- lack of timely assistance provided to the Americans in Benghazi
- failure of the Veterans Administration to adequately care for our troops
- failure to allow our troops to take the necessary actions to win a war, unnecessarily putting them in harm's way

36. Private gain over public service

When politicians and bureaucrats use their position as public servants for personal gain, several bad things happen, including the creation of uneven playing fields, a violation of their oath to public service, the diversion of public resources away from critical public needs, the tacit encouragement of others to do the same, and a loss of public confidence and moral authority to lead. In a 2015 Pew study, 74 percent of those surveyed said that "most elected officials put their own interests ahead of the country."[308] These are examples of intellectual helplessness created by public corruption scandals:

---

[305] Catherine McIntyre, "Should Doctors be paid a premium for assisting deaths?" *Macleans*, July 12, 2017, http://www.macleans.ca/society/should-doctors-be-paid-a-premium-for-assisted-deaths/.

[306] John Stonestreet, "Suicide and the Logic of Utility," BreakPoint, August 16, 2017, http://www.breakpoint.org/2017/08/breakpoint-suicide-and-the-logic-of-utility/.

[307] Thomas Sowell, "A 'Duty to Die'?" Townhall, May 11, 2010, https://www.townhall.com/columnists/thomassowell/2010/05/11/a-duty-to-die-n936572.

[308] "Beyond Distrust: How Americans View Their Government," Pew Research Center.

- the US Navy's "Fat Leonard" scandal in which a Malaysian contractor offered bribes, kickbacks, and gifts to top navy brass in exchange for contracts, false payments, and access to ship schedules[309]

- the Clinton Foundation pay-to-play scandal

- the IRS's intentional targeting of conservative groups who disagreed with the policies of the Obama administration.

- illegal surveillance and unmasking of American names to damage the political opposition

- failure of government agencies to hold Wall Street and other institutions accountable for their contributions to scandals like the 2008 subprime mortgage crisis

- failure to make meaningful changes to the political system so manipulations and private gain can continue (e.g., campaign finance, congressional exemptions from laws they create)

- extremely excessive prices paid in government procurements

37. Immigration mat

Immigration is not a four-letter word. America has been and continues to be the world's melting pot. We encourage and welcome anyone who wants to commit to becoming a fully integrated American. We have an established process for citizenship to safeguard our country. An immigrant must accept and be assimilated into the moral-cultural, political, and economic values of America. Immigrants can retain their heritage, but they must surrender their national identity and become an American at the door. Speaking of doors, each of our homes has one. Would anyone rationally

---

[309] Craig Whitlock, "Fat Leonard Scandal expands to ensnare more than 60 admirals," *Washington Post*, November 6, 2017, https://www.washingtonpost.com/investigations/fat-leonard-scandal-expands-to-ensnare-more-than-sixty-admirals; and Kari Hawkins, "Federal employees charged with putting public service above private gain," US Army, August 7, 2017, https://www.army.mil/article/191934/federal_employees_charged_with_putting_public_service_above_private-gain.

allow a complete stranger who knocks on one's door to come in and stay with one's family? One would rightly consider it his/her duty to protect one's family first and then assist the stranger if one reasonably can. When we change the immigration process from a welcome mat of assimilation into a doormat of accommodation, we become intellectually helpless in addressing a variety of problems. Note these examples:

- A 2017 report from the Federation for American Immigration Reform (FAIR) detailed that American taxpayers pay an estimated $135 billion annually for its approximately 12.5 million illegal aliens, while only collecting $19 billion in taxes, resulting in a $116 billion deficit.[310]

- State and local prisons/jails do not routinely provide the federal government statistics on how many illegal aliens are present in their facilities. Of the approximately fifty-nine thousand aliens in federal prisons, nearly 95 percent are unlawfully present in the United States.[311]

- Previously arrested and undeported illegal immigrants who are released back into American communities.[312]

- The children of illegal immigrants automatically becoming Americans because they were born in the United States.

- The increased probability of terrorist activity: San Bernardino, Boston, Orlando, New York.

---

[310] Matt O'Brien and Spencer Raley, "The Fiscal Burden of Illegal Immigration on United States Taxpayers," Federation for Illegal Immigration Reform, September 27, 2017, https://fairus.org/issue/publications-resources/fiscal-burden-illegal-immigration-united-states-taxpayers.

[311] Katie Pavlich, "DOJ Releases New Numbers: One-in-Five Federal Prisoners are Foreign Born, Most Illegal Aliens," Townhall, December 21, 2017, https://www.townhall.com/tipsheet/katiepavlich/2017/12/21/doj-releases-new-numbers-oneinfive-federal-prsoners-are-foreign-born-n2425834.

[312] Stephen Dinan, "20,000 illegals with criminal convictions released into U.S. communities in 2015," *Washington Times*, April 27, 2016, https://www.washingtontimes.com/news/2016/apr/27/hoeland-secuurity-releasing-thousands-illegal-immigrants/.

- Gross anomalies in culture such as an American citizen being arrested for hunting or fishing without a license, but not an immigrant for entering and remaining in the country illegally.[313]

38. Economically unsustainable government pensions

The mission of government is to provide public services to its citizens in an effective and efficient manner. Efficiency includes the reasonable payment of salaries and pensions for government workers. Over the past two decades, many local government agencies have approved lucrative pension plans for their employees, far above what the private sector provides. For instance, many public safety employees were given pension plans like the 3 @ 50 formula. This formula allows a public safety employee to retire at age fifty with annual pay equal to three times the number of years of service for the rest of his/her life (e.g., a fifty-year-old police officer with thirty years of service could retire with 90 percent of his/her pay for life—three times thirty years). Another extreme feature of the pension formula was its retroactivity. When the new pension formulas were approved, it was retroactive to the beginning of the employee's career. This feature allowed newly retiring employees to receive the increased pension formulas without ever having to pay any of the increased costs of the plan for prior years. While new laws have been passed to partially mitigate this situation, their full mitigating effect will not be realized until those who received the lucrative plans retire in twenty or thirty years. The following are examples of the intellectual helplessness created by these decisions:

- The domino effect of other jurisdictions succumbing to pressure to approve these higher formulas to "keep up with the Jones" or theoretically lose public safety staff to other jurisdictions that did approve these increased formulas.

- The resulting economic devastation to governmental budgets, including the bankrupting of cities like Stockton (CA), Riverside (CA), and Detroit (MI) as a direct result of approving higher pension formulas.

---

[313] Jeff Foxworthy, comedy routine.

- The increasing of taxes to pay for the cost of new pension plans, as well as the reduction of traditional government services. A researcher for Stanford University's Institute of Economic Policy Research wrote that government "employer pension contributions are projected to roughly double between 2017 and 2030, resulting in the further crowd out of traditional government services."[314]

- The early retirement of a jurisdiction's most senior staff, decimating the ranks of leadership and the subsequent promotion of people before they are ready.

39. Mission failure of the grand experiment in democracy

The United States' political-economic system of democratic capitalism is based on certain moral-cultural assumptions. It only runs on the fuel of voluntary virtue. Remove virtue and one spends all day trying to pop the clutch of democratic governing. Eventually the Band-Aids, bailing wire, and duct tape run out, and so does the grand experiment of democracy. Imagine for a moment the specific things you really enjoy doing in life. Then think about whether these things would be possible or at least significantly reduced without democracy. Democracy is a relationship. It is the *consent* of the people to be governed by their elected representatives. When we step out on that relationship, bad things happen, much of which cannot be regained. Examples of the consequences of democratic infidelity include the following:

- law enforcement agencies whose actions/inactions promote unequal justice under the law
- hostile Supreme Court and Cabinet nomination processes
- overreach of the judiciary
- bypassing the lawmaking process by the issuance of executive orders
- sustained lack of *progress* by a *Congress*
- inept regulatory and bureaucratic processes

---

[314] Joe Nation, "Pension Math: Public Pension Spending and Service Crowd Out in California, 2003–2030," Stanford Institute for Economic Policy Research, October 2, 2017, https://siepr.stanford.edu/research/publications/pension-math-public-pension-spending-and-service-crowd-out-california-2003.

- deficiencies in military readiness
- rule breaking by those charged with enforcing laws
- misuse of technology, causing America to go from "one nation under God" to "one nation under surveillance"[315]
- failure to provide adequate security for citizens because law enforcement has its hands tied behind its back
- attitudes and policies that foster dependence/victimhood rather than independence/initiative

Examples of Intellectual Helplessness in the Business Arena

> *There is a great deal to be said about the view that all corporate institutions*
> *have a kind of corporate soul, an identity which is greater than the sum*
> *of its parts, which can actually tell the part what to do and how to do it.*
> *This leads to the view that in some cases at least, some of these corporate*
> *institutions—whether they be industrial companies, governments or even*
> *churches—can be so corrupted with evil that the language of 'possession' at a*
> *corporate level becomes the only way to explain the phenomena before us.*
> —N. T. WRIGHT

Business is the fuel that propels democratic capitalism. As Adam Smith envisioned, free enterprise is the motivation to invent, the freedom to produce, and the enjoyment of the social and economic rewards by both the producer and the consumer. When business ceases to fulfill its profit and public service roles, the gas tank of democracy dries up and its engine seizes to a halt. The following specific examples demonstrate the presence of intellectual helplessness in the business arena:

40. Management diseases and disorders[316]

Just as with physical health, business managers and their organizational cultures have diseases and disorders that negatively impact economic health. People who run businesses bring their intellectual baggage into the workplace. This baggage includes personal, interpersonal, and behavioral

---

[315] Guinness, *A Free People's Suicide*, 191.

[316] Steven Danley and Peter Hughes, *Management Diseases and Disorders: How to Identify and Treat Dysfunctional Managerial Behavior* (Lulu Publishing Services, 2016).

deficiencies that impede an effective and efficient workplace. Businesses also have cultures that result from the amalgamation of management personalities. The operating systems implemented to run the business reflect its cultural values. Here are some specific examples of intellectual helplessness created by deficient management personalities or cultures/systems:

- illegal lobbying and bribery of public officials, such as the case of Jack Abramoff, who was convicted along with twenty-one others—including White House officials and members of Congress—for mail fraud, conspiracy to bilk public officials, and tax invasion

- financial, environmental, and health care disasters created by corporate greed (e.g., Enron accounting scandal, British Petroleum's oil spills, Mylan's excessive pricing of its EpiPen, Wells Fargo's fraudulent customer charges, Volkswagen's fraudulent emissions tests)

- hiding and inadequately dealing with malfeasance to protect the company's reputation (e.g., Catholic Church protecting its priests who sexually molested minors)

- decisions made to not protect the public good due to a fear of litigation (e.g., CBS corporate initially deciding not to cover the story of the tobacco industry's intentional actions to get cigarette smokers addicted to nicotine after the industry threated to sue the company if the story aired)

- promotional decisions based on loyalty over competence and its subsequent proliferation down into the ranks of the organization

- firing and disciplining of legitimate whistle-blower employees for pointing out work-culture deficiencies[317]

---

[317] "List of whistleblowers," Wikipedia, https://en.wikipedia.org/wiki/List_of_whistleblowers.

41. The tail of technology wagging the big dog of business

Technology should be a tool designed and used by business to accomplish mission-centric goals. When this is forgotten, the process becomes reversed and the goals are determined by what the technology can accomplish. The use of technology should be guided by philosophical and moral considerations prior to its use. Examples of technology that can create intellectual helplessness include the following:[318]

- the creation and inappropriate use of military weapons (e.g., "swarm warfare," where vast numbers of drones are programmed to act in unison; enhanced chemical pathogens)

- attempts to create and implement biological experiments that re-create life or attempt to improve the human species without proper ethical vetting (e.g., cloning; artificial life forms with synthetic DNA)

- the illegal use of surveillance technology (e.g., NSA surveillance scandals; brain-hacking techniques from wearable devices that measure EEG waves; employers requiring their employees to wear technology that records everything they see and say, and tracks their movements)

- society coming to a near standstill when the electricity goes out (e.g., computers, gas stations, air conditioners, traffic lights, appliances)

- "ransomware," where an entity holds your data hostage until to you pay your bills

---

[318] Jessica Brown, "Reilly Center releases its 2018 top 10 list of ethical dilemmas in science and technology," University of Notre Dame, December 7, 2017, https://physorg/news/2017-12-reilly-center-ethical-dilemmas-science.html; and Jessica Baron, "Reilly Center releases 2017 list of emerging ethical dilemmas and policy issues in science and technology," *Notre Dame News*, December 20, 2016, https://news.nd.edu/news/reilly-center-releases-2017-list-of-emerging-ethical-dilemmas-and-policy-issues-in-science-and-technology; and "10 Emerging Ethical Dilemmas in Science and Technology," *Bioscience Technology*, December 8, 2014, https://www.biosciencetechnology.com/news/2014/12/10-emerging-ethical-dilemmas-sci.

- "medical ghost management," in which pharmaceutical companies hire firms to perform their clinical trials, write up the research, find academics to put their names on publications, place it in journals, and create and run their marketing campaigns, which can create significant conflicts of interest

- programming a computer to predict with high accuracy whether or not someone will manifest criminal behavior; "sentencing" software, where Americans are in some cases being sentenced in a court of law with the help of an algorithm

- the "robot priest," where computer-programmed priests or robots help you with your spiritual needs

42. Customer disservice

Not that long ago, it was a basic management tenet that the "customer is king." This tenet has slowly eroded due to changing cultural trends in such areas as one's ethics, primary focus (us vs. me), definition of success (intangible vs. tangible), commitment (long vs. short haul), and work ethic (producing a surplus vs. doing just enough to get by). These examples demonstrate intellectual helplessness in serving customers:

- intentionally not providing an outlet for customer complaints
- immediately threatening customers with being sent to collections for a first late payment
- waiting on hold for several minutes or being endlessly transferred
- initially denying all complaints or making it so difficult to resolve an issue that, hopefully, the customer will just give up
- product development driven by corporate, not customer, preference

43. Virtue signaling[319]

Virtue signaling, a new term, indicates a business's support for a social cause, in the hope that it will produce increased sales revenues. In cases

---

[319] John Stonestreet, "Corporate Virtue Signaling," BreakPoint, February 21, 2017, www.breakpoint.org/2017/02/corporate-virtue-signaling/.

where business firms pony up a revenue match for a cause, it can be a win-win situation. However, far too often, virtue signaling is typically a self-glorifying faux virtue for manipulative profit. Businesses do not necessarily have to believe in the cause, or even plan on doing anything specific to support it. Tragically, these advertising campaigns force complex social issues into thirty-second sound bites, oversimplifying and stereotyping them. They are often attempts to dubiously capitalize on current events to publicize virtuous feelings about an issue. Examples of this type of intellectual helplessness follow:

- Taxi competitor Lyft taking advantage of Uber by continuing to run its service during the taxi strike in New York City over President Trump's immigration order.[320]

- Major corporations and the NFL threatening to boycott doing business in North Carolina due to its legislature passing a bill requiring people to use the public restroom corresponding with the sex on their birth certificate.[321]

- Toiletry and household cleaner giant Proctor and Gamble's new "My Black is Beautiful" campaign depicting a black mother warning her daughter, a new driver, what to do *when* she gets pulled over by the police.[322]

- In an answer to a question no one was asking, Facebook founder Mark Zuckerberg stated, "If you're a Muslim in this community, as the leader of Facebook I want you to know that you are always

[320] Phillip Wegmann, "Lyft's virtue signaling threatens to wreck the car service," *Washington Examiner*, January 30, 2017, http://www.washingtonexaminer.com/lyfts-virtue-signaling-threatens-to-wreck-the-car-service/article/2613376.

[321] Mitch Hall, "The Left's Huge Double Standard for Corporate Speech," the Federalist, April 7, 2016, http://thefederalist.com/2016/04/07/the-lefts-huge-double-standard-for-corporate-speech/.

[322] Michelle Malkin, "Proctor & Gamble's Identity-Politics Pandering," Townhall, August 2, 2017, https://www.townhall.com/columnists/michellemalkin/2017/08/02/proctor--gambles-indentitypolitics-pandering-n2363170.

welcome here and that we will fight to protect your rights and create a peaceful and safe environment for you."[323]

- McDonalds inverting the "M" in its logo to "W" on some of its stores' signage to signal its support of International Women's Day.[324]

44. Short-term thinking

Our fast-paced society often encourages focus on the now, with only cursory consideration of the future and almost no consideration of the past. Things have become throwaways in many areas of life. Indeed, many products (e.g., clothes, cars, appliances) are now built to last only a couple of years in order to reduce their price and/or allow the customer to change products after they get tired of them in a few months or years. This focus on the now has migrated from things to other areas of life, such as business relationships. These examples illustrate the short-term thinking in business that creates intellectual helplessness:

- British Petroleum oil spills in Alaska and the Gulf Coast that resulted from poor operating decisions based on time and cost cutting pressures, that ultimately killed people and wildlife, destroyed vast stretches of the environment, closed surrounding businesses, and resulted in billions of dollars in cleanup costs and regulatory fines

- focusing almost exclusively on communicating electronically rather than face-to-face with colleagues and clients on issues that require significant and nuanced discussion, and the development and maintenance of personal relationships

---

[323] Nate Church, "Virtue Signaling: Mark Zuckerberg Declares Muslims Welcome on Facebook," Breitbart, December 10, 2015, http://www.breitbart.com/tech/2015/12/10/virtue-signalling-mark -zuckerberg-declares-muslims-welcome-on-facebook/.

[324] Janine Puhak, "McDonald's flips logo upside down for International Women's Day, but Twitter users aren't lovin' it," Fox News, March 8, 2018, http://www.foxnews.com/food-drink/2018/03/08/mcdonald-s'flips-logo-upside-down-for-international-womens-day-but-twitter-users-not-lovin-it.

- not addressing significant behavioral issues (e.g., sexual harassment, tardiness, poor interpersonal skills, ignoring of company policies, dishonesty) because of an employee's value to the organization

45. Short-changing the benefits of religious nonprofits

Considered as a whole, American religion is the world's fifteenth largest economy, between Russia and Australia.[325] A study conducted by the *Journal of Religion*, found that "religion in the United States today contributed $1.2 trillion each year to our economy and society."[326] This is no doubt a surprise to many people, who have never known or forgotten the importance of a religious institution's contributions to addressing social needs. Religious nonprofits fund 1.5 million social programs using 7.3 million volunteers.[327] Without these programs, the government would have to pick up the tab, bringing with it all its bureaucratic gore. Examples of intellectual helplessness in taking the work of religious nonprofits for granted include the following:

- government attempting to force religious institutions to adhere to the tenets of the sexual revolution, thus causing them to opt out of service provision

- periodic government consideration of removing tax-exempt status for religious institutions

- requiring the largest nongovernment provider of health care services in the world (church-run hospitals) to violate their freedom of conscience and consider closing their doors by requiring them to provide things like contraceptives, abortion-producing drugs, or sex-reassignment surgeries

The above forty-five specific examples of intellectual helplessness in America, unfortunately, are just the tip of the dunce cap.

---

[325] John Stonestreet, "Religion, the Great Economic Engine," BreakPoint, September 23, 2016, www.breakpoint.org/2016/09/religion-the-great-economic-engine/.
[326] Stonestreet.
[327] Stonestreet, "Religion, the Great Economic Engine," BreakPoint.

PART III

Turning the Lights Back On

Chapter 7

Suggestions for Thinking Clearly

The primary task of the perfected intellect is to bring order to knowledge. The perfected mind stretches itself around facts and discerns their relationships.
—James Sire

I did try and find a heresy of my own; and when I had put the last touches to it, I discovered that it was orthodoxy.
—G. K. Chesterton

Nothing pains some people more than having to think.
—Martin Luther King, Jr.

Let us endeavor, then, to think well, this is the principle of morality.
—Blaise Pascal

Now that we have examined the extent of society's intellectual helplessness, it's time to consider potential means to address this epidemic. The following recommendations provide suggestions for intellectual excellence—clear thinking that will result in the robust analysis of information, development of better options, quality decisions, and implementation of efficient and effective solutions. Each suggestion includes a list of life observations to support the efficacy of the suggestion.

Suggestion 1: Conform one's thoughts to reality

Reality is the way things are. Clear thinking starts here. It involves the integrity of accepting and addressing what is concretely there and experienced.

It is not first determining what one wants and then manipulating circumstances to achieve one's desires. Here are some of the more important things that are real and therefore true:

There is an order to things.

There is an orderliness to the universe that is continually being discovered and reaffirmed. It is present in every aspect of life. There is design in every living thing. There are beginnings, middles, and ends to every story. There are linkages to people, places, times, and events. Once we understand this, we begin to be on the lookout for the coherency that we instinctively know is there, as our minds consciously and unconsciously search for connections.

Supporting observations from life:

- Mathematical equations can explain all of physical reality. The original Apollo astronauts wouldn't orbit the earth until the math proved it could be done.
- Viewing nature under the microscope clearly demonstrates structure, sequence, and process.
- The ubiquitous presence of "if-then" precepts.
- Foundational ordering structures, such as numbers (1, 2, 3), scales (do, re, mi), and grammar (subject, predicate, noun, verb, adjective).
- The replication of the concept of male/female coupling for creating mechanical structures: electrical, mechanical, and plumbing parts; screws and nuts; pistons and cylinders; pipes and elbows; roof gutters and downspouts; electronic cables and jacks; electrical plugs and outlets.
- The necessity of morals and manners for a functional society.

The dilemma of human nature and the certainty of evil.

Blaise Pascal said, "Man is the glory and shame of the universe."[328] How does one explain that humanity is at the same time capable of incredible accomplishment and the worst atrocities? The "humans are basically good"

---

[328] Blaise Pascal, *Pensees*, 434.

theory is easy to rationalize because we don't want to admit the other, darker side of our nature. However, both natures are present and active in each of us. This is not news to those with clean spectacles. That is why, as Chuck Colson wrote, "Government is, in a sense, God's response to the nature of people themselves."[329] The Declaration of Independence begins by explaining why the founders wanted to separate from England. The US Constitution then goes about building a government walled in by checks and balances designed to distribute the good parts of our nature and to ration its bad parts.

The year 2017 is a good example of the binary character of human nature on display. On the positive side of the ledger are these:

- improvements in medicine, such as potential treatments for ALS, Huntington's disease, and repairing the skin of burn victims
- humanitarian relief efforts by citizens and first responders to calamities, such as hurricanes (Texas, Louisiana, Florida), shootings (Las Vegas), rebuilding a burned-down mosque (Texas), and fires (California)
- all eyes to the sky to view the 2017 solar eclipse
- Syria and Iraq liberated from ISIS, worldwide improvements in bringing electricity to people, a reduction in extreme poverty, a reduction in child mortality, and a reduction in teenage pregnancy rates
- a Florida high school starting a club so no one has to eat lunch alone

On the negative side of the ledger are these:

- mass shootings and terrorist events in Las Vegas, Fort Lauderdale, and New York
- intensified political party divides and the resulting stalemate on addressing critical national issues
- intensified nuclear threats from North Korea and Iran
- intensified social unrest related to race, gender, and religion

---

[329] Colson, *God & Government*, 102.

- government bureaucrats circumventing the desires of a new presidential administration by promoting ideological agendas rather than the common good
- outpourings of sexual harassment allegations in the workplace
- the worsening of the media's creation and distribution of fake news

Not addressing the dual nature of humanity (i.e., good and bad) and the certainty of evil always results in severe consequences. In many ways, 2017 was a year of reckonings—dealing with the consequences of poor choices that contributed to the occurrence of the items in the negative list above. Unfortunately, this generation continues to relearn human nature and evil the hard way, still hoping for a competent humankind benevolently ruling the planet. All the efforts to continue to view evil as an exception, or random interruption, did was give liquor to the sentry of democracy while on night duty. Evil walked by as the guardian slept. The dilemma of human nature and the certainty of evil are such important truths that below I have provided corroborating views of venerated thinkers from differing backgrounds on the subject:

- Theologian Ravi Zacharias: "The skeptics of our time forget that human depravity is at once the most empirically verifiable fact that is and, at the same time, the most intellectually resisted."[330] This begs the question: if humanity cannot be trusted to accept depravity as a verifiable fact, how can we be fully trusted with anything else?

- Author Charles Colson: "Every human being has an infinite capacity for self-rationalization and self-delusion."[331]

- Scientist Daniel Kahneman: "Social scientists in the 1970s broadly accepted two ideas about human nature. First, people are generally rational, and their thinking is normally sound. Second, emotions such as fear, affection, and hatred explain most of the occasions on which people depart from rationality. Our article challenged both

[330] Ravi Zacharias, *Beyond Opinion* (Nashville, TN: Thomas Nelson, 2007), 206.
[331] Charles Colson, "The Problem of Ethics: Speech at Harvard Business School," BreakPoint, January 1, 1992, 6, http://www.breakpoint.org/features-columns/articles/ntry/12/9649?tmpl=component&pri.

assumptions without discussing them directly. We documented systematic errors in the thinking of normal people, and we traced these errors to the design of the machinery of human cognition rather than to the corruption of thought by emotion."[332]

- Professor Allan Bloom: "Human nature, it seems, remains the same in our very altered circumstances because we still face the same problems, if in different guises, and have the distinctively human need to solve them, even though our awareness and focus have become enfeebled."[333]

- Author Russell Kirk: "Human nature suffers irremediably from certain grave faults ... Man being imperfect, no perfect social order ever can be created ... Because of human restlessness, mankind would grow rebellious under any utopian domination, and would break out once more in violent discontent—or else expire of boredom ... To seek utopia is to end in disaster ... All that we reasonably can expect is a tolerably ordered, just and free society ... The ideologues who promise the perfection of man and society have converted a great part of the twentieth-century world into a terrestrial hell."[334]

- Theologian Reinhold Niebuhr: "For all the centuries of experience, men have not yet learned how to live together without compounding their vices and covering each other 'with mud and with blood.'"[335]

- Author G. K. Chesterton: "The sane man knows that he has a touch of the beast, a touch of the devil, a touch of the saint, a touch of the citizen. Nay, the really sane man knows that he has a touch of the madman. But the materialist's world is quite simple and solid, just

---

[332] Kahneman, *Thinking Fast and Slow*, Introduction.

[333] Bloom, *The Closing of the American Mind*, 380.

[334] Russell Kirk, "Ten Conservative Principles," The Russell Kirk Center for Cultural Renewal, http://www.kirkcenter.org/kirk/ten-principles.html, 3.

[335] Reinhold Niebuhr, *Moral Man & Immoral Society: A Study in Ethics and Politics* (Louisville, KY: Westminster John Knox Press, 1932), 1.

as the madman is quite sure he is sane … Madmen and Materialists never have doubts."[336]

- Professor and author C. S. Lewis: "One almost hears the incessant whispering, tattling, lying, scolding, flattery, and circulation of rumours. No historical readjustments are here required, we are in a world we know. We even detect in that muttering and wheedling chorus voices which are familiar. One of them may be too familiar for recognition."[337]

There is a practical necessity for God.

Lacey once asked me if I thought God looks out for people. I guess he does. I say He's just about got to. I don't believe we'd make it a day otherwise.[338]
—FROM THE MOVIE *ALL THE PRETTY HORSES*

We are in a fight against ourselves. On one hand, we exist within an orderly universe that provides peace and prosperity under certain conditions. It can be seen by those with clear eyes, a humble heart, and a willing spirit (i.e., clear thinking and rational acting). Yet, on the other hand, we all struggle with a powerful desire and societal prodding for autonomy, believing that we know better and can make a more fruitful existence under systems created by humans. And so our dilemma continues to play out, with the resulting struggles being broadly labeled as the history of humankind.

Even at this crossroads, however, there is common ground. Consider that philosophy exists because of the human requirement for answers, regardless of one's worldview. Why is it that both those who believe in God and those who don't involuntarily have the *same* life questions? Why do we all feel compelled to explain existence and meaning? Why do nihilistic philosophers spend their "finite" time contemplating and advocating for nothingness, or refuting something they believe doesn't exist? Why spend one's valuable time thinking, writing, and speaking about what's not there?

---

[336] G. K. Chesterton, *Orthodoxy* (Orlando, FL: Relevant Media Group, Inc., 2006), 13—14.
[337] C. S. Lewis, *Reflections on the Psalms: The Celebrated Musings on One of the Most Intriguing Books of the Bible* (New York: Mariner Books, 1958), 73.
[338] *All the Pretty Horses,* Drew's Script-O-Rama, http://www.script-o-rama.com/movie_scripts/a/all-the-pretty-hourses-script.html.

Why do some believe that human personality could have come from impersonality (random, impersonal creation)?

While it is not possible to scientifically prove (or disprove) the existence of God, it is a widely shared proposition among people from different philosophical perspectives that it is necessary for God to exist (literally or figuratively) in order to make a functional society possible. One would expect that claim from people with a religious commitment. But what about from Immanuel Kant (skepticism: God can't be rationally demonstrated by science or reason); Jean Paul Sartre (secularism: there is no God, no design, and no purpose to life); and Sir Julian Huxley (atheism)? Kant postulated that even if we cannot know God exists, for practical purposes we must live as if he does exist if ethics and society are to be possible.[339] Sartre did not believe in God but wished it wasn't that way.[340] Huxley acknowledged, "Somehow or other, against all one might expect, man functions better if he acts as though God is there."[341]

One area in which humans function better is in personal stability. University of California Irvine Director of Medical Ethics Aaron Kheriaty noted, "We now have a sizable body of medical research which suggests that prayer, religious faith, participation in a religious community, and practices like cultivating gratitude, forgiveness, and other virtues can reduce the risk of depression, lower the risk of suicide, diminish drug abuse, and aid in recovery. To cite just one finding from a growing body of medical research on this subject, Tyler VanderWeele of Harvard's T. H. Chan School of Public Health recently published a study of suicide and religious participation among women in the U.S. Against the backdrop of increasing suicide rates, this study of 89,000 participants found that some groups remain protected from the rising tide of despair and self-harm. Between 1996 and 2010, those who attended any religious service once a week or more were *five times less likely to commit suicide*."[342]

Along these same lines, author Dennis Prager said that while God's existence/nonexistence cannot be proven, "what is provable is what happens when people stop believing in God:

---

[339] R.C. Sproul, *The Consequences of Ideas*, 131.
[340] Sproul, 181.
[341] Sir Julian Huxley in *Trilogy* by Francis Schaeffer, 95.
[342] Kheriaty, "Dying of Despair," 6.

- Without God, there is no good and evil.
- Without God, there is no objective meaning to life.
- Life is ultimately a tragic fare if there is no God.
- Human beings need instruction manuals.
- If there is no God, the kindest and most innocent victims of torture and murder have no better a fate after death than do the most cruel torturers and mass murderers.
- With the death of Judeo-Christian values in the West, many Westerners believe in little. That is why secular Western Europe has been unwilling and therefore unable to confront evil, whether it was communism during the Cold War or Islamic totalitarians in its midst today.
- Without God, people in the West often become less, not more, rational. If there is no God, the human being has no free will. He is a robot, whose every action is dictated by genes and environment.
- If there is no God, humans and 'other' animals are of equal value.
- Without God, there is little to inspire people to create inspiring art.
- Without God, nothing is holy.
- Without God, humanist hubris is almost inevitable.
- Without God, there are no unalienable human rights.
- 'Without God,' Dostoevsky famously wrote, 'all is permitted.'"[343]

One of the areas most impacted when people stop believing in God is how men relate to women. In a theistic (particularly Judeo-Christian) worldview, men and women are created differently but are of equal importance and value to God. Both need each other and are to respect each other in word and deed. This worldview provides a workable framework of male-female relations based on mutual respect, interdependence, and obeying God's commands. In contrast, without this framework, it is a question of personal power and who (male or female) has it. By definition, this framework is unsettled, with men and women perpetually jockeying for dominance over the other. There is no transcendent basis for reconciling

---

[343] Dennis Prager, "If There is No God," Townhall, May 4, 2017, https://townhall.com/columnists/dennisprager/2008/08/19/if-their-is-no-god-n807351.

"the bright clean ideals of gender equality and the mechanisms of human desire."[344]

There are opportunities for good.

Evil is easy; good requires effort. Fortunately, there is an abundance of opportunities every day to spread light and life to a needy world. The opportunities are not found in a book but in the dramas of everyday life. They are casting calls to fill the part of giving to raw need. Giving is a win-win activity. It is the gym for the exercise of the heart and soul. As NBA executive and author Pat Williams wisely noted, "Service to others is the rent we pay for living."[345]

Supporting observations from life of those in need:

- infirmed seniors
- disabled veterans
- mentally ill
- homeless
- abused children
- victims of crime
- rehabilitation of criminals
- environmental stewardship
- educational tutoring
- holding babies in the maternity ward

Suggestion 2: Commit to acknowledging and accepting the truth

Once we accept reality, we are in a good position to communicate truth (i.e., accurate descriptions of reality). Truth is our only solid anchor and guide. Without it we are perpetually lost and adrift without legitimate purpose. Our instincts confirm truth when we see it. Dallas Willard noted that "truth is a very simple concept that only very bright people can confuse

---

[344] Stephen Marche, "Opinion: The Unexamined Brutality of the Male Libido," *New York Times*, November 25, 2017, http://www.cetusnews.com/life/Opinion-%7C-The-Unexamined-Brutality-of-the-Male-Libido.
[345] Pat Williams with Jim Denney, *The Success Intersection: What Happens When Your Talent Meets Your Passion* (Grand Rapids, MI: Fleming H. Revell Company, 2017), 182.

for us."[346] Given the many lures of false advertising, it is necessary to be committed to finding the truth so we are not distracted by the counterfeit. Willard agreed: "It is a fact that one can be logical only if one is committed to being logical as a fundamental value. One is not logical by chance."[347] W. Jay Wood adds to the conversation, listing four intellectual virtues he believes are necessary for acquiring the truth: "inquisitiveness, teachableness, persistence, and humility."[348]

There are many ways to test for the truth. One way is to apply a proposition to a problematic area and observe the results. Truth begets power; it is the right key to the lock—it works. Another indicator of truth is that its presence can sometimes stir considerable emotion. Generally, the truer a thing is—particularly if it points out a fault or error in judgment—the higher intensity of emotion that results from those who stand to lose if the truth is exposed. Another way to test for truth is to notice how its absence makes things much more complicated and contentious. An absence of truth also results in a notable absence of the intellectual virtues listed above, leading instead to "ignorance, arrogance, decadence, and debauchery."[349] This is particularly true when there is an absence of humility. As James Sire noted, "All intellectuals are in love with ideas; not all intellectuals are in love with the truth ... Intellectuals are not always right, even when—especially when—they think they are absolutely right ... Without humility, every virtue becomes a vice."[350] Willard identified a three-step plan for humility: never pretend, never presume, and never push.[351]

Supporting observations from life about the characteristics of truth:

- Truth utilizes love rather than manipulation.
- Truth encourages cooperation and community.
- Truth addresses the root causes over the symptoms.
- Truth breeds confidence rather than skepticism.
- Truth prefers introspection over flattery.
- Truth allows for freedom of conscience rather than coercion.

---

[346] Willard, *The Divine Conspiracy Continued*, 93.
[347] Willard, *The Great Omission*, 183.
[348] W. Jay Wood in *Habits of the* Mind by James W. Sire, 107.
[349] Wood, 113.
[350] Wood, 77.
[351] Willard, *Renewing the Christian Mind*, chapter 38.

- Truth allows one to ask for help.
- Truth simplifies rather than complicates.
- Truth doesn't need a marketing campaign.

Suggestion 3: Concentrate on fulfilling one's needs (not wants)

Humankind has multiple needs that, when met, positively impact our ability to function effectively in the world. Maslow's Hierarchy of Needs model[352] remains an effective tool to use for identifying our needs:

- self-actualization—reaching one's full potential, purpose, meaning, morality, behaving and relating to oneself, others, nature, and the cosmos
- aesthetic—beauty, order, creativity, design, and art
- cognitive—knowledge and understanding, predictability
- esteem—confidence, achievements, respect from others, connections, and need for individuality
- love and belonging—friendship, family, affection and love, connections
- safety—health, employment, property, family, stability
- physiological—air, food, water, shelter, clothing, sleep, activity, sex

Unfortunately, many of these needs have been superseded by "wants" that are inadequate substitutes. Examples of wants we feel we can't do without include, but are not limited to, smartphones, the Facebook confessional and bloviator, unlimited choice, immediate fulfillment, and the desire for multiple simultaneous stimuli. The unmitigated pursuit of our wants distracts us from our lifelong journey of significance and in meeting our real needs.

One easy way to distinguish needs from wants is to ask *why* one needs something. If it is really a need, the answer to the *why* question will be specific and legitimate. In contrast, if the primary reason for doing something is because one wants to do it, it is obviously a desire.

---

[352] Wikipedia, "Abraham Maslow," https://en.wikipedia.org/wiki/Abraham_Maslow.

Supporting observations from life regarding needs and wants:

- meeting one's needs produces satisfaction; continually chasing one's wants produces neuroses
- overcrowded jails due to fulfilling wants that are illegal
- chasing one's needs encourages interpersonal relationships; chasing one's wants encourages impersonal shortcuts and increases loneliness
- divorce on demand
- the current hookup culture
- spending a large portion of one's paycheck on booze, drugs, or gambling

Suggestion 4: Recognize and productively address one's intellectual limitations

C. S. Lewis urged, "We must take our ignorance seriously."[353] And so we must if we are to locate and avoid the landmines of life. Unfortunately, this is another area of mental resistance. Our inward, intangible thought processes are not like our outward, tangible behaviors. Our thinking limitations are obscured and therefore easier to ignore and hide. Our clandestine intellectual limitations are, however, of critical importance as recognized by multiple sources:

- Daniel Kahneman: "A puzzling limitation of our mind: our excessive overconfidence in what we believe we know, and our apparent inability to acknowledge the full extent of our ignorance and uncertainty of the world we live in. We are prone to overestimate how much we understand about the world and to underestimate the role of chance in events."[354]

- Andy Crouch: "Most people, most of the time, will get more predictions wrong than right. Our inability to accurately anticipate the direction of cultural change is one of the most commonly

---

[353] Lewis, *Christian Reflections*, 166.
[354] Kahneman, *Thinking Fast and Slow*, Introduction.

affirmed realities of human existence—and one of the most commonly ignored."[355]

- James Sire: "Intellectuals are both limited and fallible. Bias, preconceived but erroneous ideas, hasty skipping over relevant details, inordinate desire for a given outcome, fear of the implications of an idea, unwillingness to accept the consequences of correct reasoning: all of these and more stand in the way of the mind's reaching a worthy judgment. True intellectuals, therefore, reach their conclusions with deliberate humility and caution."[356]

- C. S. Lewis: "Nothing is more obvious than that we frequently make false inferences: from ignorance of some of the factors involved, from inattention, from inefficiencies in the system of symbols which we are using, from the secret influence of our unconscious wishes or fears."[357]

- Blaise Pascal: "The world is a good judge of things, for it is in natural ignorance, which is man's true state. The sciences have two extremes which meet. The first is the pure natural ignorance in which all men find themselves at birth. The other extreme is that reached by great intellects, who, having run through all that men can know, find that they know nothing, and come back again to that same ignorance from which they set out; but this is a learned ignorance which is conscious of itself. Those between the two, who have departed from natural ignorance and have not been able to reach the other, have some smattering of this vain knowledge and pretend to be wise. These trouble the world and are bad judges of everything."[358]

- Kahneman: "The illusion of skill is deeply ingrained in the culture of the industry. Facts that challenge such basic assumptions—and

---

[355] Crouch, *Culture Making*, 191–192.
[356] Sire, *Habits of the Mind*, 84.
[357] Lewis, *Christian Reflections*, 67.
[358] Pascal, *Pensees*, 327.

thereby threaten people's livelihood and self-esteem—are simply not absorbed. The mind does not digest them."[359]

This is the bad news we don't talk much about, let alone admit, because we don't like the answer. We like to believe we are smarter than this. In fact, some people like to believe, without any foundation of prior intellectual or experiential acumen, they are qualified to pass moral judgments on past leaders and undemocratically revise and tear down history to suit their cause. This ignorance belies a basic fact of life that human beings have significant and debilitating intellectual stumbling blocks that we must acknowledge and address. These are dangerous people who don't know what they don't know.

Supporting observations from life of our intellectual limitations:

- Sure things that failed: the Titanic, "The earth is flat," Y2K, Hillary Clinton.
- The idea that white people are smarter than everyone else.
- The Chicago Cubs are cursed and cannot win the World Series
- Father knows best.
- Common behavioral pitfalls: confirmation bias (seeking information to confirm what one already believes); loss aversion (tendency to prefer avoiding losses over acquiring gains); framing bias (different decisions reached based on how one frames a situation); and recency bias (drawing present conclusions based only on the recent past).

Suggestion 5: Balance facts and emotions in one's thought processes

There are two ways to know things: intellectually (facts) with our head and emotionally (feelings) with our heart. Both must be courted to properly analyze a situation and make an informed decision. Francis Schaeffer suggested that "scientific proof, philosophical proof, and religious proof all follow the same rules. Proof consists in two steps: (1) the theory must be non-contradictory and must give an answer to the phenomenon in

---

[359] Kahneman, *Thinking Fast and Slow*, chapter 20.

question, and (2) we must be able to live consistently with our theory."[360] Albert Einstein also weighed in: "It would be possible to describe everything scientifically, but it would make no sense; it would be without meaning, as if you described a Beethoven symphony as a variation of wave pressure."[361]

The intellect allows the use of logic and reason to analyze and form conclusions based on facts. This allows us to trust by verification. The emotion provides us with intuition, values, morality, and relationships. This allows us to have faith and desire justice, and to give and receive love, loyalty, and forgiveness.

It is imperative that we avoid the use of either extreme facts or feelings in our thought processes. Science (facts) is only a portion of a much broader field of knowledge. If "science is our only source of knowledge, and science only gives us knowledge of facts and not of value, then distinguishing good and evil can only be a matter of arbitrary preference."[362] On the other side, feelings are volatile, fleeting, and changing. Committing to action based solely on feelings buys one a ticket on the roller coaster of life. Succinctly put, when an evaluation is based on all facts, there is only justice, without mercy. Conversely, when evaluation is based on all feeling, it offers all mercy, with no justice.

Supporting observations of the unbalanced utilization of facts and emotions from life:

- sanctuary cities that factually ignore immigration law and emotionally allow those in the country illegally to be protected and receive free public benefits
- child custody decisions based solely on the emotion of wanting to maintain the biological family rather than considering the quality of care and safety of the child
- emotional vigilante "justice" versus factual law and order by the proper authorities
- emotional and factual issues related to right-to-life and pro-choice issues

---

[360] Schaeffer, *Trilogy*, 121.
[361] "Albert Einstein," Goodreads, "Popular Quotes," https://www.goodreads.com/quotes/tag/science?page=2.
[362] Johnson, *The Right Questions*, 110.

- decisions to get married based on emotions versus factual circumstances
- decisions about going into significant debt based on emotional wants versus factual needs

Suggestion 6: Test the meaning and validity of ideas

There are several ways in which one can test the meaning and validity of ideas before they are implemented. James Sire[363] and Ravi Zacharias identify some helpful ways.[364] Sire suggests asking three basic questions to clarify what is meant by an idea and to test its practical applicability to life:

1. What does the idea say?
2. What does it mean to the author and to those first intended to read or listen to it?
3. What does it signify for my life (what should I learn and apply from this)?

Zacharias offers the following approaches:

- Logical consistency: Can the idea be logically stated and defended? Does it affirm views that are self-contradictory? Does the logic hold up when pushed to its logical end?
- Empirical adequacy: Is there corroborating evidence to make the case beyond a reasonable doubt? Has the idea been implemented before? If yes, what were the results?
- Experiential relevance: Can the idea be successfully applied in real life because it conforms to the way things really are?

Supporting observations from life of failing to test the validity and meaning of ideas:

- false acceptance of the view that the earth is flat
- false acceptance of the view that crime is only an economic or racial issue

---

[363] Sire, *Habits of the Mind*, 152.
[364] Ravi Zacharias, *Can Man Live Without God*, 123–124.

- believing that people should be required to have mandatory health care
- the illogical implementation of bureaucratic procedures in which the mentally ill are expected to function normally (example: please read, understand and adequately fill out this ten-page legal form)
- "participation" trophies
- the inefficacy of unlimited choice, tolerance, and autonomy

Suggestion 7: Identify the elements of a solid strategic foundation for life and/or business

As the saying goes, if one doesn't know where one is going, any road will get one there. A strategic foundation provides individuals and groups with a destination and an approach for the most efficient and effective route to get there. It includes identifying a vision, mission, strategic goals, strategies, and values in the accomplishment of those goals. Establishing a formal strategic foundation demonstrates intentionality about knowing what one wants, and a commitment to get there. Here is a brief description of these critical pieces of foundational information:

- Vision: The overarching purpose for what one is trying to achieve— the "why." It must be big enough to require continuous effort and meaningful enough that one doesn't stop trying to achieve it. Examples might include loving your family well, eradicating hunger, providing affordable transportation in one's community, securing citizen safety, and so forth.

- Mission: The specific contribution made toward the fulfillment of one's vision—the "what." Examples: being present and available to one's family, contributing to the eradication of hunger by establishing facilities and stocking food resources, contributing to providing affordable transportation by starting a bus service, and contributing to securing citizen safety by establishing a private security firm.

- Goals: The establishment of general targets that will result in significant movement toward accomplishing one's mission—the "general how." Strategic goals should be multiyear objectives that keep one focused and committed over time. Examples: dedicate two weekends per month to quality time with family, establish and maintain a homeless shelter and food bank by achieving the following goals: provide shelter to 75 percent of the homeless in-our-city, provide food to 90 percent of those in need in our city, establish and maintain positive relations with government and regulatory groups in the city, establish and maintain positive relationships with the community, and establish and maintain an effective fund-raising capability.

- Strategies: Identification and implementation of specific tasks that will result in the accomplishment of one's goals—the "specific how." Examples: schedule specific time on one's calendar for family, design and construct a homeless shelter with a food bank, schedule time with each city council member at least once every three months, hold community meetings at least once every six months, and hire a manager to establish a fund-raising capability.

- Values: Establishing the values that set the parameters for what is acceptable versus unacceptable behavior in the accomplishment of one's mission.

Once established, the strategic foundation will serve as the intellectual map to reach one's desired destination. This foundation will also provide a framework in which every decision can be evaluated. All considerations should be "mission-centric."[365] All decisions regarding such things as projects, purchases, commitments, resources, personnel, and organizational structure should be based on whether and to what degree they align with the organization's or one's personal mission, goals, and value statements. If a proposed action does not align with one's mission, it likely should be discarded and not pursued, even if it's a quality idea.

Supporting observations from life of not being mission-centric:

- saying yes to every good thing without sufficient time and resources to make it a productive endeavor

---

[365] David W. Gill, *It's About Excellence: Building Ethically Healthy Organizations* (Eugene, OR: WIPF & Stock, 2008).

- the illegitimate belief that the unspoken purpose of a company or family is to meet one's own needs
- employees or spouses chasing differing definitions of success
- employees, students, and children not onboarded or raised with common values
- implementing strategies that do not align with one's goals or mission

Suggestion 8: Devote sufficient time to "noodle" the important stuff

Most people in America seem to have little free time. Jobs, kids and their activities, community organizations, and the increased demands created by technology have us moving a mile a minute—a very fast minute. Nearly everything is expected now, now, and now. This "drinking water through a fire hose" approach leaves us little time to thoughtfully reflect and respond to the bigger issues that have large consequences: marriage, children, large purchases, job changes, new hires, new organizational structure, discipline, prayer/meditation, community involvement, and so on. Seek to schedule specific time to perform one's due diligence regarding these issues. Resist the pressure to make big decisions when more information and time is needed to digest and reflect on the ramifications of important choices. Say "no" more often than "yes" when forced to make impromptu decisions. Marinated meat tastes much better than the microwaved version.

Supporting observations from life of devoting insufficient noodle-time:

- not reading the Affordable Care Act before voting on it
- President Trump's first executive order on immigration
- saying "I do" to Henry VIII
- impulse purchases on expensive items
- believing that Trixie is really interested in you for you
- not thoroughly analyzing the impacts of making changes to the traditional family structure, which has existed for millennia

In addition, don't forget that the important stuff includes thinking about what is good with the world. Noodling the positive stuff is essential for balance and mental health. A very good suggestion from the Bible is, "Whatever is true, whatever is noble, whatever is right, whatever is pure, whatever is lovely, whatever is admirable—if anything is excellent or praiseworthy—think about such things."[366] It clears and focuses the mental palate.

Supporting observations from life in noodling the good:[367]

- Swedish historian Mark Norberg breaks down global indicators of human flourishing into nine categories: food, sanitation, life expectancy, poverty, violence, the state of the environment, literacy, freedom, equality, and the conditions of childhood. In nearly all categories, there have been vast improvements.
- Phillip Collins, columnist for London's the *Times*, noted that the proportion of the world's population living in extreme poverty had fallen below 10 percent for the time, and global carbon emissions from fossil fuels had failed to rise for a third year running.
- In the *New York Times*, Nicholas Kristof noted falling global inequality, and child mortality being roughly half of what it had been as recently as 1990.

Suggestion 9: Have an appropriate definition of success

Each person has his/her own idea of success. These definitions are generated by such things as one's worldview, positive and negative life experiences, and personal goals and desires. As Dr. Seuss might say: some choose to shoot for the stars, some choose to drive fancy cars, some want to live on Mars, some want it poured in jars, some swing for pars, some want to win wars, and some wind up behind bars. Definitions of success create expectations that are filled, partially filled, or unfulfilled. The outcome of expectations met or unmet in large measure impacts one's attitude and outlook on life and one's sense of accomplishment. Thus, it is important to select an appropriate barometer of success.

One's definition of success will be radically shaped by one's primary philosophy: the philosophy of us or the philosophy of me. Even for those

---

[366] Philippians 4:8, Bible, New International Version.
[367] Oliver Burkeman, "Is the world really better than ever?" *The Guardian*, July 28, 2017, https://www.theguardian.com/news/2017/jul/28/is-the-world-really-better-than-ever.

who do not choose it, I think most would agree that the best definition of success is based on the philosophy of us. Taking care of *us* can mean a lot of things, but in the most basic form, I think would include three things: developing good character and reflecting it to a needy world; positively contributing to the wise stewardship of our planet and its resources; and helping each other, especially those in critical need who cannot take care of themselves. What is common in these goals is a commitment to sacrificial love: a straining to be the best person one can be, working diligently to preserve our environment (moral-cultural, political, economic), and going the extra mile for those in need. The affirming news here is that when you make success about relationships, rather than yourself and your individual wants, it dramatically increases your chance for success because people will readily help you help others. N. T. Wright has observed this is because we intuitively know that "self-giving love turns out to have a power of a totally different sort from any other power known in the world."[368] Therefore, creating a definition of success that involves others, as well as your personal good, is life-affirming and satisfying. One compact but powerful example of a good definition of success is "to do justice, to love kindness, and to walk humbly with your God."[369]

Supporting observations from life of having an appropriate definition of success:

- success being measured by one's faithful efforts, not in uncontrollable outcomes
- success being a well-lived journey, not necessarily the destination
- success in telling the truth, not being measured by results
- success being achieved when one productively helps others
- success not being the exclusive accumulation of fame, money, adulation, or power, which typically renders people unhappy, afraid, and alone
- success not being measured in the acquisition of things as an insatiable pursuit

---

[368] N.T. Wright, *The Day the Revolution Began: Reconsidering the Meaning of Jesus's Crucifixion* (New York: HarperOne, 2016), Kindle edition, 252.
[369] Micah 6:8, Bible, New American Standard Version.

Suggestion 10: Mentally prepare for ridicule and suffering

Thinking well purifies, clarifies, unencumbers, motivates, and distinguishes. It stands out and calls for change from the way things are to the ways things should be. This is threatening to any status quo of institutionalized mediocrity. Being intellectually virtuous will encourage change and the movement of people and resources to the common good, rather than toward the continuation of personal empires based on false claims and unhealthy dependencies. The exhibition of one's virtue will often be an unwelcome mirror to those in the status quo and, at times, will result in ridicule and suffering to dirty or destroy the reflection. Unfortunately, for many power-orientated people, they have two primary self-focused concerns: (1) getting to the top, and (2) staying there. They will want to keep the world in their grip. They will fight back.

Therefore, if thinking clearly is a priority, one must mentally prepare oneself for the coming battles. If it is, then be smart and begin making a list of survival "life jacket" items:

- Be sure of and committed to one's point of view as inherently worthy of sacrifice.
- Professionally attempt to build support for one's point of view both at line and executive levels.
- Ensure that one crosses every t and dots every i, not providing detractors with any ammunition.
- Be able to clearly and cogently articulate one's ideas in writing.
- Get rest and exercise regularly; learn stress management techniques.
- Discuss the situation and seek the emotional support of family and friends.
- Build a rainy-day fund to address unforeseen setbacks.
- Identify potential secondary employment options.

Supporting observations from life of having to mentally prepare for ridicule and suffering:

- women's suffrage and the 1960s civil rights movement in which their advocates endured significant hardship and physical, mental, and emotional pain

- legitimate whistle-blowers who risk loss of employment and peace of mind
- "drain the swamp" advocates who seek to change the culture and power structures within Washington, DC
- freedom-of-conscience advocates who are unfairly targeted and labeled because it is often easier to attack a person rather than a good idea
- students who are graded unfairly or targeted on campus because they hold conservative viewpoints
- bosses who suddenly initiate discussions with solid employees about "being a team player," "looking the other way," "not rocking the boat," or "watching one's back"

Chapter 8

Suggestions for Acting Rationally

What matters most in life is not knowledge, but character.
—A. G. Sertillanges

The insight of this principle should be shocking: we only know what we act on, or we only believe what we obey.
—James Sire

With a clear thought process, we are now positioned to act rationally. Actions are where the rubber meets the road. While thoughts can be compartmentalized and placed under lock and key, once one acts, the cat is out of the bag. Sometimes, this is no small matter. Who hasn't been in a situation where one knew exactly what should be done and yet was afraid for various reasons to do it? Knowledge takes one to the right door; courage opens it to see what is on the other side and to walk through it.

The following are suggestions for acting rationally in the implementation of well-thought-out ideas and the decisions reached:

Suggestion 1: Pursue and be loyal to the truth

Loyalty is an often-misapplied word. It has a primary and a secondary context. In its primary context, it means loyalty to *something* that one is bound by pledge or duty. Synonyms include: fidelity, devotion, piety, faithfulness, and steadfastness. In its secondary context, it can refer to allegiance to a *person*.

As a confirming example of our intellectual helplessness, this distinction has been mostly transposed in today's world. We tend to be dyslexic loyalists. When we speak of loyalty or disloyalty, it is usually in the context of loyalty to a person, usually the loyalty of someone else to ourselves. We say this with the expectation that a loyal person is someone who will be submissive to us, even to the extent of acquiescing to our unethical demands. This context completely misses the concept of loyalty. Loyalty is first and foremost to an idea worth being committed to, such as democracy, family, faith, and truth. It is centered on an idea rather than a human being primarily due to the fickleness of human nature.

We remain on solid ground when the object of our loyalty is the truth. "People do not expect perfection, but they do expect reality."[370] This frees us to individually and collectively be loyal to the common good rather than the shackles of an individual, keeping us well grounded and working in the same direction.

Doing what one knows to be right often requires courage. Francis Schaeffer rightly noted, "There is no romanticism as one seeks to move a man in the direction of honesty."[371] Hungarian psychiatrist Thomas Szasz observed, "Clear thinking requires courage rather than intelligence."[372] This courage can be activated by the knowledge that when one does the right things, and cooperates with reality, it will produce superior results and positive change, because truth is immutable, unconquerable, and inevitable. Lord Moulton said, "The greatness of a nation, its true civilization, is measured by the extent of its obedience to the unenforceable."[373]

The finding and applying of truth is also a renewable mental energy source and a reward unto itself. Sire observed that it "is only to those who are willing to do the truth that the truth itself comes. Virtue is rewarded by knowledge."[374] Commit to the truth even if no one else will. Be the oasis in the desert that people will flock to.

Examples of people who pursued and remained loyal to truth:

- Martin Luther
- Founding Fathers

---

[370] Schaeffer, *Trilogy*, 166.
[371] Schaeffer, 144.
[372] Thomas Szasz, Quotery. Accessed June 25, 2017, http://www.quoetery.com/quotes/clear-thinking-requires-courage-rather-than-intelligence.
[373] Lord Moulton in *A Free People's Suicide* by Os Guinness, 7.
[374] Sire, *Habits of the Mind*, 78.

- Abraham Lincoln
- William Wilberforce
- Martin Luther King Jr.
- Pope John Paul II
- Nelson Mandela
- Muhammad Ali
- Caesar Chavez
- Hacksaw Ridge combat medic Desmond Doss
- Mother Teresa
- Walter Cronkite
- Arthur Ashe
- Jesus
- (Add your own truth teller)

Suggestion 2: Become and select qualified leaders

Quality leadership is the most important ingredient for any institution (family, government, business). The tone is *always* set at the top. Children/ subordinates should be guided by parents/leaders who are competent and have the family's/organization's best interests at heart, not merely their own. Children/subordinates take their cues from the top, emulating those traits that are rewarded.

When less than competent people are placed in positions of leadership, it provides outlets for their deficiencies to spread and mutate. Often the loyally incompetent are selected as wingmen to conceal information, limit dissent, and manipulate consensus. As a remedy, T. S. Eliot encouraged that society "must see that ablest artists and architects rise to the top, influence taste, and execute the important public commissions; it must do the same by the other arts and by science; and above all, perhaps, it must be such that the ablest minds will find expression in speculative thought. The system must not only do all of this for society in a particular situation—it must *go on* doing it, generation after generation."[375]

Quality leaders dramatically increase the chances for success because they have a clear focus on others, rather than a clouded focus on themselves. Dallas Willard said it nicely: "A leader can serve the public good

---

[375] T. S. Eliot, *Christianity and Culture* (San Diego, CA: A Harvest Book, Harcourt Inc., 1939), 117–118.

well, only if those individuals routinely act in ways that supremely promote the specific public good for which their particular leadership position exists. Further, leaders make a positive impact, only if they are prepared to sacrifice their own personal gain, monetary or otherwise, for that good. Last, leaders serve the common good only if they are appropriately vigilant in ensuring that members of their own peer group overwhelmingly conform to these moral ideas even when self-sacrifice is required."[376]

Leadership also requires an appropriate possession and display of humility. Montesquieu said, "Great men who are moderate are rare."[377] Humility doesn't assume that one knows it all, and seeks to get all the information necessary to make an informed decision before acting. As G. K. Chesterton said, "The moment you step into a world of facts, you step into a world of limits."[378] Humility also accepts accountability. Author and pastor Chuck Swindoll lays out four qualities of people of accountability:[379]

- vulnerability—capable of being wounded, shown to be wrong, even admitting it before being confronted
- teachability—a willingness to learn, being quick to hear and respond to reproof, being open to counsel
- availability—accessible, touchable, able to be interrupted
- honesty—willingness to admit the truth no matter how difficult or humiliating the admission may be, hating all that is phony or false

In short, leaders must internally become the kind of people who naturally and habitually think and act in an others-orientated fashion.

Examples of qualified leaders:

- political examples: George Washington, Thomas Jefferson, Abraham Lincoln, Winston Churchill, William Wilberforce
- economic examples: Adam Smith, Charles Coffin (General Electric), Katherine Graham (Washington Post), James Burke

---

[376] Willard, *The Divine Conspiracy Continued*, 61.
[377] C.L. Montesquieu, Baron de Secondat; *De l'Esprit des lois* (Paris, France: Garnier Freres, Libraires-Editeurs Kissinger Legacy Reprins, 1874), 6.28.41.
[378] Chesterton, *Orthodoxy*, 29.
[379] Charles Swindoll, *Living Above the Level of Mediocrity* (Waco, TX: Word Books, 1987), 127.

(Johnson & Johnson), George Merck (Merck & Co.), Bill Allen (Boeing)[380]

- moral-cultural examples: Mother Teresa, Mahatma Gandhi, Nelson Mandela, Martin Luther King Jr., Billy Graham, Pope John Paul II

Suggestion 3: Remain within one's strategic foundation or assigned role/lane

Strategic foundations have been established in each arena (moral-cultural, government, business) of the democratic-capitalistic system to provide the necessary checks and balances against the desire for unilateral control by any one group. Each arena must competently fulfill its individual role to ensure the success of the entire system. As T. S. Eliot said about checks and balances, "The universality of irritation is the best assurance of peace."[381]

In the moral-cultural arena, we have the institutions of family, media, religion, and education to provide philosophical, ideological, and practical checks and balances over governmental and business power. Each moral-cultural institution has a strategic foundation with specific roles and responsibilities created for the good of society. The family procreates and raises children; the media provides accurate news; religion/philosophy are the schools of love (i.e., seeking the good); and education is the transmitter of knowledge and wisdom.

In the governmental arena, America's strategic foundation is delineated in the Declaration of Independence and the US Constitution. The Declaration of Independence proclaims that we are created beings that have been unalterably bestowed certain fundamental rights. The US Constitution is the supreme law of the land. It is the instruction manual, power distributor, and the policies and procedures for maintaining our republican form of democracy. The Bill of Rights is our statement of values.

In the business arena, each organization has a formal strategic/business plan (vision, mission, goals, strategies, corporate values) that delineates its purpose and guides its choices, actions, and motivations. Without this guide, employees begin fermenting their own definitions of success, which

---

[380] Jim Collins, "The 10 Greatest CEOs of All Time. What these extraordinary leaders can teach today's troubled executives," *Fortune*, July 21, 2003, http://archive.fortune.com/maganizes/fortune/fortune_archive/2003/07/21/346095/index...
[381] Eliot, *Christianity and Culture*, 133.

leads to differing and inevitably exclusive styles and methods of achieving that success. Business is designed to provide corporate and individual wealth for economic security, and to diversify the interests and power of the republic. On a side note, Dallas Willard observed that business is one of the most powerful forces for necessarily bringing the world together, recognizing that "we're going to have to love one another or die."[382]

In each of these arenas, every decision and subsequent action must be filtered through the mission-centric requirements of each strategic plan. The players in each arena must stay in their own lane of competence and authority—business and government institutions should not culturize employees/citizens; moral-cultural and government institutions should not create wealth; moral-cultural and business institutions should not provide national security; and so on. Decisions and actions in each arena should be made or not made, or taken or not taken, based on their comportment with their respective strategic plan.

Suggestion 4: Avoid extreme actions

As a general rule, one should avoid extremes. Hypo/hyper, over/under, or in/out are not generally descriptors with positive connotations. Too much or too little of most things create problems. Liberals usually have more questions than answers, while fundamentalists usually have more answers than questions.[383] Beware those who advocate for extreme actions. They usually request your sacrifice for their gain. As James Sire noted, "Mistaken ideas always end in bloodshed, but in every case, it is someone else's blood."[384] Additionally, extreme actions do not usually bring fulfillment. It may satisfy an immediate want, but it rarely fills a long-term need.

A positive step toward avoiding extreme actions/reactions involves setting up established boundaries ahead of when they are needed. Possessing a made-up mind on boundaries, prior to the temptation, gives one the best chance of fighting the beast de jour. Having to find and implement the *no* word while in the throes of extreme pain or pleasure is a tough ask.

Another positive step in avoiding extremes is to refrain from compelling anyone to believe or act in a certain way in ordinary circumstances.

---

[382] Willard, *Renewing the Christian Mind*, chapter 16.

[383] Dr. Bryan Crow, conversations with my pastor.

[384] Albert Camus, quoted in *Habits of the Mind* by James Sire, 212.

While this might seem obvious, it is a habitual response in many self-serving philosophies, dogmas, and selfish pursuits. Legitimate and positive pursuits request one's voluntary and free consideration of something without the loss of fundamental human rights; illegitimate and negative pursuits mandate acceptance and enforce penalties against those who do not comply.

One more positive step in avoiding extremes is to monitor one's emotional responses to positive and negative events. Generally, it is a good rule of thumb to refrain from extreme highs or lows as a reaction to events. When experiencing a huge success, celebrate with humility; when you have a huge defeat, demonstrate perspective and gratitude for opportunities. Tomorrow is another day, and forgetfulness is a social reality.

Examples of areas in which to avoid extreme actions:

- avoiding either extreme of eliminating religious freedom of speech and consciousness from the public square, or the government establishing a national religion
- adjudicating punishment that is either too harsh or too lenient
- treating victims like criminals or criminals like victims
- treating the physically or mentally disabled as disposable
- avoiding narcissism or self-loathing

Suggestion 5: Develop good habits

Many of the things we want to change in our lives are simply the result of cultivating bad habits: smoking, incessant cursing, overeating, excessive drinking, speeding, and others. Developing bad habits preconditions us to respond in certain ways to certain things, allowing the undesired action to occur before our mind kicks in to weigh its options. One of the ways to kick a bad habit is not to repeatedly tell oneself how bad the bad habit is. One already knows that. The point is to replace it with a good habit or virtue. James Q. Wilson offers a valuable insight: "By virtue, I mean habits of moderation action; more specifically, acting with due restraint on one's impulses, due regard for the rights of others, and reasonable concern for distant consequence … Virtue is not learned by precept, however; it is learned by the regular repetition of right actions; by acting rightly with respect to small things, we are more likely to act rightly with respect to large ones."[385] It can be a painstaking process, but it works. Every time one gets into a situation that triggers the bad habit, one must stop and consciously decide to respond in a specific, more productive way. E. Michael Jones commented on the stakes involved: "The mind is like a window. It is transparent only when it is clean."[386]

Wilson also recognized that developing good habits is essential to achieving the good society. "The essential first step is to acknowledge that at root, in almost every area of important public concern, we are seeking to induce persons to act virtuously. Not only is such conduct desirable in its own right, it appears now to be necessary if large improvements are to be made in those matters we consider problems."[387]

One bad habit to overcome is the placement of self-interest over the common good. If nothing else, prioritize the common good for practical reasons. Nothing maximizes one's chance for success more than doing something for others. Daniel Kahneman offers two creative exercises (good habits) to help in doing things for the right reasons on a corporate level, which could also be applied in one's personal life:

- Before an issue is discussed, all members of the group should be asked to write a brief summary of their position. The standard practice of open discussion gives too much weight to the opinions of those who speak early and assertively, causing others to line up behind them.[388]

- Premortem—when the organization has almost come to an important decision but has not formally committed itself, gather for a brief session with a group of individuals who are knowledgeable about the decision. The premise of the session is to "imagine that we are a year into the future. We implemented the plan as it now exists. The outcome was a disaster. Please take 10 minutes to write a brief history of that disaster."[389]

---

[385] Wilson, *On Character*, 22.
[386] E. Michael Jones, *Degenerate Moderns: Modernity as Rationalized Sexual Misbehavior* (San Francisco, CA: Ignatius, 1993), 258.
[387] Wilson, *On Character*, 22.
[388] Kahneman, *Thinking Fast and Slow*, chapter 24.
[389] Kahneman.

These two approaches have common threads. One, they isolate individual thought from group thought to ascertain what individual people really think. Two, they assist in examining all aspects of an issue before implementation in a time-efficient manner. And three, they build consensus before proceeding and unity if things don't work out.

Examples of developing good habits:

- practice intellectual hospitality in the form of ethical and respectful debate
- demonstrate manners in all encounters
- vet for character and skill in making employment decisions
- replace carbohydrate snacks with healthy and great-tasting fruits and vegetables
- walk short distances rather than driving
- dwell first on the positive before the negative
- practice meditation and/or prayer
- "do unto others as you would have done unto yourself"

Suggestion 6: Learn about America's heritage

A significant contributor to our intellectual helplessness has been the expunging, ignoring, or downplaying of the fundamental tenets of America's political/economic/cultural heritage, in favor of the obscure, trivial, or less worthy. It has been a faux pas of massive proportions, currently having severe, negative ripple effects in every area of American society. America is filled with young people who have no idea how their well-being relates to the ideas, commitments, and supreme sacrifices of the past and present. Such ignorance renders them less able to develop a sufficient gratitude or sense of duty necessary for committing to actions that sustain their country's well-being. They are forever the demanding customer and never the diligent waiter. Somewhere along the line, we have been bamboozled into believing that while our democratic-capitalistic system may falter from time to time, it will never fail. Fat, dumb, and blisteringly ignorant are not the traits for a sustainable legacy.

Another severe educational deficiency has been our neglect in teaching our youth logic, reason, and analytical skills. Perhaps this has occurred because some people falsely believe that truth is relative. Relativism is akin to dropping our kids in the wilderness without a point of reference, compass, or map, and hoping they find their way home. Risky business.

One cannot love and defend that which one does not understand. Immigrants made America; America is now making immigrants. *E Pluribus Unum* is now *E Unum Pluribus*. We must return to our roots and, experience both the intellectual and emotional majesty of the original pursuit of true freedom. We must understand and appreciate the degree of personal risk and sacrifice taken by our ancestors for us. We must understand their dynamic combining of unique and beautifully crafted new systems of governance and economics, and ponder their vulnerability, as they placed these creations on the mantel of history to see if a higher power would bless them and form a more perfect union from it.

Perhaps this suggestion of teaching America's heritage, more than any other, can most effectively address the radical polarization that is tearing our country apart. Diversity has been taken to a debilitating extreme. Unity around common, uplifting, and eternal principles is needed to bring us back together. It is also needed to internalize an appropriate critical response to those attempting to deviate from our grand structure, which was built on the highest aspirations of humankind. We need to return to the daily liturgical repetition of our commitment to "liberty and justice for all." This will activate an automatic choke reflex when we see proposals that contemplate violating these principles and help prevent that from happening. Required reading and discussing of our "democratic scriptures" out loud might just recouple the cars on the liberty train. Cogent education will help us find our way home. Our story must be repeated and inculcated in the heart of every American. Once we know it intellectually and emotionally, we can love it unconditionally. If one has a *better* idea that produces real life, liberty, and happiness, let one speak now or forever hold his/her peace.

Suggestion 7: Establish, uphold, and reward standards

Standards are necessary for any civilized society to function. Without them, there is unmitigated self-interest leading to anarchy. If there are no standards, nothing matters, and society becomes the survival of the most depraved. A lack of standards also communicates apathy, and that doesn't even work for tyrants who demand power and subservience.

Human beings routinely utilize all kinds of ways to rationalize their unseemly behavior. One way is to unconsciously refuse to admit one's problems because admitting them could be too painful and significantly damage one's psychological stability. A second way is to consciously lie and pretend the behavior didn't occur, hoping the issue will be dropped. A third way is to believe one's destiny is absolute; therefore, one should not be held to the same rules as other mortals. A fourth way is to claim that everything is relative; therefore, there should be no standards (unless of course you violate mine). Another way is to rationalize that if no one else is adhering to any standards, doing so would put one at a competitive disadvantage. Another rationalization is culturally based, looking the other way on egregious violations of morality in other environments because that is what is done and accepted in that culture.

If we want to live a life of meaning and decency, there must be worthy standards that command our attention and respect, and lead us to the achievement of the good society. Fortunately, American standards have already been established (e.g., "liberty and justice for all"). We just have to own them. Positive movements toward accomplishing these goals should be rewarded; negative movements away from them should be admonished, particularly by those who claim to be standard bearers while having no standards. Without encouragement and recognition, people lose the motivation to live up to standards when things get difficult. Without enforcement and accountability, standards are a waste of time and put good people at a competitive disadvantage. A solid approach to follow in upholding standards is to be people affirming and detrimental behavior nonaffirming. This demonstrates respect for both the person and the principle.

Examples of ways to uphold standards:

- address fake news
- follow facts to their logical conclusion(s) and hold accountable those responsible for moral-cultural, political, and economic scandals
- discontinue celebrity behavioral exemptions
- address educational freedom of speech violations
- discontinue the ubiquitous use of profanity
- hold sanctuary cities accountable for violating the law
- celebrate masculinity and femininity differences and their complementary necessity

Suggestion 8: Implement balanced and reality-based solutions

Human beings are both a thinking (analytic) and feeling (emotional) species. We are at our best when we consider both the intellectual and emotional ramifications of decisions. As a result, we should think with our heads and feel with our hearts, and then we should search for a solution that combines the best of both. This approach works in every area of life:

Moral-cultural:

- philosophy: ensure the freedom to worship as one chooses and to follow one's conscience
- family: support parents in raising and protecting their children
- education: accept university students based on qualifications rather than sociological ideologies
- news media: insist that news programs accurately reflect what people did and why they did it
- arts media: produce arts that depict reality with skillful, artistic expressions of beauty

Government:

- offer services that address both one's practical and emotional needs
- implement solutions that meet the needs of the community as a whole, and use public resources in an efficient, cost-effective manner
- make decisions that are competent and fair
- enforce land planning that meets community development needs while protecting the environment

Business:

- provide quality customer service
- ensure an honest day's pay for an honest day's work
- implement solutions that turn a profit and meet a community need
- make decisions that fulfill both the letter and spirit of the law

Suggestion 9: Pick one's battles

Picking one's battles is critical. There are simply too many problems in today's world to tackle everything that comes one's way. One suggestion for picking one's battles is to adhere to the "mission-centric" concept of pursuing only those actions that align with one's stated priorities. Another suggestion relates to knowing when to take a firm stand on an issue, "In essentials, unity; in non-essentials, liberty; in all things, charity [love]."[390] Another obvious but unfortunately less utilized practice these days, is to make sure one's facts are straight before tackling an issue. It is not helpful to become just another person who doesn't know what he/she doesn't know.

In picking one's battles, also be sure that the implementation of one's viewpoint will result in progress—that is, change toward the positive. Progress can be best ensured when one's recommendation is a balanced solution that enhances the common good, rather than a lopsided proposal that only benefits a few.

Examples of picking one's battles:

- refrain from being the world's policeman
- for tweet's sake, Mr. President
- don't "poke the bear" unnecessarily
- only speak when one can improve upon the silence
- render to Caesar what is Caesar's, render to God what is God's
- when in doubt, choose less government over more government

Suggestion 10: Take action

Much of our culture adopts a wait-and-see, don't-ruffle-anyone's- feathers, live-and-let-live attitude toward life. While this may sound nice, it isn't a practical strategy—or even one adhered to consistently by those who espouse it. What they really mean is live and let live until your living interferes with their living; then *you* must change. In things that matter, one must decide and act. Productive life requires it. Participatory democracy is

---

[390] Rupertus Meldenius, quoted in "In Essentials Unity, In Non-Essentials Liberty, In All Things Charity," Mark Ross, Ligonier Ministries, https://www.ligonier.org/learn/articles/essential-unity-non-essentials-liberty-in-all-things-chartity.

not possible without it. When we don't act, many times our inaction results in the problem returning later, only in a form far more difficult to solve.

A helpful general philosophy is to shoot for an approximately 20/80 percent plan/act ratio. Limit approximately 20 percent of one's time to the planning phase, and dedicate the rest to implementing a solution. Of course, this must be adjusted when addressing extremely critical projects in which someone may only get one chance at something, dictating more time spent in the planning process.

Another suggestion to utilize during implementation is polite determination. It is okay to be tough, but not unkind—a sort of "rough and humble" approach. Action requires commitment and drive, and sometimes a firm but judicious nudge to get started. Being willing to act demonstrates conviction and usually lessens the need to prove oneself again.

Unfortunately, many people today want to put out as little effort as possible. One strategy they use is to hide their inaction by using semantic mysticisms as calculated strategies to camouflage their inadequacies. These mysticisms are verbal phrases designed to sound like competency is present or that activity is taking place, when, in truth, there is neither. Those who use these phrases are verbal magicians willing to say whatever people want to hear, with no intention of doing what they say. They behave as if saying something makes it so. Take for instance the Hollywood sexual harassment and abuse scandals. The vast majority of those in the entertainment industry stood silent and failed to point out or take action against the harassment, blacklisting, and sexual abuse that was happening all around them. Yet this same group now supposes it has the moral authority to shame the behavior it previously ignored, and the audacity to portray their public feelings of concern as proof of ethical action.

Another strategy used today is to immediately dismiss an idea that one deems as requiring too much effort to implement. Although it may be hard to take action, if one is willing, others will be willing to follow.

Examples of issues that require definitive action rather than just discussion:

- ensuring racial and gender equality
- enforcing weapons treaties with Iran and North Korea
- holding accountable those who cross red lines (e.g., Syria)
- dealing with illegal immigration

- restoring confidence in government institutions (executive, legislative, judicial) by holding people accountable
- establishing and maintaining a safe work environment
- holding accountable those who make false accusations
- ending fake news

PART IV

Concluding Remarks

Chapter 9

Danger in Front of the Horizon

Now there arose up a new king over Egypt, which knew not Joseph.
—Exodus 1:8

Hopefully, the foregoing chapters have provided a reasonable basis to conclude that intellectual helplessness is an epidemic within American society, leaving us susceptible to the dissolution of our political-economic system of democratic capitalism. This book has provided evidence to suggest that this impoverished condition is the result of random changes in culture, as well as calculated strategies of those pursuing power to "repurpose" American systems in order to accomplish their ends and means. I believe one such movement seeks to form an American monarchy of the elite. This is the haunting danger in front of the American horizon. It is a vast and disappointing departure from America's original elite, the Founding Fathers. They were perhaps the wisest collection of American souls ever assembled at one time, and it was their desire that power be intentionally distributed among various groups as a check and balance.

The Pursuit of an American Monarchy

Periodically, America has toyed with the idea of monarchy. Twice in his remarkable career, George Washington withstood the pressure to become an American monarch. At the end of the American Revolution, with all the country's power and resources under this authority, General Washington resigned his military commission. At the end of his second term as president, this man who helped create American government—by virtue of being our first president was a walking and talking precedent—again voluntarily chose to step aside. This was a gesture considered so profound that King George III of England proclaimed him "the greatest character of the age." Washington withstood the temptations of his time because he thought clearly and acted rationally. He knew his heritage and what he and others had created, with divine inspiration. He also knew his humanity. And he knew his and his fellow countrymen's hopes and dreams. Thinking clearly resulted in sacrificial obedience to a calling beyond himself and a faith in providence to secure success beyond what artificial means could attain. It was in this framework of faithful perseverance, that Washington beat back the attempts to make him a king.

The Catalyst for the Here and Now

Since then, America has persevered through many trying and tumultuous times that have tested our democratic-capitalistic system:

- The American Civil War resulted in the succession of southern states from the Union over the issue of slavery. Tragically, 620,000 troops lost their lives because this injustice was not properly addressed at the American founding.

- The second Industrial Revolution and Gilded Age brought the prosperity of gold discoveries and the railroads' transport of people and products, alongside the extensive problems created by massive immigration and the closing of the frontier.

- The Progressive Era saw an increase in industrial wealth set against the problems created by industrialization, urbanization, corruption in government, and entry into World War I.

- The Great Depression and the resulting national poverty were dealt with by dramatic changes in government responsibilities through the New Deal and our entry into World War II.

- The Allied Forces' victory in World War II saved us from the evils of fascism, but the war's conclusion was secured by a technology of historic destructive force that everyone wanted. The post-World

War II era brought prosperity, infrastructure improvements, and further migration of the US population westward. Eventually, however, the unabated discussion of postwar global territory issues contributed to the spreading of communism in Korea, Vietnam, and Cuba, during a nuclear age filled with the apprehension of "duck and cover" drills.

But perhaps democratic capitalism's greatest challenge has come from the storm waves of intellectual helplessness created by the severe culture changes of the 1960s. This decade experienced mounting national anger over troops dying in the faraway jungles of Vietnam for apparent political motivations, the daunting realization of "mutually assured destruction," and the civil rights issues and assassinations at home, which played heavily on the minds of Americans and resulted in cultural chaos across the country. Some of America's youth chose to fight back with demonstrations and civil disobedience; some chose to check out with drugs, draft dodging, or hibernation. In this environment, loyalty, sacrifice, and moderation appeared superfluous and limiting to many young people. The cognitive dissonance of what they had been taught about their country and what they were observing from its leaders was disillusioning and debilitating. Eventually, this generation had to get jobs to support themselves and their families. As they entered the workforce, many brought with them a mixture of uncertainty about the continuation of civilization; a growing distrust of government, business, and moral-cultural institutions; and underdeveloped occupational and moral skill sets from their paralysis over existential concerns.

Over the past few decades, the youth of the 1960s have matriculated into the leadership positions of society. Many figured out how to rise to the top despite their limited occupational and moral skill sets: they changed the rules.

- The acceptance of perception as a substitute for reality. One doesn't really have to be qualified or care about an issue; one just needs to give the impression of being qualified or concerned.

- Stacking the organizational deck of leadership with the loyally incompetent so the rules will not apply to those at the top.

- Use of the compliant loyally incompetent to indoctrinate an entrenched elitist minority worldview into society's moral-cultural, government, and economic systems.

- The use of dishonesty and deception as accepted strategies and weapons to harm those who disagree with the elite.

- Changing society's overall mission of achieving the common good to achieving the individual good (from organizational health to individual wealth).

Put succinctly, the elites have focused on worshipping themselves. This unadvertised mission change has produced ongoing distortions in our constitutional democracy. While our citizens still pledge their allegiance to "one nation, under God, indivisible, with liberty and justice for all," the underlying machinations of an entrenched elitist minority dismantle this pledge one brick at a time. These distortions are the source of our injustices and the catalyst for the suppression of truth. Many in the 1960s generation accepted the Faustian bargain that if one cannot trust society to do the right thing, then one might as well be on top and look out for number one. Their fanaticism of the self has now fully blossomed at the top of many organizations. Many believe or insist that to ensure their comfortable survival, the truth *is* them; it is what they say it is. This strategy clears the way for the full realization of *me* socially, economically, and politically. In this environment, saying and doing whatever it takes to benefit oneself is considered wise and self-preserving; sacrificing for those who do not care about one is foolish and self-destructive. In the implementation of this approach, the Declaration of Independence and US Constitution are still displayed on the wall, but in the back rooms of decision-making, "We the people" has been replaced with "Us the Elite." It is the ultimate bait and switch. I'm here for me, and over there for you.

Promises the Elite Will Never Keep

Thus, the elite are attempting to create an American society in which the people relinquish complete control to the government, based on the premise that the government knows best and the promise that it will look after our interests. In short form, I believe this was the referendum of the 2016 presidential election: abdication to an entrenched elitist minority or not.

Notwithstanding the election results, current events indicate that we would be mistaken to think that the outcome of the presidential election put an end to the hopes of an elite monarchy. The elite's anger from its electoral loss is so palpable that it has rendered its constituents (hopefully) temporarily insane. They are irrationally willing to hurt the country (and inevitably themselves) to ensure that President Trump and populism is either neutered or euthanized. They were so close to controlling power—all the branches of the government (executive, legislative, judiciary) and several of the moral-cultural institutions (education and media, substantive control; family and philosophy/religion, partial control by legislation), and they were working on the business sector through government influence and organizations like the Clinton Foundation. Their proximity to, without crossing, the finish line of an informal American monarchy was so devastating to them that it has resulted in the left's adoption of the mother of all ends-justifies-the-means revolts. Frighteningly, there is nothing that is out of bounds for the elites at this point—nothing that they won't do to retain power and achieve "me-vana."

Of course, the only trouble with the elite's governing proposal is that it will not work on a number of levels. First, giving complete control to an insensitive, ill-responsive, and distant government will not make things better. It will only result in the continuation of a politicized bureaucratic monopoly, whose minds have been sharpened to only one point of view over the past eight years. It opens the van door outside the schoolyard and beckons the children to see the magic trick of wealth without work, knowledge without research, fame without skill, integrity without conviction, and power without domination. With each step forward, we become dangerously close to abduction and disappearance.

Second, the elite who claim to care, do care, but primarily about themselves. They call themselves *elite* for a reason. Like Yogi, they believe they are "smarter than the average bear." The minute you or I become a burden, we will be dropped like a hot potato before receiving any condiments.

Third, once our political-economic system approaches collapse due to its inability to fund and implement a monarchist or socialistic type system, the most likely outcome will be anarchy and totalitarianism. America is already a heated powder keg of emotions. The minions of the elite have already shown their intentions through violent rioting, attempts to shut down freedom of speech at freedom-of-speech franchises (i.e., universities), verbal threats to destroy the White House and harm the first family, and unprecedented negative media coverage littered with unsubstantiated opinion masqueraded as fact. In contrast, the ultra-right has not been heard from, yet. If something were to happen to President Trump (impeachment or physical harm), "Katie, bar the door." I tragically would predict a high probability of widespread violence inflicted upon the elite. I worryingly believe this is where the end game is heading for those who seek to usurp constitutional democracy from public ownership. "Of, by and for the people" will not quietly relinquish itself to "of, by and for the elite," not after the people having spoken in the 2016 presidential election about what they don't want. If people want change, vote for somebody else in the next election. That's the way we roll.

Taking Care of De-*mom*-cracy

The idea of America has been the hope of the world in modern times, a concrete expression of what is possible when humanity cooperates with divinity. It's like an outreached hand to save one from the rough seas of life and an invitation to walk on the water. America has stood as a beacon for what is possible when we look after one another.

But now she is tired and sitting down, weary from the meddling of unqualified management and the lack of respect shown to one's heritage, aghast at the current environment of name calling from within a brothel. She knew it was coming. It is always coming with humans. She has seen it before. After wiping tears from her eyes, she is writing letters, making phone calls, sending emails, and snapchatting to all who will listen. Do you want true freedom? Are you willing to sacrifice for it? Will you respect reality and cooperate with its truth? Are you willing to discern good from evil? Will you uphold standards? Will you take care of your mother?

America was founded as "one nation under God" precisely so it wouldn't be one nation under humankind. For over two centuries, it has been the imperfect perfection of freedom. Adjustments for time and circumstance are provided for as a mechanism within our Constitution so it can be done in a sensible and orderly manner. But whole scale change violates the law of noncontradiction. America is defined. When its definitions are circumvented, it is no longer America. If we want to replace her, we should at least have the respect and courtesy to rename her.

As for me, I am going the distance with the original pledge: "And for the support of this Declaration, with a firm reliance on the protection of divine Providence, we mutually pledge to each other our Lives, our Fortunes and our sacred Honor."[391]

Think clearly and act rationally, my friends.

> *Some believe that it is only great power that can hold evil in check. But*
> *that is not what I've found. I found it is the small things. Everyday*
> *deeds by ordinary folk that keeps the darkness at bay.*
> —GANDALF THE GREY, *THE LORD OF THE RINGS*

> *Love is our most mature act as human beings.*
> —EUGENE PETERSON

---

[391] Declaration of Independence, July 4, 1776.

About the Author

I have multiple occupational passports in a variety of fields. In the public sector, I worked thirty-three years as a practitioner and executive for the County of Orange, California, in several departments. The County of Orange serves the sixth-largest county populace in the United States with more than eighteen thousand employees and a $6 billion annual budget. The significance of county government for many people is relatively obscure but critically important. Counties are the regional service providers for nearly every important aspect of daily living in areas like public safety (law enforcement, district attorney / public defender, courts, probation); social services (welfare, child protection); health care (mental health, disease prevention, correctional medical); recreational services (parks and beaches); personal services (birth/marriage/death certificates, real estate transactions, property taxes); transportation (airport, roads, harbors); voting; and public works (flood control, waste management, permits and licensing, construction). Providing these critical services in a public-sector environment is a constant challenge, particularly with five term-limited elected officials in charge. Sometimes there are high fives (votes), low fives, or no fives. Sometimes there are three high fives and two low fives. At other times, there are sharpened knives and running for one's life.

Some of my assignments at the county included chief human resources officer, performance audit director, director of administration for a variety of departments, chief of organizational assessment/development, and the high-wire frontline jobs of regional landfill manager and go-to personnel investigator, just to name a few. It should also be noted that I am a survivor of the county's 1994 bankruptcy, which at the time was the largest municipal bankruptcy in US history. In my assignments from the shop floor to the C-suite, I spent time, in one form or another, in nearly every functional area of the county. For my work in performance audit, the county was awarded Harvard's highly competitive Kennedy School/Ash Center for Democratic Government and Innovation 2012 "Bright Ideas" recognition.

Academically, I earned a master's of business and public administration, and a bachelor's degree in political science from the University of California at Irvine (UCI). I serve as a lecturer at UCI, teaching a "Business and Government" class. In 2016, I coauthored a book with Dr. Peter Hughes entitled *Management Diseases and Disorders: How to Identify and Treat Dysfunctional Managerial Behavior*. The book has received critical acclaim from Kirkus, BlueInk, and Foreword Reviews.

In the private sector, I am president and CEO of SD Consulting, Inc., which specializes in human resources, performance auditing, and organizational assessment and rehabilitation. In my younger days, I worked for United Parcel Service (UPS) and the Dr. Pepper Bottling Company, which I thank for helping to finance my college education.

Additionally, I was a thirty-year NCAA and high school basketball referee, where instant feedback was a blessing and an occupational hazard.